# Solidarity: A Normative Principle

## European Monographs Series Set

---

### VOLUME 116

---

*Editor*

Prof. Andrea Biondi is Professor of European Law and Director of the Centre of European Law at King's College London

*Introduction & Contents/Subjects*

As the process of European integration assumes an increasingly complex character, the EU legal system continues to undergo sweeping changes. The European Monographs series offers a voice to thoughtful, knowledgeable, cutting edge legal commentary on the now unlimited field of European law. Its emphasis on focal and topical issues makes the series an invaluable tool for scholars, practitioners, and policymakers specializing or simply interested in EU law.

*Objective*

The aim is to publish innovative work appealing to academics and practitioners alike. The result is an original and ongoing library of detailed analyses, theories, commentaries, practical guides, and proposals, each of which furthers the cause of meaningful European integration. Cumulatively, the series may be regarded as a 'work in progress' engaged in building a sharply defined representation of law in Europe.

*Readership*

Academics and practitioners dealing with EU law.

*The titles published in this series are listed at the end of this volume.*

# Solidarity: A Normative Principle

Guido Alpa

 Wolters Kluwer

*Published by:*
Kluwer Law International B.V.
PO Box 316
2400 AH Alphen aan den Rijn
The Netherlands
E-mail: lrs-sales@wolterskluwer.com
Website: www.wolterskluwer.com/en/solutions/kluwerlawinternational

*Sold and distributed by:*
Wolters Kluwer Legal & Regulatory U.S.
920 Links Avenue
Landisville, PA 17538
United States of America
E-mail: customer.service@wolterskluwer.com

*Printed on acid-free paper.*

ISBN 978-94-035-3596-8

e-Book: ISBN 978-94-035-4146-4
web-PDF: ISBN 978-94-035-4156-3

Printed in the Netherlands.

# Table of Contents

Table of Contents

# Introduction

There is a continuity between ideas, values, and principles that are accredited at a given historical moment in a given society and the legal forms it adopts to organise relations between individuals and between individuals and the state. If law in the objective sense is a system for distributing power, a system for distributing wealth, a system for governing peace and war, a system for allocating individual and collective rights, a system for administering justice and regulating – or as we prefer to argue today – regulating the market, it cannot be thought that law as a science and as a technique can be divorced from culture, the world of ideas, politics and the other social sciences. This prejudice, which originated in the nineteenth century, at a time when constitutions were concerned with legitimising the power of authority and even defining its divine origin, and civil codes were limited to settling conflicts between owners, lasted until almost the end of the twentieth century, and, to read certain history and philosophy books today, right up to the present day. But if a century ago this prejudice could be considered well-founded, today it no longer is. And yet if we scrutinise the literature that has been gathered in certain areas, we can find that this prejudice is practised so widely that it is not even perceived, indeed, that it is considered a natural component of research. This has been the case with the idea of solidarity: for a long time absorbed into the world of ideas by scholars of history, philosophy, political science, and sociology, it has proceeded as if it were extraneous to law and law were extraneous to its definition.[1] But from reflexive law, which is content with a notarised function of history, we have long since moved on to militant law. Ever since the principle of solidarity entered the constitutions, law has been given an active task in defining subjective legal positions and relations with the state. And the state, in its various guises as an organisational system, as a 'welfare state' or as a market operator, has taken on complex tasks designed to guarantee fundamental rights and redefine the role of the individual in society, ensuring not only dignity but also a job, housing, a healthy environment, a sufficient income and a secure future.[2]

---

1. Zoll, *Solidarity: Equality and Difference 2000*, Trad. it., Bologna, 2003.
2. Rodotà, *Solidarietà. Una utopia necessaria*, Roma-Bari, 2014; and already, Lipari, *Diritto e valori sociali*, Roma, 2004.

1

Today, we live in a post-democracy in which multinational corporations prevail over the free market, digital platforms over the rules of national legal systems, the debasement of the individual to a mere consumer of goods and services is taking place, uncertainties towards technological challenges are being felt, the frontier of fundamental rights is being pushed back, and the crisis of the European Union (EU) is being feared.

The Preamble of the Charter of Fundamental Rights states that the Union, this great supranational edifice is founded on 'the indivisible and universal values of human dignity, freedom, equality and *solidarity*; (...) the principles of democracy and the rule of law', placing 'the individual at the heart of its action by establishing the citizenship of the Union and creating an area of freedom, security and justice (...)'. This great institution, created to 'promote balanced and sustainable development', is today looking for a more secure future and a stronger glue. Of all the values on which it is founded, *solidarity* appears to be the most ethereal, in some ways even the most equivocal, even though it can boast, like the others, an august tradition.[3] Its meaning has been the most changeable and certainly, the most abused: on this expression, or on similar expressions, the tables of individual freedoms and fascist corporatism, liberal constitutions and the spirit of the Nazi people, the Christian spirit of brotherly love and socialist humanism have been built from time to time. Given its ductility, some scholars have come to the conclusion that it is useless or dangerous. But this argument is not conclusive.[4]

*Solidarity* is not only a value-principle endowed with philosophical and moral significance,[5] but it is also a value-principle with *legal content*, and therefore *preceptive*, instrumental to the realisation of social ends. Decoding solidarity, in order to fully understand its potentialities, misrepresentations and mystifications has therefore become, today more than ever, a task entrusted to jurists: a difficult task since we are all aware that that value is based on a *utopia*, Stefano Rodotà emphasised, albeit a *necessary one*. This is why solidarity, with respect for private autonomy and collective interests, must be 'reinvented'.

The vast literature on the subject obviously counts contributions of great impact and usefulness in the Anglo-American world, where, however, solidarity is seen above all under the lens of the 'common good', or of the dialectic between communitarianism and particularism, as well as under the guise of aspirations for social justice. In the French-speaking world, where solidarity appears coupled with fraternity, this term

---

3. Leneuf, *Solidarity, a Legal Concept? Study of the Concept in the Charter of Fundamental Rights of the European Union*, in ERPL, 26, 2014, pp. 91 ff.
4. *See* the thorough research by Stjerno, *Solidarity in Europe*, Cambridge, 2005 and Supiot (cur.), *La Solidarité: Enquête sur un principe juridique*, Paris, 2015.
5. In the extensive literature, *see* in particular the final chapter of Rorty, *Contingency Irony and Solidarity*, Cambridge, 1989. Habermas, *Solidarity among Strangers: Interventions on Facts and Norms*, Milan, 1997; Sparti, *Difficult Cohabitations: A Note on Habermas and Multiculturalism*, in Quad. Sociologia, 2002, pp. 29 ff.; Cunico and Bruzzone (eds), *Solidarietà: una prospettiva etica*, Sesto S, Giovanni (Mi), 2017; AA.VV., *Perseguire il bene comune: come solidarietà e sussidiarietà possono operare insieme*, Pontif. Acc. Sc. Soc., Acta, no. 14, Vatican, 2008.

recalls the revolutionary ideals, the sociological currents of the nineteenth century, and the radical solidarism of the early twentieth century.

In research on the subject, legal aspects are mostly neglected, being ancillary to philosophical or political aspects. Hence the need to counterpoint metagi-legal studies with a narrative that, starting from the earliest constitutions, documents the interweaving of norms with ideas and values. Different paths could be chosen to accomplish this task: the evolution of the concept of property, or that of person, or of contract, or of harm, or of democracy, or of power, or of sovereignty. In today's difficult and calamitous times, it seemed more appropriate to rethink the principle of solidarity as the reason for living, living fully and not just surviving, in a social agglomeration we call a community.[6]

From a lexical point of view, the expression does not say much, if not a singularity. It does not often happen that a term with a specific and circumscribed technical meaning in the world of law conquers a much wider space and extends over time, enriching its meanings and overcoming the narrow confines of its origin. 'Solidum' is one such term: as is often repeated, it derives from another term, solidum, which in addition to designating a noun, also indicates an adjective: in its direct meaning, it indicates a portion of concrete substance, essentially different from that which is liquid or airy, and in its translated meaning it means full or 'whole'. In the world of law, it is connected with the concept of debt, i.e., with one of the forms in which debt can be configured: the debtor 'jointly and severally' (as was already the case in Roman law) is the debtor who has contracted the obligation together with other debtors to the same creditor; the creditor may, at his or her choice, demand fulfilment of the obligation in full even from only one of them, and the latter must fulfil it, without prejudice to his or her right of recourse against the others. The tradition of Roman law has transmitted this formula to us, from which certain corollaries immediately emerge: whoever is held jointly and severally has a debt, that is, is the holder of a passive subjective situation, and this debt is not individual, singular, but shared with others.[7] The situation presupposes a dual relativity: the debtor's relationship with the other joint debtors and all together and singularly with the creditor. Debtors jointly and severally thus experience a common contingent situation. From the legal language, still found in this meaning in the Encyclopaedia of Diderot and D'Alembert, the term solidarité was transposed into common language and acquired a meaning – still very generic – of mutual responsibility. It is a French word, and from French it is transposed into the Italian language; Niccolò Tommaseo records it in his dictionary in 1847 as an 'ugly Frenchism'. At the same time, it conquered the German language (Solidarität) and the English language (solidarity).

---

6. Paugam (cur.), *Repenser la solidaritè*, Paris, 2007.
7. Article 1200 Code Civil (1804); Article 1186 c.c. it. (1865) according to which 'the obligation is joint and several for the debtors when they are obliged to the same thing, in such a way that each can be compelled to pay in full and the payment made by one alone releases the others towards the creditor'.

# CHAPTER 1

# History of a Term, of Architects and Artifices

## §1.01    FOREWORD

The polysemy of the term *solidarity* depends on its rich history, which runs through philosophy, with theories on social cohesion, is coloured by the foundations of sociology, with the division of social labour, takes root in workers' and trade unionist culture at the turn of the nineteenth century, and becomes the promoter of the Church's social doctrine, it became the protagonist of a political season in France with the seizure of power by the radicals, it became entrenched in fascist and Nazi ideology with corporate solidarity and comradeship, and conquered the post-war constitutions to become the banner of the welfare state, fundamental rights, equality in the substantial sense and the social and economic policy of the EU.

It is an honourable history, which justifies the vast literature that has been gathered in the West on this subject. And it is also understandable that one appropriates the term and its history if aspirations, values, feelings and intentions are gathered behind that term. To the point that anti-historical projections are also attempted, with anachronistic inductions aimed at ennobling the past.

Spy of these curious and interesting elaborations is the reconstruction of the evolution of the concept of solidarity over the centuries. We have spoken of the solidarity of the ancients and the solidarity of the modern.[8] But it is clear that one can identify many parallel histories of solidarity that correspond to as many meanings of the term. This opens up unsuspected scenarios, from the history of charity and altruism, which are articulated in a horizontal relationship between private individuals, to the history of public care of the sick, orphans, the insane, epileptics, lepers, the elderly, the invalids, the maimed, lavished by public authority, in a vertical relationship: from the first conceptions of common life and relational relations in the Greek

---

8. AA.VV., *Solidarities Ancient and Modern*, P. Merlin ed., Rome, 2017.

polis to the complex articulations of power in Roman society, and again in the history of religions, and the interweaving of religion and power in the Middle Ages.[9]

The idea of political, economic and social solidarity referred to in contemporary constitutions, however, took shape with the Enlightenment.[10]

It is now worthwhile to consider the evolutionary lines of the concept of solidarity by taking into account the cultural backgrounds and regional origins of scholars, and then by taking into account direct sources, rather than their sometimes uncritical reproduction so frequently found in studies on the subject.

An external consideration of this copious literature makes us aware that the succession of the protagonists of thought and the succession of events that mark the history of the concept passes, for German scholars, through France and Germany, neglecting Italy;[11] for French scholars, it is formed and developed only in France, as if there was not, in the eighteenth and nineteenth centuries, an osmosis of ideas and projects that overcame territorial, linguistic, political and religious barriers.[12] It is very important to reconstruct from phase to phase the cultural humus in which the idea of solidarity matures because it is precisely that humus that then contributes to making it a juridical concept in the modern sense, in which the passage from voluntariness, gratuitousness, self-sacrifice, generosity, charity, to duty – of contribution, of support – to the rights connected with the Welfare State[13] is felt. In addition, it is necessary to verify in what context the term is used, and how it gradually with its polysemic use ends up being transformed.

The idea of solidarity constitutes a cultural laboratory used to achieve different and often contradictory ends: hence the caution with which it is often surrounded, not to mention the discredit of those who preach its ambiguity and thus its uselessness.

## §1.02    THE ORIGINS OF MODERN SOLIDARITY

Scholars are conflicted as to the identification of the sources of the concept of solidarity as a translation of the principle of common responsibility of debtor subjects, which codifies its original legal meaning traceable in the sources of Roman law. Most, when speaking of *political* solidarity, refer directly to the Enlightenment and Voltaire.[14]

However, there is a specific antecedent: Rousseau in demonstrating how from the state of 'good savage' man creates, in addition to the family, community, appeals to feelings rather than reason, and thus combats the principle of sociability.

The principle of sociability, the cornerstone of all previous meditations and the basis of the moral science of duties, although accepted as true and forcefully re-launched by the major European Enlightenment circles as the ultimate foundation of civil society, was resolutely denied by Rousseau in favour of the thesis of the dispersion

9. Rodotà, *Solidarietà, supra*, pp. 5 ff.
10. Zoll, *Solidarity, supra*, pp. 19 ff.
11. *Ibid.*, passim.
12. Blais, *La solidaritè. Historie d'unn idée*, Paris, 2007.
13. Mengoni, *Diritto e valori*, Bologna, 1985; Stjerno, *supra*, pp. 338 ff.
14. Laitinen, *Solidarity*, in Enc. Of Philosophy and Social Science, London, 2013.

and isolation of the human being: 'Wandering in the forest, without industry, without speech, without domicile, without war, and without association, without any need of his fellows, as without any desire to harm them, perhaps even without ever recognising any one individually, the savage man', he pointed out, 'subject to few passions, and sufficient to himself had only the feelings and knowledge suited to such a state'.[15]

In this sense, Rousseau denies both the principles of morality of the neo-stoics such as Grotius and Pufendorf, as well as religious morality based on the Gospel and the Epistles of St. Paul, which legitimise civil authority as deriving from the divine will:

> On the basis of the social pact we have given existence and life to the body politic; we must now give it movement and will by *legislation*, since the original act by which this body is formed and united does not yet establish anything about what it must do to preserve itself [...]. Certainly, Rousseau pointed out, 'all justice comes from God, he alone is its source; but if we knew how to accept it from such a height, we would have no need of either government or laws. Undoubtedly there is a universal justice emanating from reason alone, but this justice, in order to be accepted among us, must be reciprocal [...]'. Agreements and laws are therefore necessary to link rights to duties and bring justice back to its purpose.[16]

With different accents and on the basis of different arguments, Kant also theorises the emergence of society from a secular perspective: his most famous sentence in this context is taken from the pages that theorise perpetual peace: 'The solidarity of mankind is not only a beautiful and noble sign, but a pressing necessity; a to be or not to be; a matter of life or death'.[17]

And a few years later, in his treatise *The Metaphysics of Moral*,[18] he speaks of *duties*: towards God, towards oneself, towards other men. And as to these, he distinguishes duties of love, i.e., charity, gratitude, sympathy.

## §1.03    THE FRENCH MODEL: THE ENLIGHTENMENT

Mirabeau (1789) and Danton (1793) had used concepts such as 'solidarité' and 'solidaire' in the National Assembly in a sense that is at least somewhere between the legal meaning of joint and several liability and the more recent[19] meaning of the principle of sociality. It thus went beyond the principle of co-responsibility that Diderot and D'Alembert had included in the *Encyclopaedia*.

One should not omit the passages on fraternity and solidarity laws that appeared on the French political scene in the most crucial years of the Revolution. We note here

---

15. Rousseau, *Discorso sull'origine e i fondamenti della disuguaglianza fra gli uomini*, in *Discorsi*, edited by L. Luporini, Milan, 1997, p. 128; on this point, *see* Ferrone, *Il problema Rousseau e i diritti dell'uomo. La pratica politica dei diritti tra natura e cultura, individuo e comunità*, 'stato di pura natura' e società civile, in *Studi francesi*, 2012, pp. 221 ff.
16. Rousseau, *Del contratto sociale*, (1792) Milan, 2014, p. 294.
17. Kant, I., *Per la pace perpetua. Progetto filosofico* (1795), in I. Kant, *Scritti politici*, Turin, Utet 1956, pp. 283-336.
18. A work that was written between 1787 and 1788: *see* now the Italian translation, Roma-Bari, 1989.
19. Brunot, *Histoire de la langue française*, Paris, 1905.

an extraordinary fact, which the historians of solidarity do not grasp, and which instead has not escaped the attention of jurists. Indeed, one finds in the meshes of ordinary legislation – not in constitutional texts – rules that can be considered the expression of a primordial nucleus of social solidarity, such as those concerned with ensuring work for all, or a pension for those who can no longer work, or those combating poverty and coming to the aid of *citoyens malheureux*.[20]

The revolutionary ideas were, however, overtaken by events: and already by 1795, solidarity laws were reduced in scope, and then supplanted by the great 'silence' of the years of the Empire: this is how Michel Borgetto expresses himself, in reconstructing on a juridical level the concepts of fraternity and solidarity, considered homologous and therefore fungible: it will be necessary to arrive at the July Monarchy and then at the Republican Constitution of 1848 to find the idea of *fraternity* reinvigorated.[21] The social state *in nuce* and the juridical concept of fraternity will however become the expression of another political conception, the variegated but powerful one of socialism, first on the political level and then on the juridical level. Fraternity or solidarity become the prerogative of socialist thought, in France and Germany.

Saint-Simon believes that it is physiological feelings that weld human relationships together, and Fourier replaces Christian *caritas* with the physical relationship of love. Finally, in 1848, solidarity triumphs as 'social catechism'[22] and at the end of the nineteenth century, it pervades the political programmes of socialists and radicals. This is the most linear path of a term – value – concept that, as is already evident from what has been said (and will be explored in more detail below), frays into many meanings.

## §1.04     REVOLUTIONARY FRATERNITY

The triad of revolutionary values – liberty, equality, fraternity – actually boiled down to the binomial *liberty-equality*, fraternity not even being mentioned in the preamble, which is worth quoting word for word:

> The representatives of the French people constituted in the National Assembly, considering that ignorance, oblivion or contempt for the rights of man are the sole causes of public disasters and the corruption of governments, have resolved to set forth, in a solemn declaration, the natural, inalienable and sacred rights of man, so that this declaration constantly present to all members of the social body, may incessantly remind them of their rights and duties; that the acts of the legislative and executive powers may be treated with greater respect by being compared at all times with the purpose of every political institution; that the claims of the citizens, founded henceforth on simple and incontestable principles, may always result in the maintenance of the Constitution and the happiness of all. Accordingly, the National Assembly recognises and declares, in the presence and under the auspices of the Supreme Being, the following rights of man and citizen:

---

20. Borgetto, *La notion de fraternité en droit public français*, Paris, 1993, pp. 189 ff.
21. Borgetto, *supra*, pp. 232 ff.
22. Blais, *La solidarité. Histoire d'une idée*, Paris, 2007, p. 50.

We owe to Auguste Comte the idea that pervades the development of the meanings and role of solidarity during the modern age: society is based on consensus, both in its static structure, which imposes order, and in its dynamic structure, which seeks progress.[30]

'From the scientific point of view [...]', he writes, 'this mother idea of universal social solidarity becomes here the inevitable consequence and indispensable complement of a fundamental idea declared [...] to be adapted in a high degree to the study of living beings. With scientific rigour, this idea of consensus is by no means, without doubt, strictly specific to such a study, and presents itself directly as having to be, by its very nature, necessarily common to all phenomena, but with great differences in intensity and variety, and, consequently, in philosophical importance. Indeed, it can be said that wherever there is any system, there must consequently exist a certain solidarity [...]'.

This concept circulates with great insistence in the world of ideas, whether taken as a cementing factor in society, as a moral canon for each individual, or as a sign of recognition and affiliation for those in the same situation of hardship, poverty and exploitation. Studies of philosophy, politics and the new science, sociology, contribute to creating the favour for solidarity, which goes beyond the pages of scientists to appear in legislative texts: its acquisition in the French constitutional text of 1848 with the substratum that animates its meaning, *fraternity*, implies the passage from the philosophical to the juridical level, and solidarity/fraternity becomes a concept of *positive law*. It brings together two aspects, the right and the duty: the right, in the sense that the citizen must find in the community, hence in the state, the guarantor of his survival, defence, work, health and old age; the duty, in the sense that each citizen, on the basis of his means, must contribute to the needs of the community. The uprisings of 1848 marked the end of the Restoration and incorporated the ideals of a democracy more attentive to social needs. The Constitution of the Second Republic, in addition to textually introducing fraternity as one of the symbolic values of France and the new regime, repeatedly insists on fraternity as the rule of relations between state and citizen and between citizens:

   VI – Mutual duties oblige citizens towards the Republic, and the Republic towards
        its citizens.
   VII – Citizens must love their country, serve the Republic, defend it at the cost of
        their lives, share in the burdens of the State in proportion to their fortunes; they
        must secure by work the means of existence and, by provision, the resources for
        the future; they must contribute to the *common welfare by helping one* another
        *fraternally*, and to the general order by observing the moral and written laws
        that govern society, the family and the individual.
   VIII – The Republic must protect the citizen in person, the family, religion, property,
        work, and put the education indispensable to all men within everyone's reach;
        it must, by means of *fraternal assistance*, ensure the existence of needy citizens

---

30. *Cours de philosophie positive* (6 vols, 1830-1842) and the *Système de politique positive* (4 vols, 1851-1854).

either by providing them with work within the limits of its possibilities, or by giving, in the absence of the family, subsidies to those who are not in a condition to work. In view of the fulfilment of all these duties, and for the guarantee of all these rights, the National Assembly, faithful to the traditions of the great assemblies that inaugurated the French Revolution, decrees in the following manner, the Constitution of the Republic.

Even more explicit, though purely propositional, is the text that Charles Renouvier composed for Hippolyte Carnot, the *Republican Handbook of Man and Citizen, 1848*,[31] in which solidarity and fraternity are illustrated in two different yet coherent meanings: solidarity is a law of humanity, no man is good intelligent happy while others suffer; fraternity is the rule of society, for which the Republic recognises the right to work, to social education, to associate among workers, to share property until wage labour disappears.

France certainly owes the primacy of the *legal concept of solidarity/fraternity* to France.

On a political and philosophical level, the ideas that were spreading at that time in Germany thanks to Lasalle's studies and in Italy, thanks to Mazzini's thought, are driving forces. It is more difficult here, however, to trace the mention of that concept in legal texts. Frédéric Bastiat[32] also proclaims the relevance of fraternity, not, however, as a juridical concept, but first and foremost as an instrument of social cohesion that implies *collective responsibility,* and then as a sentiment that founds mutual aid, charity and social altruism. The juxtaposition of solidarity and responsibility will be emphasised at the end of the century by Leon Bourgois in his construction of the social structure based on solidarity.

The French model had imposed itself throughout Europe through the strength of ideas and the success of revolutionaries. The Second Republic[33] had the language of the jurist and a socialist heart,[34] it combined democratic order with socialist aspirations and had stubbornly created an associative and cooperative network preaching a life of collaboration, solidarity, and mutual aid to support the humble and oppressed; in other words, it had realised – and not only on paper – the socialist ethos.[35] Hence his capture also by the popular classes.

---

31. Reprinted edited by Agulhon, Paris, 1981; Hawkins, *Charles Renouvier and the 'Conservative Republic' in France, History of Political Thought*, 33(1) Spring 2012, p. 145; aude Biais, *Au Principe de la République: le cas Renouvier* (Paris, 2000); the collection of essays in *'Renouvier: philosophie politique', Corpus: revue de philosophie*, 45, ed. Marie-Claude Biais (2003); Logue, *Renouvier, Philosopher of Liberty* (Baton Rouge, LA, 1993); Dobuzinskis, *Defenders of Liberal Individualism: The Forgotten Intellectual Founders of the French Third Republic*, 7 Eur. J. Political Theory, 2008.
32. *Harmonies economiques*, Brussels, 1850.
33. Agulon, *France in the Second Republic, 1848-1852*, Rome, 1979.
34. Agulon, *supra*, p. 160; and *see* Soldani, *La duplice sconfitta della Seconda Repubblica in Francia, Studi Storici*, July-September 1979, Year 20, No. 3 (July-September 1979), pp. 667-677.
35. Agulon, *supra*, p. 106.

## §1.06 THE GERMAN MODEL

This is the reason why Marx violently and sarcastically criticises the 1848 revolution because he understands that it was not the socialism of the books and the chair, the theories were embodied in the social reality of the time.[36]

According to Marx, the alliance between Republicans, Democrats and Socialists had favoured the petty bourgeoisie, not the proletariat. But he was wrong. More recent studies have pointed out that in those years 'the workers saw themselves as a united and united social force, which posed the need – in the political terms of democracy – for their own direct and no longer mediated participation in government. The demo-soc alliance substantially responded to this demand',[37] and it is precisely in that political grouping that the origins of the French left are to be identified: the Second Republic is the source from which radicalism, socialism and Blanquism spring. And it was precisely thanks to these currents that the doors were opened to the spread of Marx's thought.[38]

These were years of great ferment: the first organised working class was being formed, made up of workers and artisans, who not only demanded work and bread but also to be able to participate democratically in the government of the nation. Universal suffrage, already acquired in France with the February revolution, was becoming a constitutional seal between democracy and socialism. Equality was no longer merely formal but was realised through the improvement of citizens' social and economic conditions. And through political debate in which individuals were protected by workers' associations and social cooperatives.

Hence the conclusion that 'in this context, it is not surprising that, even later, France proved to be substantially impervious to the penetration of Marxism: Guesde's attempt to transform the Parti ouvrier – which rejected electoral alliances with the middle classes – into a centralised political structure in line with Marx's theories was defeated by the preference given to Paul Brousse and Benoît Malon, both advocates of a peaceful evolution towards socialism. Likewise, the attention paid by Malon, and later by Jaurès, to the ideal motives of history shows how the revolutionary tradition in France contrasted with the assumptions of scientific socialism'.[39]

In short, Marx could not see the February Revolution as the realisation of socialist ideals because he thought that flaunting universal fraternity meant renouncing the class struggle.[40]

---

36. Berenson, *Populist Religion and Left-Wing Politics in France, 1830-1852*, Princeton, 1854, cited by De Francesco, *Democratici e socialisti in Francia dal 1830 al 1851: Il Politico*, 1986, Vol. 51, No. 3 (1986), pp. 459-494.
37. De Francesco, *supra*, p. 461.
38. On the legacy of banquism, however, there are divergent ideas that highlight the distance of Blanqui's theories from Marx's, despite what Marx said: De Francesco, *supra*, p. 461. On the gradual and deficient Knowledge of Marxian thought in Italy *see* Hosbawn, *Preface* (1965) *in Marx, Forme economiche precapitalistiche*, trad. it., Roma, 1967, pp. 7 ff. The Grundlisse were composed in the years 1857-1858: see AA.VV., *I Grundriss di Karl Marx. Fundamental outlines of political criticism 150 years later*, Pisa, 2015.
39. De Francesco, *supra*, p. 494.
40. Zoll, *Solidarity*, *supra*, p. 47.

Marx in the Manifesto uses the term solidarity to give foundation to the bond between proletarians all over the world and does not admit it instead, and this is obvious, as a bond between all citizens, or even worse, between all classes.[41]

It was up to Lassalle to recover the concept of solidarity, as elaborated in France, at the expense of the fraternity/fraternity that circulated in the works of the utopian socialists.

Lassalle is a very influential German philosopher in the middle years of the century, also famous in France, where he stayed for a long time. Lassalle, a left-wing Hegelian, points to the state: according to his belief 'in a democratic system of universal suffrage, socialism could only advance if the working class knew how to associate itself, found cooperatives, and be supported by the state. This path would lead to the transition from the capitalist to the socialist model, transforming bourgeois society into a reality based on equality and self-management'.[42]

For Lassalle, in short, only an alliance between state and workers could overcome capitalism and defeat the selfish and individualistic bourgeois society; this alliance had to be formed through direct universal suffrage, in which Lassalle saw the possibility for workers to conquer the bourgeois state and transform it from within: it was a sort of 'revolutionary Hegelian reformism'.[43] Those ideas were warmly welcomed in Italy, even though they were opposed by Marx for reasons not dissimilar to those already put forward by the French coryphaeus of socialism.

In the years of the philosophical and political construction of the concept of solidarity, there are therefore already many facets to it. But the consolidation of this concept is achieved with its legal configuration, which on the principle of solidarity founds the constitutional cornerstones of society: universal suffrage, in the new constitutional law, shapes a new society in which a bridge is established between the individual and the state through individual labour and workers' associations and work and consumer cooperatives.

Along this line, both French radicalism and socialism throughout Europe will develop. These are the years of the First International and scientific socialism has not yet defeated the other epiphanies of this ideology.

In every country in Europe, these ideas are developed, and each country has its own peculiarities. In Italy (and elsewhere), the thought of Giuseppe Mazzini emerges strongly and with great success.

### §1.07    BROTHERHOOD AND SOLIDARITY IN THE THOUGHT AND ACTION OF GIUSEPPE MAZZINI

Scholars of the political evolution of the idea of solidarity only make quick references to Mazzini's thought. Zoll only fleetingly mentions it once, in connection with the

---

41. *Ibid.*, p. 57.
42. Antonini, *Ferdinand Lasalle et les deux internationale*, Cahiers Jaurès 2014/2-3 (N° 212-213), pp. 153 à 163. On Lassalle's contribution to the construction of the concept of solidarity *see* Zoll, *supra*, pp. 37 ff.
43. *See* the entry Lassalle Ferdinand, in *Enc.italiana*, 1933 (edited by Beccari).

meeting in Berne in 1834 of Italian, German and Polish 'radicals' for the signing of the Act of Fraternisation of the Young Europe. The word fraternity is used here both with regard to equality and humanity and with regard to equality and people.[44] A little more generous is the analysis of Blais, who recalls the connection between humanity and nation in Mazzini's writings on the 'Young Switzerland' of 1836, and the movement on the Young Europe founded in 1848; he also recalls his apostolate in exile in London where he had, at a distance, his first confrontation with Marx, and his appeal to the republicans in the name of European solidarity made in 1855 together with Kossuth and Ledru-Rollin.[45]

But Mazzini deserves much more.[46] You may or may not like his smoky way of writing appeals, his romantic rhetoric, the connection of God and People, but you cannot ignore the enormous political influence he had throughout the nineteenth century in Italy, in England, in the irredent lands, and, in the middle years of the century, even in France and Germany. His persuasive and impressive oratory, his ascetic life, his total selflessness, his generous heroism, made him the 'apostle of the people'.[47] His impact on the political life of the peoples of European empires, of nations stifled in their aspirations for independence, of revolutionaries hunted down, imprisoned and executed by absolute powers, is unparalleled in the history of the Risorgimento. The interpretation of his figure, and his legacy, as well as the instrumentalisations to which he was subjected, especially during Fascism, have made him a figure regarded with caution. But it would be anti-historical to deny its relevance and fail to appreciate its central role also in the construction of the concept of solidarity.

In truth, Mazzini does not only focus on solidarity but also on *fraternity*, a word that speaks to the heart and expresses feelings of unity that are stronger than solidarity. By their very nature, men are brothers. Brothers are consanguineous, they come from the same family, they express 'by nature' an indelible bond.

Germany, Poland and Italy are the first nations Mazzini seeks to unite and bring to independence, which is to be achieved at any cost, even through the use of violence, of demonstrative attacks, of aggression against illibertarian autocrats. His credo is based on the principles of a universal moral law, which has freedom, equality and progress as its pillars. He speaks of solidarity between peoples, in defence and offence. He insists on considering the individuals who are part of the three associations as brothers: 'each of them will fulfil the duties of brotherhood with the other'.[48] Life is considered a mission, *duty* its supreme law.[49] A single, free and independent Italy is the goal of men united by brotherhood.[50]

The category of *duty* is, perhaps for the first time, at the centre of political thought and constitutional law.

---

44. Zoll, *supra*, p. 46.
45. Balis, *supra*, pp. 67, 81, 83.
46. Falco, *Mazzini and the Constituent Assembly*, Genoa, 1972.
47. An objective reconstruction of the figure can be found in AA.VV., *Giuseppe Mazzini*, in *Edizioni della Voce*, Rome, 1972.
48. Act of Brotherhood, *supra*, in *Giuseppe Mazzini*, edited by Ghisalberti, Milan 1972, p. 195.
49. *Ibid.*, p. 209.
50. *Ibid.*

The constitutional principles, which Mazzini places at the foundation of the Roman Republic, are based on equality liberty and fraternity, which also concerns the brotherhood of peoples. Property is inviolable, everyone has a duty to contribute to the expenses of the Republic.

Although they are almost coeval, it is interesting to note the differences between the text of the Constitution of the Second Republic and the text of the Roman Constitution. As much the former is insistent on the concept of work, as the latter ignores it; as much the former recreates the premises of the welfare state, albeit embryonic, as the latter insists on the protection of other interests.

Mazzinianism was the first conduit for the penetration of political interests into the class movement, but when the movement evolved, Mazzinianism was pushed to the margins.[51] It cannot be said that Mazzini was in the true sense socialist, although his action in the International was initially very much involved;[52] but he certainly gave the idea of solidarity and the idea of fraternity revolutionary content with his thought.[53]

Mazzini is not materialistic. However, he only protects property if it comes from labour. But he is against class hatred, is republican, does not suppress authority if it comes from the people democratically, believes in God and respects religions. A little too much to hold Marx in esteem, who, apart from the early days, ends up regarding him as a dangerous, confused and inconclusive corrupter of the working.[54]

Starting with duties, rather than rights, is the beginning of a political project in which freedom and equality are values that must be earned and go beyond material well-being. It is about duties to God, to Humanity, to Country, to Family, to oneself:

> Why do I tell you about your duties before I tell you about your rights? Why, in a society where everyone, voluntarily or involuntarily, oppresses you, where the exercise of all the rights that belong to man is constantly robbed from you, where all unhappiness is for you, and what is called happiness is for the men of the other classes, do I speak to you of sacrifice, and not of conquest, of virtue, of moral improvement, of education, and not of material well-being? This is a question that I must make clear before going on, because in this lies the difference between our school and many others that are preaching in Europe today; then, because this is a question that easily arises in the irritated soul of the suffering worker. We are

---

51. Arfé, *Storia del socialismo italiano* (1892-1926), Turin, 1965, p. 17.
52. Galante Garrone, *L'incontro con il sansimonismo*, in *Giuseppe Mazzini* cit. pp. 60 ff.; De Felice, *Mazzini e il socialismo*, ivi, pp. 67 ff.; Lotti, *L'operaismo mazziniano nella 'questione sociale'*, ivi, pp. 71 ff.
53. 'Mazzini fought for an increase in wages and a reduction in the working day, advancing the idea of establishing special forms of credit for workers to facilitate their access to ownership of the means of production. The negative phenomena of the European economy are indicated in the recurring production crises, which have repercussions on wages and lead to the progressive worsening of workers' lives. The increasing integration of the European markets, rather than contributing to the economic progress of the various countries, aggravates the living conditions of the inhabitants, preventing the realisation of a fairer distribution of wealth and revealing the deceitful aspect of free trade.' Dell'Erba, *Giuseppe Mazzini*, in *Il contributo italiano alla storia del pensiero*, Rome, 2013).
54. Levi, *La filosofia politica di Giuseppe Mazzini*, Bologna, 1917; Salvemini, *Mazzini*, Roma, 1925; A. Galante Garrone, *Filippo Buonarroti e i rivofuzionari dell'Ottocento*, Torino, Einaudi 1972, it whose last chapter is dedicated to Buonarroti and Mazzini. By the same author, *L'incontro con il sansimonismo*, in *Mazzini vivo*, Bari, Centro librario, 1973, pp. 27-33.

poor, slaves, unhappy: speak to us of material improvements, of freedom, of happiness. Tell us whether we are condemned to always suffer or whether we must in turn enjoy. Preach Duty to our masters, to the classes who are above us and who, by treating us like machines, monopolise the goods that are due to all. To us, speak of rights: speak of ways to claim them; speak of our power. Let us have our existence recognised; then speak to us of duties and sacrifice. This is what many of our workers say, and they follow doctrines and associations that correspond to their desire; not forgetting only one thing, and that is that the language invoked by them has been held for fifty years without having yielded a minimum of material improvement to the condition of the workers.

The concluding words are very effective:

'You are free and therefore responsible. From this moral freedom, descends your right to political freedom, your duty to win it and keep it inviolate, the duty in others not to undermine it.' One cannot therefore consider Mazzini a romantic revolutionary.

Mazzini founded the first Italian political party.[55] His idea of fatherland, the values of brotherhood, concord, solidarity are the factors that Alberto M. Banti has brought together in the so-called Risorgimento canon.[56]

The question has been asked whether his insistence on brotherhood is not the result of his affiliation with Freemasonry. But the question is still open: Mazzini's myth has lent itself to appropriations from all sides and of all colours.[57] However, it is a fact that as early as the beginning of the eighteenth century, when the new creed spread in Germany and then gradually throughout Europe, (secular) brotherhood joined the religious brotherhood, an initiatory bond was created, the bonds between members were strengthened, but also the commitment to charity.[58] It is a commitment that corroborates the political one, to which Mazzini's apostolate is circumscribed, but which is always attentive to the precarious situation of the workers.

## §1.08    SOCIALISM AND THE LEGAL CULTURE

At the end of the century, new directions appear in the cultural scenario of jurists, one dictated by political reasons, the other by scientific reasons. The political reasons are

---

55. Della Peruta, *Nazionalità e Risorgimento fino alla rivoluzione del '48*, in Niccolò Tommaseo e Firenze. *Atti del Convegno di studi* (Firenze, 12-13 febbraio 1999), edited by R. Turchi and Volpi, Olschki, Florence, 2000, p. 9. 5 *Un Italiano [G. Mazzini], D'una letteratura europea*, in 'Antologia', XXXVI (1829), November-December, pp. 91-120; *Del dramma storico*, 'Antologia', XXXIX (1830), July, pp. 37-53 and XLIV (1831), October, pp. 26-55.
56. Banti, *La Nazione del Risorgimento. Parentela, santità e onore alle origini dell'Italia unita*, Einaudi, Turin, 2000. By the same author *L'onore della nazione. Identità sessuali e violenza nel nazionalismo europeo dal XVIII secolo alla Grande Guerra*, Einaudi, Turin, 2005 and the volume of Storia d'Italia. Annali 22; *Il Risorgimento*, edited by A.M. Banti and P. Ginsborg, Einaudi, Turin, 2007.
57. Giarrizzo, *Massoneria e Risorgimento*, 'Hiram' 1999 no. 2 pp. 43-46; Angelo Mattioni co-author of the book *La fraternità come principio di diritto pubblico*, Marzanati (Author), Mattioni (Author) ed. Città Nuova, 2007.
58. Novarino & Rosso, *Solidarity and Initiatory Path: Freemasonry's Commitment Against Old and New Poverty*, Rome, 2018.

mainly connected to the rise of the 'fourth state', whose class consciousness is stimulated by the works of socialist exponents, the anarchist current, the Marxist current, and the humanist current. Mass industrialisation opened up new economic and social problems: the abandonment of the countryside and urbanisation, agrarian backwardness and worker exploitation, the harassment of farm labourers and struggles to reduce working hours, the fight against illiteracy and the exploitation of women and minors, the demand for wage improvements, social security guarantees for accidents, illness and old age. It is the history of Italy that intends to move towards a role as a European-level nation with colonial ambitions.

These political ferments gave rise to the first social legislation, the 'legal socialism' movement, the solidarist movement informed by the Church's social doctrine summarised in the encyclical *Rerum Novarum*, the movements that attributed to law an ameliorative and corrective power for mankind in which human justice is illuminated by the light of faith and goodness. The rulings of the 'bon juge Magnaud' are the most prominent symbol of this.

But the great scientific discoveries and the spread of Darwinism and organicistic conceptions of society cast a new light on legal science: law is considered the form of a 'living organism'.

Scientism and scientific positivism so strongly influenced the science of criminal law that it became a benchmark throughout Europe.

Civilists are also attracted to these movements, the most important of which is legal socialism, which is, however, short-lived. The others are even more short-lived.

Only recently has an accurate assessment of legal socialism been offered.[59] The bibliographic research[60] prepared for this critical reflection enumerates an impressive production that includes writings by leading exponents, such as those of Salvioli, Cimbali, D'Aguanno, Vanni and Vivante, as well as occasional adhesions, such as those of Brugi, Cogliolo, Gianturco, Barassi and Polacco, which are accompanied by the works and interventions of economists, natural and social science scholars and, of course, political scientists.

One of the merits of this direction is the methodological innovation, which consists precisely in bringing the jurist out of the empty and sterile chrysalis of formalisms to take cognisance of the real facts, forcing him to enter into dialogue with other exponents of the social sciences; the jurist must make himself available to modify his own vocabulary and conceptual categories in confrontation with the other social sciences.

This too is a sign of Italian originality, which succeeds in transforming the germs thrown by isolated foreign scholars into movement, into a cultural and reforming direction.

At the end of the century, Giuseppe Salvioli's first contributions emerged, including the lecture for the inauguration of the academic year at the University of

---

59. Sbriccoli, *Elementi per una bibliografia del socialismo giuridico italiano*, Milan, 1976.
60. Grossi coordinated the most complete and accurate research on this season in two volumes of the Quaderni fiorentini (Il socialismo giuridico, II/IV, 1974-1975); *see also* Alpa, *Diritto civile. Due secoli di storia*, Bologna, 2018.

Palermo on 9 November 1890; these were accompanied by Nani's critical writings. Immediately the controversy was ignited with a corrosive essay by A. Loria who criticised the way jurists dealt with social problems; it was a condemnation of innovative jurists. It was Loria who coined the label 'juridical socialism', which then also came into use abroad. The terminology is taken from Engels and Kautsky's polemic against Menger in the Neuezeit of 1887; in France, this expression will only be used from 1904. Loria sarcastically examined the proposals of socialist jurists in the pages of the most important journal of the time, La scienza del diritto privato; and in the same journal, Vidari and D'Aguanno replied to him.

Despite the harsh criticism, the movement took shape: Enrico Cimbali intervened shortly afterwards with Il diritto civile e il proletariato (Civil Law and the Proletariat) and Icilio Vanni in his lecture of 15 January 1894 on the practical function of philosophy and contemporary socialism; A. Labriola countered them. Labriola; Sorel also spoke; Vivante made it the subject of his inaugural speech at the University of Rome on 8 November 1902. Gioele Solari gives philosophical dignity to the discussion, which covers the individualist and socialist conceptions of private law. Only the volume on the first profile is published, the second will be published posthumously. The debate between proponents and critics continues, and among the critics, Sergio E. Panunzio stands out in particular, E. Bruni's book, *Socialism and Private Law*, and Donati's book, *Il Socialismo giuridico e la riforma del diritto*.

The translations of the volumes by the Austrian Anton Menger constitute the most significant reference point for the Italian jurists animating the movement.

It was a time of great intellectual as well as political ferment: it was precisely in those years that the works of Rudolf von Jhering, who fought abstract conceptualism, and those of Kantorowicz, who paved the way for the free-law movement, saw the light in Germany.

The state model advocated by Anton Menger is the democratic labour state: a state in which the social demands of the proletariat are met with reforms, not revolutions, with a balanced settlement of conflicting interests, with the peaceful and gradual distribution of land ownership and industrial profit. It is a state in which there is no overpowering of one class over the others and the system rests on two pillars: property and labour. Goods are divided into three categories: consumer goods, utilitarian goods, and capital goods. This is an innovation of great moment because until then the distinction – also known to jurists – was only relevant from a formal point of view, of the ownership of the right, without regard to the content or the doctrinal distinction of the resources, but above all with regard to their economic and social function: on consumer goods (as constructed by legal science: Code civil, Articles 1874 and 1892; Allgemeines bürgerliches Gesetzbuch (ABGB) § 301, Cod.civ.it. Article 1819; Bürgerliches Gesetzbuch (BGB) § 92), the right of private property is exercised; on utilitarian goods, which are worn out but not consumed, such as dwelling houses, parks, gardens, libraries, there must not be a right of full ownership, but a right of usufruct; on instrumental goods (or means of production, as economists call them) that serve to produce other goods (such as agricultural land, etc.) individual rights cannot insist, but only collective rights.

Menger then goes on to describe the systems of distribution of these goods; they are subjective, automatic and objective systems, linked to the right to the full appropriation of the product of labour by the provider.

In light of this project, which takes up Marxian ideas, albeit not in their entirety, Menger critically examines the categories of private law in light of a tempered socialism.

The rules contained in civil codes allow the master to dismiss the worker with impunity, the landlord to evict the tenant, the trader to use his economic power to harass the customer. In the private organisation of labour, the system of contract law is functional to the exploitation of the working classes; in contrast, in the organisation of social labour, within the framework of the democratic labour state, goods are distributed according to the above-mentioned criteria and the equal position of the contracting parties is re-established in the contractual discipline. The main defect of our bond law, Menger observes, 'is that the freedom of the contracting parties is in many cases only apparent, and this is especially evident in the wage contract, which is almost always concluded between the poor and the rich'.

Consistent with this premise, he proposes to regulate successions, which, instead of encompassing all types of property, are limited to individual estates. Menger also favours legitimate succession over testamentary succession, which he admits only in the absence of legitimators. The limitations on the testator's will are justified by the energy of handing down basic economic resources to the family unit.

With regard to the family, in all the codes of the time organised with the authoritarian pyramid model that excludes the wife from decisions and responsibilities, Menger – in favour of free love – is concerned about the legal position of women: women have their own 'right to existence', their own right to work and their own free disposal of property. Children must be taken care of by the state; to illegitimate children, Menger ensures a position equal to that of legitimate children. It is a legal reform project that tends to repair social injustices but also to recover the dignity of man, in all his roles, within the family, the work organisations, the community. A modern project, which will wait more than half a century to be realised, even if not explicitly, in the liberal-democratic constitutions of the post-Second World War period.

It is understandable, then, why the dialectical materialists do not appreciate Menger's thought: he challenges the idea of law as a superstructure that underlies Marxian thought but also underlies historicism, and believes that law can have a propulsive, not exclusively notarial, function for the improvement of social relations: the transformation of private law can lead to the realisation of a democratic and socialist state. Associated with the political component is the 'social' component and above all the critical component, which exerts important pressure at the time on the renewal of the method of analysing civil law institutions. It is an innovative and appreciable vision, even if it sins of pan-Giurism: Menger's entire construction is contained in the one and only juridical perspective because 'law is a political instrument for the exercise of social power' and the state is an instrument for the distribution of economic power and freedom, as well as a guarantor of the fundamental economic rights that are the right to the integral product of labour, the right to existence, and the right to work.

Menger's discourse based on legal arguments is intended for jurists and is therefore marred by a twofold weakness: it may not be considered well-founded in law, but above all, it appears to lack a concrete and articulate foundation of a political-institutional nature, since it is too labile if it is to propose a new model of social organisation. In short, it was a 'techno-bureaucratic state organisation in which almost all power was concentrated in the executive and almost all social life was absorbed by the state'. More. His convinced statism could not find adherents either among the advocates of scientific, revolutionary or anarchist socialism, because the proposals appeared too modest and compromising, incapable of radically changing the status quo; nor, of course, among the advocates of the free market.

Cimbali's ideas would have had no better fate either. In his case, it was also a question of method: impressed by the new techniques and the organicistic conception of society, Cimbali coined curious definitions of property, contract, and possession; they were affected by one and the other, and led to conclusions that were difficult to perceive.

His conception of the state also appears ambiguous, oscillating between a legitimising or interventionist conception and an oppressive one.

The openness of jurists to the social sciences, to critical reflection, and to the demands of the oppressed, however, highlights the selfish spirit shared by the civil codes of the nineteenth century.

The individualism of the 1865 civil code, the subject of an admirable essay by Gioele Solari, is the target of the cultural militancy of Giuseppe Salvioli, one of the greatest legal historians of the time. It is a class-based, bourgeois code that dictated the rules of civil society in a unified Italy. It is no coincidence that Salvioli's criticism of the Italian code anticipates the criticism levelled at the Code civil by French jurists on the occasion of the first centenary celebrations. Well-founded criticisms, of which much has been said. What is targeted is the legal dimension that exalts the selfishness of the individual to the detriment of the interests of the community, which Salvioli calls 'social interests'.

To resolve this issue, the right balance must be found between the individual and the collective, between authority and freedom, between individual well-being and collective improvement. The criterion-value that Salvioli identifies is solidarity. Solidarity 'is the law of the physical world and the law of human society. Social life is an ensemble of intersecting solidarities. Man is not isolated, but lives, works, produces, possesses, insofar as he is in the midst of other men, to whom he must coordinate his action. Just as every good comes from society, so every act must have a social value, a social function. Hence the norm of life and the ethical ideal must consist in the composition of interests'. The scientific basis of solidarity is work, or rather, the dimension of social work, according to the theorisation of Durkheim whose work saw the light in 1899.

The dissemination of socialist ideas in the world of law, a world no longer entrenched in form and no longer describable in terms of abstract formulas, is also entrusted to minor thinkers, to marginal authors, to honest if unoriginal militants. An example of this is the essay on Socialism and Private Law by Enrico Bruni.

This book is divided into two parts: one, which constitutes the theoretical framework, discusses the essence, content and forms of socialism and social reforms; the other deals specifically with the evolution of private law, and proposes an analysis of the fundamental institutes reread in a socialist perspective. Bruni's main interlocutor is once again Anton Menger, to whom he acknowledges the 'most organic conception that socialism (...) has given until his time'. But Bruni discussed the ideas of many other jurists in whom he recognised socialist yearnings or at least humanitarian values such as Barassi, Chironi, Cimbali, Cogliolo, Gabba, Salvioli, Scialoja, Stammler, Vadala-Papale, Venezian, Vidari and Vivante.

Bruni is an ardent supporter of the 'socialists of the chair', of the exponents of non-materialistic socialism with an economic content; he places legal socialism alongside it, of which he identifies – with an inclusion that has attracted criticism today – the major exponents in the brightest figures of the turn of the century: Menger, Stammler, Sombart, Jellinek, Gierke and Duguit.

He gives an appreciable definition of legal socialism, which, in the moderation of its proposals, highlights its possible continuity with the existing legal order destined to be adapted to necessity but not revolutionary. In Cosentini's definition of legal socialism, the legislative means are 'designed to strengthen the social position of the proletariat and to introduce those reforms that do not transmit the social organism ex novo (since in every legal system, alongside the new there always persists a large part of the old) but reconcile the old constitutions consecrated by the laws with the new social needs and ideals'.

This is why, since it is not a revolutionary socialism based on class struggle, this direction will be considered 'dangerous' by materialist socialists and will be vehemently opposed and derided by them.

The reform project from within the system concerns both the adaptation of the civil code to the new requirements and the intervention of the state with special legislation. The discourse unfolds starting from the criticism of the regulation of private law, which presents, according to the expression used by Salvioli, 'social defects'; he clarifies the ideological matrix of the civil codes and insists above all on the need to recover the value of work in individual and social relations. Having then examined the programmes of reforms proposed by the socialists in politics, Bruni insists on the need to bring the legal system into line with social needs: hence the focus on the work of the Commission for the general reform of private law legislation, set up by Hon. Gallo, then Minister of Justice, with the decree of 15 September 1906.

It is a commission composed of, among others, civilists such as Bensa, Chironi, Filomusi Guelfi, Gabba, and Polacco, but also includes jurists of different training and backgrounds such as Salvioli, Scialoja, Mortara and Orlando.

The Civil Code as an instrument of legal organisation is not abandoned, but it is considered outdated in its original version. Its necessity is felt to such an extent that one wants to see *in* it, *in nuce,* even if not yet explicit, the new social ideals. Bruni's aim is to show that already in the codes of the early nineteenth century, there are anticipations of socialist ideas or at least rules that temper the protection of individual interests; examples of this are the limits placed on private property in the public interest, the inversion of the burden of proof in favour of the worker in matters of contractual liability, the introduction of objective liability for professional risk in matters of civil liability. The sampling of other legal experiences is full of suggestions and innovations. In-depth comparative analyses of the German and French legal situations enable Bruni to propose regulatory changes in the area of employment contracts in industry and agriculture, as well as in the areas of succession and family.

Hence the conclusion that the reform of private law is a component of the reform of law in the socialist sense: 'reform', not 'distortion' because reforming private law does not mean making the individual subservient to society or to a particular class, even if it is the labour class, but rather it means finding a way to reconcile 'the highest perfecting of the individual with the highest general interest'.

The position of the other exponents of legal socialism is even more moderate. But each opening caused a stir, given the demonisation of Marxism and the staunch defence of the established order advocated by liberal and conservative jurists of the time.

However, it is important to note that at the end of the nineteenth century, a new area of the legal system began to emerge, labour law.[61]

## §1.09 COOPERATION AND THE COOPERATIVE MOVEMENT

One of the most significant aspects of the application of the solidarity principle can be seen in the origins and development of cooperation, the aggregation of people who, by working together, with work cooperatives, or by procuring the essential resources for life and family, and trading them at affordable prices, with consumer cooperatives, share activities, advantages and responsibilities, which they share among all cooperators. Normally, the legal forms that these initiatives take do not correspond to those of profit-oriented initiatives.

In the business world, cooperatives take ad hoc legal forms.

Despite being an expression of the principle of solidarity, cooperativism is ignored in recent works dedicated to this theme, both from a historical and philosophical perspective, and from a political and juridical perspective,[62] even though proponents of solidarism have been at times in history and in some countries even protagonists of cooperativism, and even though the cooperative movement, from its very beginning, has set itself as an alternative line to economic liberalism and capitalist competition, which by its very nature is individualistic and selfish. Contributing one's own labour to achieve common goals, sharing benefits and responsibilities on an equal footing, devoting oneself to the activity with charitable aims, not strictly related to

---

61. Cazzetta, *Leggi sociali, cultura giuridica e origini della scienza giuslavoristica in Italia fra Otto e Novecento*, in *Quad. fior.*, 1988, no. 171, p. 154 ss.
62. Neither Stjerno, *supra*, nor Zoll. *supra*, nor Blais, *supra*, mention it.

remuneration, are all drives that collide with the construction of a free market in which opposing forces compete and are indifferent to the well-being of the members. Cooperativism thus lies in an area of thought and action very close to socialism and communitarianism, so much so that we find its expressions in the secular world of the solidarity and reformist left and in the Christian religious world.

In the first decades of the nineteenth century, one of the pioneers of cooperativism was Robert Owen, to whom we owe the foundation in England of associations with a mutualistic purpose, which had drawn up plans for social reform in the sense of solidarity. His teaching is taken up by William King, and in Germany by Viktor Huber, in Italy by Giuseppe Mazzini. Cooperativism developed extensively in France, to which Fourier and Proudhon made essential contributions.

Already in the first decades of the nineteenth century, cooperation, which spread rapidly, presented more sophisticated forms of organisation: it was not limited to producing directly or buying for resale, products made available to members at affordable prices. The Rochdale Statutes, promoted in 1844 by Owen, foresaw a minimum remuneration for the capital collected, its use in a virtuous manner, and the creation of profits reinvested in the business so that the new dimension included not only consumer and labour cooperatives, but also building cooperatives, and even cooperatives dedicated to banking, finance and cooperative activities.[63] In each country, cooperation took on particular connotations, as happened for example in the Rhineland with the spread of agricultural cooperatives promoted by Friedrich Wilhelm Raiffeisen.

The relationship between the cooperative movement and political movements oriented towards class solidarity was characterised at times by great convergence and at times by friction and opposition. Cooperatives were predominantly promoted by socialist or Catholic activists. At the end of the First World War, cooperatives also gathered veterans, small traders, small landowners, and became a fertile field for Fascism, which exploited their proximity to the working class to gain support.

After the Second World War and the advent of the Republic, cooperation found a place in the democratic regime, being even mentioned in the Constitution (Article 45 c.1): 'The Republic recognises the social function of cooperation of a mutual nature and without ends of private speculation. The law promotes and encourages its growth with the most suitable means and ensures, with appropriate controls, its character and aims.'

The history of cooperative societies is very complex and transcends the boundaries of this work. Suffice it to point out, however, that in Italy, the liberalist model has blurred the mutualist boundaries, also in order to favour competition between enterprises. In fact, a distinction was introduced between cooperatives with prevalent

---

63. An accurate illustration of the origins of the cooperative movement and its epiphanies is offered by Lama, *Cooperazione, Enc. Italiana*, 1948, *ad vocem Cooperazione*. The same entry in the Encyclopaedia edited by Lorenzoni, Lama and Vuoli (1931) is also very accurate, even if it is affected by the political climate of the time in which it was written. *See also* Borzaga and Ianes, *The Economy of Solidarity*, Rome, 2006.

mutuality – which are eligible for subsidies and facilities – and cooperatives with non-prevalent mutuality, which are not.

In a system such as the European one, in which profit aims are balanced with fundamental rights and social needs, the cooperative model could not but be viewed favourably. Hence the plan to standardise its legal forms in a single model, the European Cooperative Society (SCE).

To complete the picture, account must be taken of the solidaristic activity carried out by the non-profit organisations that make up the third sector, and the forms of enterprise that allocate their profits to support social purposes.[64]

## §1.10    WOMEN'S SOLIDARITY

The success of the term and the principle in the nineteenth century cannot be justified without taking into account the role of women in society. It was in this century that it established itself irreversibly, amidst difficulties of all kinds and at the cost of a commitment verging on heroism and self-denial. And yet one of the neglected aspects in the reconstruction of the roots of the principle of solidarity is women's solidarity, understood both in the sense of witnessing the ideas and propulsive activity of solidarity and as a feeling and bond between women, for the affirmation of rights and the fight against gender discrimination. Both perspectives are particularly important for the affirmation of the principle of solidarity.

The first perspective is less known and ploughed into than the second.

It began on the battlefields where modern nursing was established, in the care of the wounded. Florence Nightingale pioneered it, carrying out her apostolate of ideas, and dedicating herself to the care of the wounded first in the clashes between the patriots of the Roman Republic and the French troops, in Rome in 1849, and then in the Crimean War, in Scutati, in 1854. Numerous women have since dedicated themselves to medicine, biology, and the care of the handicapped. Aside from the originality of their ideas, they have also belonged to a gender considered a minority. Hence the connection between solidarity work and the defence of women's rights. Ernestina Paper and Maria Montessori are remembered, the former for caring for children and the latter for creating a teaching method that harmoniously develops child psychology. Elizabeth Garrett Anderson founded the women's hospital, and Marie Curie revolutionised physics and medicine through radiotherapy. More well-known are the women who militated in associations, trade unions and political parties to defend gender rights, from Olimpia de Gouges to the militants of the Suffragette Movement, Susan B. Anthony and Elizabeth Cady Stanton, or militated for noble causes, such as Cristina Trivulzio di Belgioioso and Annamaria Mozzoni.[65]

---

64. Conte, *L'impresa responsabile*, Milan, 2018.
65. Not to mention antifascist women, women who served in the Resistance, and women who were part of the Constituent Assembly: Addis Saba, *Partigiane. Le donne della Resistenza*, Milan, 2007; Morelli (ed.), *Le donne della Costituente*, Rome-Bari, 2007.

In our experience, anchored on equal opportunities, women's rights have been affirmed mainly in the area of employment[66] and in the regulation of the family.[67]

In other experiences, the battle for rights and in particular the battle for women's rights has even founded a current in legal philosophy, Feminist legal theory.[68]

The legal culture of women's rights is first and foremost a culture of equality and thus of emancipation; then it becomes a culture of equal opportunities; and finally a culture of difference, with regard not only to gender differences but also to those of ethnicity.

The strands of thought in which the principle of solidarity is embodied are innumerable, solidarity appears to us like a karst river, which at times disappears into the bowels of the earth and then re-emerges impetuously, splits into many branches and then lands in the constitutions in which it finds a safe riverbed.

---

66. Ballestrero, *Dalla tutela alla parità. La legislazione italiana sul lavoro delle donne*, Il Mulino, Bologna, 1979; *Donne (Lavoro delle)*, *Digesto*, IV edizione, UTET, Torino, 1990; *Le azioni positive tra eguaglianza e diritto diseguale*, in Legge 10 aprile 1991, n.125; *Azioni positive per la realizzazione della parità uomo-donna nel lavoro*, Commentario sistematico a cura di M.V. Ballestrero e T. Treu, in *Le nuove leggi civile commentate*, 1994, n.1, p. 11.

67. *See* Bessone, sub art. 29 Cost., in Branca, *Commentario alla Costituzione*, Bologna-Roma, 1976; Ferrando, *Note sull'uguaglianza morale e giuridica dei coniugi*, in *Politica del Diritto*, 1990, pp. 509 ff.ID., *Diritto di Famiglia*, IV ed., Bologna, 2020.

68. Mossman, *Feminism and Legal Method*, in Australian J. L. & Soc., 3, 1986, at pp. 30-52; Lacey, *Feminist Legal Theory*, in Oxford J. Legal Stud. 9, 1989, 383; Bartlett and Kennedy, *Feminist Legal Theory. Readings in Law and Gender*, London, 1991; MacKinnon, *Toward Feminist Jurisprudence* in *Feminist Legal Theory: Foundations*, D. Kelly Weisberg ed., Philadelphia, 1993, 427-436; Eichner, *On Postmodern Legal Theory*, in Harv. C.R.-C.L. L. Rev. 36(1), 2001; *Feminist Legal Theory*, in Reza Banakar and Max Travers eds, *An Introduction to Law and Social Theory*, London, 2002, 135-154; Levit, Verchick & Minow, *Feminist Legal Theory & A Primer*, New York, 2016.

# CHAPTER 2

# The Concept of Solidarity and the Third Way Between Socialism and Capitalism

## §2.01 FOREWORD

Beyond the legal aspects of solidarity in the law of obligations and in the debt relationship, where the roots of the term and concept are universally found, and beyond its pregnant ideal content, solidarity has been used to achieve very different ends. Hence the ambiguous contours it presents.

Solidarity evokes the altruistic feeling of *pity* for those who find themselves in a detrimental situation due to poverty, illness, old age, and status in general; solidarity is synonymous with generosity and economic aid, *charity* for those who suffer and are in destitution; solidarity is a feeling of comradeship and *connectedness*, in groups, associations, brotherhoods and economic categories; solidarity is class *bonding*; solidarity means *cooperation* within groups, between workers and employers, and internationally between states; solidarity is *alliance* between generations; solidarity is co-belligerence and economic and military *support* between states.

## §2.02 SOLIDARITY IN THE POLITICAL THOUGHT OF LEON BOURGEOIS

Leon Bourgeois stands out in solidarity studies. The reasons for this success are manifold. First, he is one of the first authors – among jurists above all, since he was a lawyer who had embraced a political career – to use the concept of solidarity to find a foundation for society. Moreover, the exaltation of solidarity allowed him to give political answers to the social demands coming from the working class, and to trade unionist and socialist claims. Solidarity, for Bourgeois, constitutes a third way compared to liberalism and socialism to arrive at social peace.

The rise of the Radical Republican Party in France at the end of the nineteenth century, first alongside the Socialist Party and then independently of it, and even in opposition to it, was achieved by placing this principle in the table of social values in order to gain popular consensus.

The political function of this principle, at the dawn of the twentieth century, did not escape Stefano Rodotà, who in his book on solidarity starts his discourse by moving from the republican ideology of the Revolution and then its developments. Solidarism is the means to give new legitimacy to the Republic.[69] Leon Bourgeois is recalled as one of the founders of solidarist thought, also thanks to the reconstruction of this political-philosophical direction that constitutes the terrain of extensive and in-depth studies in French culture at the end of the twentieth century and the first decade of the 2000s.[70] But it is Rodotà himself who points out the oversimplification of those who believe that the origins of the term in the legal lexicon, and then its use, again in legal terms, and its translation into language and political paraphernalia, have given rise to a 'legalised solidarity' that has its own autonomous development with respect to political and social solidarity.[71] In other words, while solidarity found its nourishment at the end of the nineteenth century in the studies of Comte, Leroux and Durkheim and in the pamphlets of Bourgeois, it also expanded vigorously thanks to Catholic solidaristic thought and the struggles of trade unions and parties of socialist inspiration.[72]

The influence of Bourgeois is considered rather marginal by Steinar Stjerno in his reconstruction of the post-war political thought that influenced the models of the EU, with Emile Durkheim rather being credited with giving a scientific framework to this social principle.[73] Other authors give it greater prominence: Rainer Zoll makes it the founder of the social model that strengthens the cohesion of the people;[74] Marie-Calude Blais[75] and Michel Borgetto[76] make it the coryphaeus of solidarity in nineteenth-century social philosophy and constitutional law in France.[77]

Beyond the 'chauvinism' typical of French scholars, and the appreciation for having 'rediscovered' the persuasive attractiveness of the concept of solidarity, Bourgeois' thought should not be overestimated. And on the other hand, his lack of notoriety outside France is largely understandable and justifiable. Indeed, Blais herself shows that the principle was already widely employed in the works and discourses of philosophers of politics or society at the dawn of the nineteenth century and in the second half of that century. Bourgeois's merit, if anything, was that he found a space between liberalism and socialism to channel social demands into a system that, by introducing the first affirmations of the welfare state, could contain the disintegrating thrusts of the Fourth Estate, which rightly demanded greater social justice in the face of the brutality of the treatment meted out by the 'ironworkers'. Insisting on solidarity

---

69. Rodotà, *supra*, p. 21, where the quotation from Chevallier and Cochart, *Presentation*, in Chevallier (ed.), La solidarité: un sentiment republicain? Paris, 1992, p. 5.
70. *See* in particular Blais, *supra*.
71. Rodotà, *supra*, pp. 41 ff.
72. *Ibid.*, pp. 62 ff.
73. Stjerno, *supra*, pp. 146 ff.
74. Stoll, *supra*, Ch. IX.
75. Blais, *supra*, Ch. I.
76. Borgetto, *supra*, 356 ff.
77. Radisson, *La philosophie en France au xixe siecle*, Paris, 1867, repr. 1889.

between the classes and on the commitment of each in the social aggregate could become the means to foster progress and give governments greater stability. The impression one gets is that the principle, as elaborated by Bourgeois, was successful not because of its intrinsic strength, but because of the personal political success of Bourgeois himself and the Radical Party he headed. Indeed, he was a Member of Parliament for many years, President of the Council, founder of the League of Nations, and even earned the Nobel Peace Prize.

## §2.03   BOURGEOIS' ARGUMENTS

In his booklet published in 1896 by the Librerie de la Société de la Société des Gens de Lettre Bourgeois moves from social-political ideas to describe the scientific doctrine of natural solidarity and arrive at a definition of the practical doctrine of social solidarity.

The sources he draws on are the nineteenth-century thinkers who laid the foundations of romantic political philosophy and the new science, sociology: Fouillee's Social Property, Izoulet's Modern Society (*la Cité*), Funk-Brentano's Man and his Destiny.[78] Its aim is to find a median way between individualism and socialism, between selfish property and collective property. Work is the legitimising factor of man's permanence in society, solidarity between human beings is opposed to the struggle for survival.[79] He finds a justification for this thesis in nature: taking up Charles Gide's thought, he justifies heredity, adaptation, selection, integration and disintegration as aspects of the general law of mutual dependence and universal life. He explains the contribution of individuals to common life with these natural facts. Natural society is an organism in which individuals are the individual parts. From natural solidarity, he then moves on to social solidarity. The human journey shows the emergence of moral principles, Christian charity and philosophical fraternity, which mark the progress from the philosophers of antiquity, of Athens and Rome, to the philosophers of modern times. He finds in Fouillée the justification of social bonds, of the practical doctrine of society, which is the moral rule, and Kantianly observes that man is both a means and an end, he is the unity and the part of the whole, he is the individual and the species. Following Izoulet he states that it is not the socialisation of property, but the socialisation of the person that is the solution to the social problem.[80] He distances himself from Rousseau, whom he acknowledges as having theorised the existence of a contractual bond between individuals. However, whereas for Rousseau, man is born free but the struggle for existence ends up putting him in chains – the strongest subjugating the weakest – with 'the total alienation of each associate with his or her rights in favour of the community', his doctrine of solidarity tends to make the freedom of the individual stronger in common action 'freely permitted by all'.[81]

---

78. Marie-Claude Blais retraces this history of ideas with an in-depth examination of their works: *see La solidarité, supra*, Ch. II.
79. Bourgeois, *Solidarité*, p. 16.
80. *Ibid.*, p. 27 n.1.
81. *Ibid.*, p. 30 n.1.

Fine words, but words, far removed from the scientific elaboration of the economy and society by Carlo Marx, who is never mentioned, even though his works had been circulating in France for decades.[82] Marx himself, by the way, had branded solidarity as a 'convenient abstraction from class oppositions'.[83] But neither does he discuss the ideas of Emilio Durkheim, whose *Division du travail social*, with its distinction between mechanical solidarity and organic solidarity had been published in 1893. There is no mention of Giuseppe Mazzini, although Bourgeois insists a great deal on the duty to contribute to the satisfaction of common needs. Perhaps this was because Mazzini had given an unorthodox reading of the 1848 revolution, had broken relations with the socialists, had cultivated and then broken off his relationship with Georges Sand, had theorised the union of the Young Europe that seemed to clash with the destinies of France, all events that had undermined his popularity in France.[84] Mazzini's political mystique could not fit in with Bourgeois' political projects.

But neither are the historical facts that marked the redemption of the working class examined:[85] e.g., the Anzin miners' strike of 1884, from which Zola drew material for his *Germinal*, which came out in 1885 and won great popularity; the birth of syndicalism and workers' cooperation.[86] *Solidarité* is not a scientific book, nor a book of historical analysis, but a pamphlet, not even an educated one, which picks up a few ideas offered as a viaticum to unravel an intermediate path between liberalism and socialism.

## §2.04    THE IDEOLOGICAL USE OF LEGAL CATEGORIES AND THE FALLACY OF BOURGEOIS' LEGAL ARGUMENTS

Bourgeois' political thought is enriched by legal arguments that deserve the applause of the jurists of the time.

The fourth chapter of the booklet on solidarity is devoted to 'man's debt to society' and the 'quasi-social contract'. It is the reinterpretation in simplified and original legal terms of the social foundation of the human aggregate carried out using the categories of private law, a sort of transfiguration of the legal relations arising not from the contract but from the *quasi-contract* as if it were possible to mechanically transplant technical concepts of private law relating to the debtor-creditor relationship into the field of public law and political philosophy concerning the organisation of society.

---

82. Louvrier, *Marx, le marxisme et les historiens de la Révolution française au XXE siècle*, Cahiers d'histoire, 2007, pp. 102 ff.; Sperber, *Karl Marx homme du XIX siècle*, Paris, 2007.
83. Marx & Engels, *Opera Omnia*, Rome 1960, vol. VII, p. 21.
84. Ignace, *Giuseppe Mazzini et les démocrates français: débats et reclassements au lendemain du 'printemps des peuples'*, in *Revue d'histoire du XIXe siècle*, 2008, pp. 36 ff.
85. Frader, *Femmes, genre et mouvement ouvrier en France aux XIXe et XXe siècles: bilan et perspectives de recherche*, Clio, 1996, pp. 3 ff.; Boll, Prost, Robert, *L'invention des syndicalismes*, Paris, 2020.
86. Dohet, *Le mouvement coopératif: histoire, questions et renouveau*, in *Courier hebddu* CRISP, 2018, 5-6, pp. 58 ff.

We must not forget – Bourgeois was a lawyer – that the Code civil provided for the regulation of joint and several liability with two provisions derived from Roman law:

> L'obligation est solidaire entre plusieurs créanciers lorsque le titre donne expressé-ment à chacun d'eux le droit de demander le paiement du total de la créance, et que le paiement fait à l'un d'eux libère le débiteur, encore que le bénéfice de l'obligation soit partageable et divisible entre les divers créanciers.
> Art. 1198.-Il est au choix du débiteur de payer à l'un ou l'autre des créanciers solidaires, tant qu'il n'a pas été prévenu par les poursuites de l'un d'eux.
> Néanmoins, la remise qui n'est faite que par l'un des créanciers solidaires ne libère le débiteur que pour la part de ce créancier.[87]

Bourgeois does not refer to the two provisions of the *Code civil*, but to the concept of *joint and several debts* when, making the first translation, he argues that each person, as a man, is 'indebted to all', and concludes: 'it is the cost of freedom'. In other words, man is not born to live in isolation, but in society, and therefore has natural moral debts that link him to his ancestors and descendants: 'He is born a debtor to human association. Each passing generation must make use of what it has found through the merit of nature or ancestors and must pass it on to future generations, having preserved and having to return those goods in their integrity.'[88] There is a *contract* between generations in which services, costs and profits are exchanged. It is the history of mankind that explains why everyone with his own efforts must contribute to the development of civilisation.[89]

The contract freely discussed and faithfully executed by the parties is the result of the consent of their free and equal wills; the prerequisite for this consent is the quasi-contract that founds society.[90]

On the freedom and equality of wills, there would be much to discuss, because the *Code civil's* formal definition of contract is one thing, its translation into practical and social terms is another, which Bourgeois could not hide, especially with regard to labour and agrarian contracts. But the use of the concept of *quasi-contract*, an archaeological remnant of a notion from Roman law that in unjust enrichment and the repayment of undue payments identifies a source of obligation, is astonishing.

Here Bourgeois, in a footnote, refers to legal doctrine, in particular the commen-tary to the Code civil by Aubry and Rau, who had used the quasi-contract institute to

---

87. With the 2016-2018 reform of the Civil Code, the above articles were deleted and replaced by a simplified provision that reads:

> La solidarité entre créanciers permet à chacun d'eux d'exiger et de recevoir le paiement de toute la créance. Le paiement fait à l'un d'eux, qui en doit compte aux autres, libère le débiteur à l'égard de tous. Le débiteur peut payer l'un ou l'autre des créanciers solidaires tant qu'il n'est pas poursuivi par l'un d'eux.

88. Bourgeois, Soldarité, p. 37.
89. *Ibid.*, p. 38.
90. *Ibid.*, p. 39.

justify the patrimonial liability of partners in the de facto company.[91] Indeed, the institution had been revitalised in a very relevant *affaire* decided by the Court of Cassation in 1892.[92]

Bourgeois, continuing the analogy between human society and civil law society, holds that there are common debts contracted between the members, which retroactively affect the past, so that just as the members of a common law society carry out an activity even without having signed a contract, they derive profits from it but contract debts. The debts, in the case of human societies, are to ascendants and descendants, but also to other men in the human consortium, because by living in society one acquires benefits and thus incurs debts (which the author considers natural and moral).

There is mastery in the unscrupulous use of these categories. But there is also confusion: a contract is not a quasi-contract; the moral debt of a man living in society cannot be confused with the sums of money subject to obligations to creditors. And then there is an incorrect use of the quasi-contract category as well as of the principle of legal solidarity. Of the former, because the quasi-contract gives rise to restitution for unjust enrichment, or the restitution of payment made unjustly not to the creditor but to a third party; the latter because it is hard to see why the debtor (in the social sense) should pay for all the other debtors.

One does not have to be a fine jurist to understand the fallacies of this reasoning. And yet the shifted use of the quasi-contract breaches the consideration of colleagues and politicians of the day.

One should ask oneself why this is so.

Somewhat simplistically, one could reply that it was the idea of solidarity itself that was making inroads into an incandescent political climate, which had to find a way out of the social claims of the working class. Or, that the appeal to notions of law, and to the *Code civil*, a monument of legal wisdom, reinforced on the side of prestige and coercion an idea that was used to explain the political relations at the basis of human consortium.

By examining the reactions of the time, one can better understand why Bourgeois' manipulative fantasy was not unmasked.[93] On the contrary, Bougler, in 1907, made it the pivot of his elaboration of solidarist thought.[94]

And even today, even outside the courtly confines of French culture, Bourgeois enjoys sympathy because, as J.E.S. points out. Hayward points out, 'despite its theoretical fragility, its practical programme was inspired by and appropriate to the

---

91. Zachariae, *Cours de droit civil français*, in *Revue et augmenté par Aubry et Rau*, Brussels, 1850; Aubry et Rau, *Cors de droit civil français d'aprs la méthode de Zachariae*, Paris, 1897-1922.
92. The case did not concern the de facto company, but the enrichment of the landowner who had produced wheat in large quantities thanks to the chemicals purchased by the tenant farmer who had been dismissed (Cour de Cassation, Reg. 15 juin 1892, in D. P.92.1.596, s. 93.1.281 with note by Lassè. Aubry and Rau expand the principle to de facto societies, in which the partners get rich by working, together, but also contract debts with creditors).
93. Andler, C. (1897), *Du quasi-contrat social et de M. Léon Bourgeois*, in *Revue de métaphysique et de morale*, t. 4, n° 4, pp. 520-530.
94. *Le solidarisme*, Paris, 1907.

political and social needs of a society in transition between individualism and non-interventionist liberalism and statist socialism, just as economic liberalism had ensured the transition from corporatism and mercantilism to free enterprise, to laisser faire, laisser passer'.[95] Hence the indulgent consideration of Stefano Rodotà[96] and the in-depth quotation dedicated to him by Pietro Costa in his history of citizenship in Europe.[97]

The prominence given in these pages to Bourgeois is not equal to the depth of his thought, which remains quite superficial, but is rather justified by the relevance he had in the society of his time.

## §2.05  SOLIDARITY IN DURKHEIM

Indeed, it is Durkheim who deserves the credit for giving scientific foundation to the concept of solidarity. Beyond the romantic theses, a few years before Bourgeois' *pamphlet*, he prints the work that will constitute the consolidation, after Comte's seeds, of the new science, sociology as a branch of knowledge, the science that studies the foundations of society. Durkheim finds them in the division of social labour. Solidarity is understood in a dual sense: *mechanical* solidarity is the bond that unites men from the beginning of their existence on Earth and is composed of beliefs, feelings, and collective values.[98] Social rules, the division of power, property and goods, and the division of *labour* arise from living together. Everyone's contribution to the well-being of society is given by work; coexistence, with its stratifications, implies social differentiation. It is *organic* solidarity. This is the point of transition from the romantic conception, which is still alluded to in Bourgeois' thought, to the scientific conception of the principle: the moral rules, unlike what Bourgeois thinks, do not coincide with social change, morality is segmentary, and in order to bring it back to unity, it is necessary to work on acculturation, so that human brotherhood corresponds to a concrete, effective ideal of social equality, not just boasted about or found in fragile legal categories constructed to solve problems of a different nature.

## §2.06  DUGUIT, GURVITCH AND LÉVY

The innovations posted by the founders of sociology find their counterpoint in the works of the founders of the new constitutional law.

---

95. *The Official Social Philosophy of the French Third Republic: Léon Bourgeois and Solidarism,* Cambridge, 2008. This does not detract from the fact that Léon Bourgeois was also an able politician on the international scene, from the League for Nations to the creation of international arbitration: *see* Tixier, *The Legacy of Léon Bourgeois: From the Solidarist Doctrine to the Emergence of International Arbitration* 1; Justin Quinn Olmstead (ed.), *Reconsidering Peace and Patriotism during the First World War,* 2017. And *see also* Audier, S. (2007), *Léon Bourgeois: Fonder la solidarité,* Paris, Michalon, 122 p. Audier, S. (2010), *La pensée solidariste: Aux sources du modèle social républicain,* Paris, Presses Universitaires de France.
96. Rodotà, *Solidarietà, supra,* p. 62.
97. Costa, *Civitas,* vol. 3, Rome-Bari, 2001, pp. 74-81.
98. Durkheim, *supra,* p. 124.

The state, positive law and positive law are the subjects of the first work with which Leon Duguit builds the constitutional law of the Third Republic,[99] and at the same time the edifice on which his progressive ideas are grafted, which refer to the social tasks of the state, the social aspects of law, and the regulation of the social relations of 'civilised peoples'. It is also the response to the German theories of public law of C.F. von Gerber, Georg Jellinek, and Paul Laband, based on the subjective public rights that citizens claim vis-à-vis the state, the pivot of the 'construction of a "system" of public law of the functional nation-state, in a decidedly conservative and state-authoritarian sense, aimed at the preservation of a hegemonic social bloc from the threats of conflict'.[100] The modern state is the holder of a nation's sovereignty. 'State sovereignty is an objectively limited power, which is exercised in the general interest. It is a power exercised over persons, who are not in all respects subordinate, that is, over free men.' Duguit insists on social rule, which is founded on the value of solidarity. It is not the contract that founds society, but society, the human aggregate that uses the contract to give a constitution to individual relations.[101] It is not artificial theories that clothe relations between individuals with abstract legal forms that account for the real relations between individuals. Civil law is in daily conflict with the needs of individuals and must therefore adapt to them. Human consortium cannot be founded on individual rights, because modern man 'is a social product' and law 'is social, exclusively social'. Objective law and subjective law are just concepts that we use because they are useful, but they must not make us lose sight of the rule of law that is a rule of social behaviour, it is the rule of the social division of labour illustrated by Durkheim. And since social facts are those consciously willed, the social rule is the product of human will:[102] objective law is therefore an objective power of will, which cannot be described as Jellinek claims in dialectical terms between public and private subjective rights. And even the legal act, thought of as the expression of individual will, is not such if it is not a social act, an act that is expressed through the division of social labour. It thus tends to realise solidarity.[103] The individual act satisfies private interest, private selfishness, but is recognised by law insofar as it does not violate a social purpose.[104] The individual act, the manifestation of will directed to a legal effect, has no relevance to law if it does not fulfil a social purpose.[105]

On the basis of this grid of principles, Duguit reinterprets the institutes of private law – contract, property, civil liability – and the institutes of public law: the power of rulers, the legislative will, the essential characteristics of 'positive law'. Thus, piece by piece, the dogmatic construction of the German publicists falls apart: the state has no will, it has no sovereignty, it does not create objective law. There is no collectivity other than the real collectivity of individuals, the science of law does not exist in a separate world. The rule of law fixes negative and positive duties, there must be no conflict

---

99. *L'Etat, le droit objective et la loi positive*, Paris, 1901, rsit. Dalloz, 2003.
100. Ridola, *State and Constitution in Germany*, Turin, 2016, pp. 1 ff.
101. *Ibid.*, pp. 6 ff.
102. *Ibid.*, p. 145.
103. *Ibid.*, p. 156.
104. *Ibid.*, p. 173.
105. *Ibid.*, pp. 190, 197 ff.

between individual and state interest. Solidarity expresses the coincidence of individual and social goals.

Gurvitch and Lévy continued Duguit's work. The former, by refining his ideas, together with those of Durkheim, for the affirmation of legal pluralism and social law;[106] the latter by highlighting the psychological foundations of law and the values of socialism.[107]

Georges Gurvitch's sociology of law is undoubtedly the highest expression of contemporary legal pluralism, a current of thought whose cultural and political influence is decisive.

'By *legal pluralism*', states Renato Treves in the introductory essay to the Handbook of the Sociology of Law, 'we generally mean that line of thought that is opposed in the most explicit and intransigent manner to legal statism, that is, to the conception, which arose with the rise of the modern age and affirmed above all in the age of the Enlightenment, which attributes the monopoly of political power to the state, reduces all law to state law and makes the supreme source of law reside in state law through the progressive devaluation of traditional sources such as custom, judicial decision, and the doctrine of jurists. Against statism, legal pluralism, which emerged in the age of romanticism and historicism, argues in fact that legal power does not reside in the state alone, but also resides in many other entities different from and independent of the state; that state law is not the only existing law, but that there are many other legal systems different from and independent of the state; that state law is neither the only nor the main source of law, but is only one of these sources and not even the main one'.[108]

This methodological direction, which finds much consensus, approaching realist philosophies from time to time, flows like an underground river in various cultural circles, surviving totalitarian experiences in France, Germany and Italy, and clashes with Kelsen's pure conception of law, with the theories of legal positivism, and above all with the dogmatics that animate formalist theories of law.

In Duguit's footsteps is also Maurice Blondel, who combines his studies in sociology and philosophy with his Catholic beliefs: the state, the fatherland, nations, the family are not absolute notions, but all the epiphany of solidarity, and humanity as a historical presence that grows and refines[109] through it.[110] Blondel's thought inspired

---

106. Gurvitch, *Sociology of Law*, transl. it., Milan, 1957.
107. Lévy, *Les fondements du droit*, Paris, 19933; Herrera, *Socialisme juridique et droit naturel. À propos d'Emmanuel* Lévy, in Les jurists face au politique, Paris, 2003, pp. 69 ff.
108. In this work, Gurvitch, as a philosopher of law, essentially equates the sociology of law with legal pluralism and the idea of social law. In terms of method, Gurvitch's sociology of law does not make use of the traditional tools of empirical sociology supplemented by the techniques and instruments of legal science, but rather refers to the principles already mentioned (legal pluralism and social law) and especially to the ideology connected with them. A critical analysis of the conceptions of the main precursors and founders of legal sociology is conducted in the work. The author then clearly distinguishes three sets of problems and focuses his exposition on them: problems of the systematic sociology of law, solved by what he calls the micro-sociology of law; problems of the differential sociology of law, the solution to which is found in the legal typology of particular groups and global societies; problems of the genetic sociology of law, analysed by means of the dynamic macrosociology of law.
109. L'action, Paris, 1937, pp. 175 ff.

Henri Schuman in his European integration project, but also Jacques Maritain, founder of integral humanism.[111]

In the same turn of the year, the ideas of Max Weber and Robert Michels came to the fore in Germany. Weber tackled the subject with in-depth anthropological and economic analyses, but as a jurist, the legal significance of solidarity and its role in constitutional law did not escape him.

Robert Michels refers exclusively to workers' solidarity[112] as 'the direct effect of class antagonisms'. Class solidarity in a given country will be all the stronger the more acute the 'economic, social, intellectual, confessional and traditional antagonisms'. In the trade union organisations, Michels sees one 'of the few possible ways today to apply solidarity in practice' and highlights the antagonistic component of solidarity, which turns out to be a mixture of altruism and selfishness, of the spirit of sacrifice and self-interest. Michels sees in the working masses of industrialised Germany 'the vanguard of the most powerful army of solidarity in this country'.[113]

---

110. Russo, *Ancient and Modern Ways of Solidarity*, Milan, 2021.
111. Soret, *Philosophies de l'Action catholique: Blondel-Maritain*, Paris, 2007.
112. *See* Ferraris & Michels, 1993.
113. *See* Michels, 1914, p. 48.

CHAPTER 3
# The Social Doctrine of the Catholic Church

## §3.01 SOLIDARITY AS A BOND FOR THE 'HUMAN FAMILY'[114]

Among the relevant factors of social aggregation and among the values cementing common life, religious sentiment occupies a central place, which, in Western Europe, is manifested in the Catholic religion, the Protestant religion and the Jewish religion. The authors who have dealt with the history of the idea of solidarity have privileged secular sources, and this is true both for the research of Marie-Claude Blais, who in France reconstructs the evolution of the principle of fraternity, later to become solidarity, ignoring Christian social doctrine, and for Rainer Zoll, who gives a nod.

But the religious influence on human behaviour and in shaping the policies of states and the EU did not escape S. Stjerno, who makes it one of the pillars of German politics and the creation of the EU.

The Scriptures are a treasure trove of ideas and precepts that paint the rules of human behaviour, the paradigmatic model that the good Christian, who is the image of God, must be inspired by and follow. The imitation of Christ marks the path of choices, sacrifices but also the joys of human life. The commandment of *mutual love*, the Pastoral Constitution *Gaudium et spes*[115] specifies, 'must inspire, purify and elevate all human relationships in social and political life. So that solidarity is understood, first and foremost, as the bond of the human family'.[116] Respect for human dignity, the protection of human rights and the guarantee of freedoms are prerequisites for all coexistence.

---

114. The Church's social doctrine is the subject of a vast literature. For initial references *see* Pontifical, *Council for Justice and Peace, Compendium of the Social Doctrine of the Church,* Rome, 2004; Sorge, *Introduction to the Social Doctrine of the Church,* 2009; Alford, *Corporate Social Responsibility and the Social Doctrine of the Catholic Church,* Milan, 2009.
115. 10: AAS, 1033 (1966).
116. *Sollicitudo rei socialis,* 40: AAS, 57 (1965).

The social doctrine of the Catholic Church began with the encyclical *Rerum novarum, in which* Leo XIII specified the Church's position on social issues in 1892. *The res novae* are the social conflicts that had broken out for the first time all over the world. The emergence of the (second) industrial revolution, urbanism, low wages, and the exploitation of the working class gave rise to shocking class conflicts. The Church can neither ignore the situation nor that the majority of the Christian people are subjected to conditions of mere survival, leading their earthly existence in misery in the cities and the countryside. The Church therefore takes a stand: on wages, which must be sufficient to meet the needs of the worker and his family; on property, which must be safeguarded; on the free market, which cannot overwhelm the essential rights of man. A new social order based on *justice* and *charity* is thus outlined.

This is an important stance. Charity, care for the sick and the poor, have always been the cornerstones of ecclesial action, but the origin of these worthy initiatives, flanked by the charity and charity of the individual faithful find their fulcrum in the Scriptures, particularly in the Christian message of love and brotherhood among men. At the end of the nineteenth century, faced with the emergence of trade unions and parties following the widespread spread of the socialist idea, the Church could not hide the urgency of intervention to mitigate the effects of the free market. It cannot admit the socialisation of land and private property, nor class hatred, but neither can it legitimise capitalist exploitation.

Written in polished language, Leo XIII's Encyclical Letter precisely focuses on the causes of political and social upheaval:

> The ardent yearning for novelty, which has long since begun to agitate the people, had naturally to pass from the political order into the similar order of the social economy. And indeed, the marvellous progress of the arts and the new methods of industry; the changed relations between masters and workers; the accumulation of wealth in the hands of a few and the widespread spread of poverty; the feeling of their own strength in the working classes, which has become more vivid, and the closer union between them; this combination of things, with the addition of the worsening customs, has led to the outbreak of conflict. The conflict is of such gravity that it keeps the souls suspended in anxious expectation and strains the wits of the learned, the congresses of the wise, the popular assemblies, the deliberations of legislators, the counsels of princes, so much so that there is no question of greater interest to the world today. Therefore, Venerable Brethren, what we have done at other times for the good of the Church and for the common salvation with our encyclical letters on Public Powers, Human Liberty, the Christian Constitution of States, and other similar subjects that seemed opportune to us to demolish fatal errors, the same thing we believe we must do now for the same reasons on the labour question.

The question is resolved by recourse to Scripture: the argument starts from the protection of private property as a natural right, given that:

> mankind, without at all caring for the few contradictors and with its eye fixed on the law of nature, finds in this same law the foundation of the division of goods; and recognising that private property is supremely consonant with man's nature and with peaceful social coexistence, it has solemnly sanctioned it through the practice of all ages. And civil laws, which, when they are just, derive their

authority and efficacy from natural law itself (cf. S. Th. I-I, q. 95, a. 4), confirm this right and secure it by public force. Nor does it lack the seal of the divine law, which strictly forbids even the coveting of another's property: Thou shalt not covet thy neighbour's wife: not the house, not the manor, not the maidservant, not the ox, not the ass, not any thing that belongs to him (Deut 5:21). Property is defended against envy, plus, it is protected by (just) law, so whoever disputes it violates law, human law, but also divine law, because property is law of nature. He who has no property, however, has labour power. Everyone has talents, and it is up to each one to spend them in the best way.

The remedies are therefore different from those proposed by socialism. First and foremost, social justice, i.e., just wages:

It is therefore the duty of the masters to leave the workman comfort and time sufficient to fulfil his religious duties; not to expose him to corrupting seductions and the dangers of scandal; not to alienate him from the spirit of family and the love of saving; not to impose on him work disproportionate to his strength, or ill-suited to his age and sex (17). Chief among their duties, then, is to give each one a just reward. But in general, let the capitalists and employers remember that human laws do not allow them to oppress the needy and unfortunate for their own benefit, or to traffic in the misery of their neighbour. To defraud then of their due wages is so great a fault that it cries out for vengeance in the sight of God. *Behold, the labourers' wages ... which were defrauded by you, cry out; and this cry has wounded the ears of the Lord of hosts* (Jas 5:4). Lastly, it is the duty of the rich not to harm the small savings of the worker either by violence or by fraud or by manifest or concealed usury; this duty is all the more rigorous, the weaker and more ill-defended the worker and the more sacrosanct his small substance.

And then charity. Charity cannot be imposed, it is everyone's duty to account for what they have had and how they have spent it:

Having satisfied necessity and convenience, it is a duty to succour the needy with the surplus. What is surplus, give alms (Luc 11:41). Except in the case of extreme necessity, these, it is true, are not obligations of justice, but of Christian charity, the fulfilment of which certainly cannot be demanded by law, but above the laws and judgments of men stands the law and judgment of Christ, who inculcates in many ways the practice of generous giving and teaches: It is more blessed to give than to receive (Acts 20:35), and he will hold that charity done or denied to the needy is done or denied to himself: What you did to one of the least of these my brethren, you did to me (Mat 25:40). In conclusion, whoever has received from the munificence of God a greater abundance of goods, whether external and corporal or spiritual, has received them for this purpose, to use them for his own improvement, and at the same time as a minister of divine providence for the benefit of others: Whoever therefore has wit, let him take care not to be silent; whoever has an abundance of goods, let him beware of being too hard-hearted in the exercise of mercy; whoever has an art for living, let him share with his neighbour the use and utility of it.[117]

---

117. S. Greg, In Evang. hom 9, n.7.

On the basis of these principles, Leo XIII dictates the rules: bearable work, suitable also for women and minors, fair pay, adequate working conditions. He also wonders whether the agreement resulting from two wills (one stronger the other weaker) is well-founded:

> However, there is always an element of natural justice, which is prior and superior to the free will of the contracting parties, and that is that the amount of the payment must not be less than the subsistence of the worker, frugal it is understood, and of upright morals. If he, forced by necessity or for fear of worse, accepts harsher pacts which, because they are imposed by the owner or the contractor, must be accepted willingly or unwillingly, it is clear that he suffers violence, against which justice protests.

Hence the legitimacy of workers' associations, and associations that elevate the dignity and uprightness of men. Legitimate, therefore, are trade unions and parties, insofar as they negotiate and thus safeguard peace: 'Let the common goods of society be administered with integrity, so that relief may be distributed to each according to need; and let the rights and duties of the masters harmonise with the rights and duties of the workers.'

Social peace is achieved through moral uprightness and soul salvation through *charity*:

> The desired salvation must be principally the fruit of an outpouring of charity; we mean that Christian charity which epitomises the whole Gospel and which, always ready to sacrifice itself for its neighbour, is the surest antidote against the pride and selfishness of the age. Saint Paul already sketched its features with those words: Charity is longsuffering, it is kind; it does not seek its own advantage: it suffers all things, it sustains all things (1 Cor 13:4-7).

The way to oppose and overcome socialism is therefore the preservation of the status quo, but with state intervention to remedy the conditions of the weak, the reduction of excessive profits at the expense of the rich, the endurance of pain and fatigue at the expense of the dispossessed, the exercise of charity as a social virtue at the expense of all, since what counts is the afterlife.

## §3.02    THE CORRECTION TO THE CHURCH'S SOCIAL MODEL

The social programme of the Church outlined in 1892 thus seems far more in-depth, and far more cultured than the proposals of the radical Bourgeois. Rather, it tends to be the response almost half a century later to Marx's Manifesto.

With the encyclical *Quadragesimo anno* 40 years later, the Christian message that founded the Church's social doctrine is renewed with a few corrections.

Pius XI reaffirms that the task of the State is not merely that of a 'guardian of order and law, but must endeavour so that by the whole complex of laws and political institutions ordering and administering the State, public and private prosperity may naturally result' (encyclical *Rerum novarum*, no. 26). Having reaffirmed freedom of association and the authorisation for Catholic workers to form their own trade unions or to join existing trade unions if appropriate, Pius XI introduces some clarifications.

First of all, the close correlation between economics and morality, since 'it would be a mistake to say that the economic order and the moral order are so disparate and unrelated to each other that the former in no way depends on the latter. Certainly, the laws, which are said to be economic, drawn from the very nature of things and from the nature of the human soul and body, establish what limits in the economic field the power of man cannot and cannot reach, and by what means; and reason itself, from the nature of things and from the individual and social nature of man, clearly deduces what end God the Creator has proposed to the whole economic order'.

Then, it confirms the protection of property as a natural right, but distinguishes ownership from use: and use must be done according to Christian teaching. As for labour, the need to give workers a fair wage is reaffirmed, the so-called Manchester economy is challenged, i.e., the free market economy that places the weak in a condition of perpetual dependence, but the theory of surplus value is also opposed:

> The so-called intellectuals approached the anguished workers by opposing an imaginary law with an equally imaginary moral principle: that what is produced and received in income, and only so much of it as is sufficient to compensate and reproduce capital, is owed by right to the worker. This error, which is more flattering than that of various socialists, who assert that all that is needed for production is to be transferred to the state, or as they say to be 'socialised', is all the more dangerous and more apt to deceive the unwary: a mild poison, which was greedily imbibed by many, whom open socialism had never been able to deceive.

The solution is the composition of the different expectations, but there is a further step from *Rerum novarum*, a redistributive instance that goes beyond the *status quo*: 'To each therefore must be given his share of the goods, and it must be ensured that the distribution of created goods, which everyone can see how uneasy it is now because of the great imbalance between the few rich and the countless poor, is brought back into conformity with the norms of the common good and social justice.'

Support for the worker and his family, balance between wages and business conditions, and the pursuit of the common good are the principles to which the social economy must adhere: a market governed by free competition is not considered the model to pursue, but rather an economy governed by the state with social justice and charity.

One senses in these words the Pastor's concern for his faithful harassed by the Great Depression. But there are also hints of corporatism: just a few years earlier the Work Charter had been approved (1926), in 1929 the Lateran Pacts had been signed, the Pope wanted to legitimise Catholic Action and therefore contested communism and liberalism, recognising that socialism had the merit of having made claims that were close to Christian ones, but based on erroneous assumptions, the denial of private property and the opposition between classes. The Pope insists on charity as a social virtue and cooperation for the realisation of better social justice.

## §3.03    SOLIDARITY AS A UNIFYING VALUE IN CATHOLIC THOUGHT

In the Protestant religion, considering all the different directions and orientations of its components[118] solidarity is preached first of all towards Catholics, and then towards Jews and other people. In the Protestant world[119] 'diakonia' is the service rendered to one's neighbour, and corresponds to what for Catholics is 'caritas' and for lay people 'solidarity'.

From the Reformation to the religious movements of Pietism and the Awakening, to which we owe the organisation of modern Christian diakonia, there are sermons, concrete initiatives, and organisations all aimed at affirming this principle.[120]

The Jewish religion also considers *brotherhood* and therefore solidarity as a precept of life. It would be necessary to distinguish between the four trends that have developed in the interpretation of the Scriptures – Orthodox, Conservative, Reformed and Reconstructionist – in order to adequately deepen the discourse, but in any case at their common basis is the consideration that solidarity is a bond that brings together not only the Jews (as a historical fact, as a condition of life, as a differential trait with respect to other religions) but also the Jews and other men. This conclusion is reached by examining the Scriptures. The analysis of the texts highlights the obligation of cooperation, of assistance, of solicitude descending from the common divine creation.[121] It is a solidarity comprising material and spiritual aspects.

---

118. Culmann, *Catholics and Protestants: A Project of Christian Solidarity*. intr. by a. Prandi Bologna, Il Mulino, 1962.
119. Villa first assembly, December 2018, which brought together the evangelical denominations: the states-general that brought together 150 delegates representing Waldensian, Methodist, Lutheran, Baptist churches, the Apostolic Church, the Salvation Army, and some free churches, delivered to the public a strongly evangelical document based on solidarity.
120. Genre, *Diakonia and Solidarity: I valdesi dalla borsa dei poveri all'Otto per mille*, Turin, 2017.
121. *Judaism and universal fraternity*, edited by the Franciscan Study Centre for Interreligious Dialogue and Cultures, 2019 (on the web); Furio Aharon Biagini, *The theme of fraternity in Judaism*, in www.etzhaim.eu/frternità; Lapide, *He Preached in Their Synagogues: Jewish Exegesis of the Gospels*, Paideia, Brescia 2001; Benamozegh, *Israel and Humanity*, Turin, 2016.

# CHAPTER 4

# Solidarity as a Normative Principle

### §4.01 FROM META-LEGAL TO CONSTITUTIONAL LANGUAGE

Of the six basic words that punctuate the chapters of the Charter of Fundamental Rights of the EU – in order, dignity, liberty, equality, solidarity, citizenship, justice – the *solidarity* that connotes Title IV is the least mentioned in legal literature and, at the same time, the least codified and certainly the least studied. To tell the truth, this term, which, as we shall see, can be declined in many ways, as a right and as a duty, as a general principle, as a concept, as a limit to individual power, or even as the foundation of human consortium, is nothing new in the vocabulary with which norms are drafted in contemporary constitutions.

But if we consider the roots of political language, which derive to us even from Greek thought, are corroborated by the thought of the Enlightenment, and develop luxuriantly in the nineteenth century, while we find all the antecedents of the terms that are familiar to us today, such as freedom, justice, citizenship and equality, and even dignity, obviously in the many and varied meanings with which these concepts have gradually been coloured, we do not always find the expression solidarity. If we wish, solidarity is expressed, albeit not fully, by other terms that are more familiar to us, such as friendship, fraternity, piety, altruism, charity, cooperation, sociality, the pursuit of the common good.

If one then considers solidarity as the joint aim of various EU actions, one discovers that it is understood in a broad sense, referring as it does to the workers' right to information and consultation within the company, the right to bargaining and collective action, the right of access to employment services protection in the event of unjustified dismissal, fair and just working conditions, prohibition of child labour and protection of young people at work, family and professional life, social security and social assistance, health protection, access to services of general economic interest, environmental protection, consumer protection.

But it is not as broad as the term might be, considering its potential: indeed, some jurists are convinced that it has been used in its most obvious and reduced meaning[122] and others that it offers only the first segment of a much longer path that the EU could, indeed should, take.[123]

Although each of the terms that can be juxtaposed to it carries a meaning that varies according to the times, places and contexts in which it is used, each of them has carved its own path in the individual conscience and in collective feeling, on the one hand, because it has more definitive and concrete contours, and on the other, because it reflects situations in which rights are involved. Solidarity has a dual aspect: it operates first in the sphere of duties and is transferred to the level of rights when it is transformed into the connective tissue of social rights, a category that comes last, after the proclamation of civil and political rights.

The analysis of the normative textual datum then becomes the starting point of a research that cannot be limited to semantic boundaries alone, but must push itself to consider the values that the term encompasses, the movements of thought that constituted its force, and the circumstances that transmitted it to us.

In order to fully understand the meaning of this term, its function in the world of law, and the potential it offers, it is necessary to go back to the origins of the ideas behind it, in order to be able to understand how it has been used by legislators, how it has been interpreted by judges, and what operations it allows jurists to perform today. From the world of ideas briefly described above, solidarity moves to the world of facts, to the world of rules, and thus becomes a *normative concept*.

Let us first consider textual solidarity in twentieth-century constitutions prior to the Italian Constitution.

As I was saying, the concept of solidarity was not discovered in the year 2000 by the drafters of the European Charter of Fundamental Rights, even though they had the great merit of naming one of its chapters after solidarity: the eye, when scrolling through the index of the Charter, cannot ignore this term, on the contrary, it is led to highlight its load-bearing role, like a pillar supporting a dome. The contents of the dome are gradually highlighted in Articles 27-38 with specific reference to labour, social security, health, the environment and consumption. To complete the picture, it is necessary to add, again in the rank of the primary sources of the EU, the preliminary provisions of the Treaty on European Union (TEU) (Articles 2-4) and the provisions of the Treaty on the Functioning of the European Union (TFEU), which have as their object (in Articles 143 ff.) employment, social policy, education and vocational training, culture, public health, and solidarity between states (Article 222).

Already by reconstructing the matters regulated under this heading, one can understand, briefly, how the expression has its own centrality in the legal language of the EU, even if, since it is not defined, its meaning can only be guessed at by linking it to the matters to which the term is connected. These are rules that are concerned with

---

122. Busnelli, *Il principio di solidarietà e 'l'attesa della povera gente', oggi*, in *Persona e mercato*, 2012 pp. 101 ff.; and previously *Solidarietà: aspetti di diritto privato*, in *Iustitia*, 1999, pp. 435 ff.
123. Rodotà, *Solidarietà, supra*, pp. 84 ff., 126 ff.

defining certain aspects of the welfare state and thus identifying the ways in which the Union protects so-called *social rights*. Even if it can be argued that solidarity is a 'vague' term, this does not mean that the rules that include it are vague: it alludes at the same time to a present situation, in which there is a constraint, and to a future situation, in which that constraint will produce its effects.

Much richer contents than those deriving from the European Charter emerge from modern constitutions, where the term is used frequently and encompasses wide-ranging, topical and project-related implications, all of which are demanding.

As we know, constitutional language, among the various languages coined by jurists, has its own peculiarity. It is solemn and declamatory, it is a harbinger of a future full of interventions and actions aimed at consolidating, improving, and developing the well-being of the citizens, it paints a table of values, it lays down the principles to which the legislator must adhere.[124]

The European Charter, although weaker – in this perspective – than the national charters, has not shirked its recognition.

The Preamble of the Charter makes precisely this clear: that the Union is founded on the indivisible and universal values of human dignity, freedom, equality and *solidarity*, and reaffirms the rights derived in particular from the *constitutional traditions* of the Member States, as well as from common international obligations. Alongside *rights, values* must be placed: common values, as the TEU puts it, are expressed by respect for human dignity, freedom, democracy, equality, the rule of law and human rights; they concern a society characterised by 'pluralism, non-discrimination, tolerance, justice, *solidarity* and equality between men and women' (Article 2). These values, reflected in the constitutional traditions of the Member States, are relevant as they are *common; as are* the rights guaranteed by the European Convention on Human Rights (ECHR), which, 'as they result from the constitutional traditions common to' the Member States, are regarded as general principles of Union law.

With the interpreter's awareness, it can therefore be said that the EU Charter and Treaty have imposed within European borders a project of social commitment that each national constitution imposes on the state and its citizens. But the recognition of this value, which is in fact a general principle, serves to unify what is expressed in the constitutions of the individual Member States in a variety of different formulas. If one carefully examines the constitutional tradition of the individual countries, one discovers in fact that, at least for the principle value of solidarity, there is no mechanical overlapping of meaning and normative scope. The common constitutional ground concerns more the objects, the subjects regulated under the title of solidarity, than the force of the normative precept. This is already evident when considering the English, customary constitutional tradition, but also emerges from the individual histories of each Member State. In many respects, the French experience is the oldest, and we can also refer to it in order to understand our own experience, but more interesting are the

---

124. *Ruggeri, Language of the Constitution and Language of Laws: Introductory Notations,* in *Osservatorio delle fonti,* 2015, no. 3, pp. 1 ff.

German experience, which only partly refers back to the first modern constitution, the Weimar Constitution of 1919, and the experiences of Portugal and Spain, which cannot be truly defined as 'traditional' because their constitutional tradition is very recent, dating back to 1976 and 1978 respectively.

We must therefore, on the one hand, preserve the characteristics of the identity – identity of the constitutional guise, in this case – of each country, with its peculiarities, and, on the other hand, acquire from those texts, as drafted, interpreted and applied, the *common content* that constitutes the postulate of the Treaty provisions of the Charter of European Rights.

This work, which is both an excavation, because it seeks to go back to the roots of terms and values, and a chisel, because it is a good methodological rule not to stop at the statement, since the interpreter must also investigate the hermeneutic result, highlights both the differences between national legal traditions and the Union's evident political design, which consists of overcoming individual differences, respecting the originality and intangibility of each person, in order to acquire a shared table of values and to project into the future a community cemented by those values.

# CHAPTER 5

# Solidarity in Early Twentieth-Century Constitutions

## §5.01    THE BASIC MODEL: THE WEIMAR CONSTITUTION

The model of contemporary constitutions, which, in addition to the tripartition of powers and the organisation of the state, also provide for a Bill of Rights in which the rights (and duties) of citizens are enumerated, can be found in the Weimar Constitution of 1919. Here, giving voice to the demands of social democratic thought, for the first time in a constitutional text an outline of a welfare state is outlined, in which, alongside political and civil rights (Articles 109-118) assigned to all citizens, rights are also enumerated that are exercised in *collective life* (Articles 119-134), religious freedom, education and education are protected, and for the first time, economic and social rights are considered in detail, in a chapter in which the analysis of relations concerning *economic life* is very extensive. It speaks of many things, in an overall design that concerns the family (Article 199), the education and training of young people (Article 122), taxation (Article 133) and participation in public burdens in proportion to one's means (Article 134), economic justice and the guarantee of a decent existence for man (Article 151), the fulfilment of property-related obligations (Article 153), the protection of large families and the possibility of healthy housing, the distribution of land (Article 155), the cooperation of the factors of production, the protection of cooperatives, and collectivised management (Article 156). These are all aims that paint a picture of a society in which, alongside the protection of individual rights, forms of collective protection are also offered, and at the same time duties are imposed that benefit the community. Even freedom of contract is mentioned and protected (Article 152).

Section 163 is particularly significant in providing that 'every German, while retaining his personal freedom, has a moral duty to use his spiritual and bodily energies in such a way as to be useful to the community. Every German must be given the opportunity to be able to provide for his livelihood through productive work. If a suitable occupation cannot be procured for him, he must be provided with whatever is necessary for his livelihood (...)'.

The insurance and social security system is already present in the wording of § 161, according to which 'The Reich organises, with the reasonable participation of the insured, a unitary insurance system for the purpose of protecting health and capacity for work, protecting maternity and preventing the economic consequences of old age, illness and accidents of life.'

It is a constitution in transition, so to speak, linking a classist and authoritarian past, such as the Wilhelminian system, to a more open and democratic present, because it is concerned with the community but not to the extent of realising aims of equality in the substantial sense. The class structure of society is taken as a given and social promotion is not contemplated, as can be seen from § 164:

> The state must promote through its legislative and administrative activities the development of the independent middle class and protect it from excessive taxation and absorption into other classes.

In any case, the provisions already configure a wide-ranging socioeconomic programme, which goes far beyond the proclamation of the rights of liberty, and combines political demands with needs related to material life, work, and the needs of each person, considered as an individual and in the family to which he or she belongs, opening up horizons that go beyond mere survival, with a view to achieving social peace.[125]

---

125. 'Article 119: The spiritual uplift, health and social development of the family is a task of the State and the municipalities. Large families have the right to adequate assistance. Motherhood is entitled to the protection and assistance of the State.
    Art. 122 – Youth must be protected from exploitation and from moral, spiritual and bodily neglect. The State and the municipalities must establish the institutions necessary for this. Welfare regulations involving coercion may only be laid down by legislation.
    Art. 133 – All citizens are obliged to perform personal services in favour of the State and the municipalities, which are imposed on them by law.
    Article 134 – All citizens, without distinction, shall contribute, in proportion to their means, to all public expenditure, in accordance with the law.
    Article 151 – The ordering of economic life must correspond to the fundamental norms of justice and tend to guarantee an existence worthy of man for all. Within these limits, the economic freedom of individuals is to be protected.
    Article 153 Property obliges. Its use, in addition to the private, must be for the common good'.
    'Art. 155 – The distribution and use of land shall be controlled with the aim of preventing abuses and of ensuring that every German has a healthy home, and that all German families, especially large ones, have a home and a family patrimony corresponding to their needs. Legislation on family property is to have special consideration for former combatants. Land property may be expropriated when this is necessary to meet the need for housing, or to promote internal colonisation, the clearing of uncultivated land, or the development of agriculture. Fedecommissums are abolished. Cultivation and utilisation of land is a duty that landowners assume towards the community. The increase in the value of land, which does not result from the use of labour or capital on the land, must be for the benefit of the community. All the riches of the soil and the economically usable forces of nature are to be placed under the supervision of the state, according to the provisions of the law.
    Art. 156 (...) the Reich may, in cases of urgent necessity and for the benefit of the public economy, provide by law for the independent assembly and management of economic

Various norms inspired our Constituent Fathers, so much so that it can be said that, even with its original aspects, the drafting of the text of the Italian Constitution took the Weimar model into account for its basic choices: a long constitution, inclusive of social rights, as well as freedom, inviolable and fundamental rights; the project of a politically evolved society, with a strong commitment by the State to promote the progress of each person and protect all social formations. The liberal economy model that had become established with industrialisation at the end of the nineteenth century was succeeded by a tempered liberal economy model, in which private property and economic initiative, while protected, must be oriented towards pursuing aims of social justice, of safeguarding the common good, to guarantee everyone a dignified existence. The Weimar Constitution is an obligatory reference point for reflecting on the meaning of democracy in the modern sense. And the insistence on this text by antifascist jurists, such as Francesco Ruffini, is significant for the relevance of that model.[126] All the more so since it saw the light after a troubled history of the German people. A history that began in 1848 with the constitutions of the individual German states, continued with the Declaration of the Fundamental Rights of the German People (the so-called Frankfurt Declaration) and the Imperial Constitution, 'the highest profession of faith of the modern liberal bourgeoisie',[127] and ended almost immediately with the abrogation of fundamental rights in 1851. The imperial constitution of 16 April 1871 ignored fundamental rights, being consistent with the Bismarckian policy of letting the citizen live undisturbed under the protection of legitimate authority (Ruffini, 40). It was only due to the insistence of the parties and the need to overcome political conflicts that it was decided to introduce, after the inglorious end of the First World War, a constitution that would take up the lofty formulas of the Frankfurt Declaration and at the same time attempt to reconcile the conflicting aspirations of the social classes.

As we know, history was not generous with the Weimar Constitution and the Social Democratic Republic came to an inglorious end. But the tragic epilogue of the Weimar Republic Constitution did not obscure its innovative aspects and merits, even though it was only able to be in force in its fullness in Germany from 1919 to 1933, and formally remained in force even under Nazism, but was emptied of its content by the torrential legislation of the totalitarian regime.

---

enterprises and associations for the purpose of securing the co-operation of the factors of production and the co-participation of employers and employees in the administration, and to regulate production, manufacture, distribution, utilisation, price levels as well as the import and export of economic goods in accordance with the principles of a specialised economy.

Production and trade cooperatives and their unions, at their request and with regard to their establishment and nature, may be included in the collective management.

Art. 161 – The Reich shall organise, with the reasonable participation of the insured persons, a unitary insurance system for the purpose of protecting health and capacity for work, protecting maternity and preventing the economic consequences of old age, illness and accidents of life.

Article 165 – Blue and white-collar workers must collaborate with employers to determine employment and working conditions and for the overall economic development of productive energies. The organisations of the two categories and the contracts concluded by them are legally recognised'.

126. Ruffini, *Diritti di libertà*, Turin, 1926, p. 38.
127. Ruffini, *supra*, p. 38.

The Weimar Constitution fascinated Italian jurists even before it became one of the reference texts for the drafting of the Italian Constitution. Although it came from a state that had lost the First World War, it became the model for almost all constitutions of European states drafted in the period between the two world wars.[128]

One of the masters of the twentieth century, Costantino Mortati, had made it the subject of a valuable study, but even today it does not cease to interest scholars, who weave in-depth discussions on it, also from the perspective of comparative law.[129]

## §5.02    THE INTERPRETATION OF THE WEIMAR CONSTITUTION

For jurists, the Weimar experience is, even today, an exceptional experience.[130] Having overcome the historicist tendency to consider it as the incubator of Nazism, and therefore destined for an inglorious end, that experience constitutes the first attempt of the twentieth century to inaugurate a modern democratic constitution attentive to social needs even though of bourgeois inclination. From 1919 onwards, those cultural trends that were the bearers of modernity asserted themselves in Germany and spread throughout the West, giving rise to a new canon in all the arts and social sciences.[131] In the text of the Constitution, we find not only the cornerstones of social democracy[132] but a formidable synthesis of the interconnection of economy and society.[133] We thus find an experience formalised in a 'paradigm'[134] in which the organisation of power, through the identification of representative bodies, is accompanied by the catalogue of rights, as recognised by the fundamental principles of the law of nations, and a framework of guiding rules of economic factors supplemented by the foundations of the welfare state, emphasising the openness of the constitution to society, 'to the real conditions of life and the web of social relations within which human freedom unfolds'.[135] Very advanced for its time, in the eyes of the contemporary jurist it appears as an extraordinary laboratory of twentieth-century democratic constitutionalism.[136]

---

128. *Ibid.*, pp. 45 ff.
129. C. Mortati, *La Costituzione Weimar,* 1946, Milan, 2019.
130. For an analysis of German constitutions *see* Lanchester, *Le costituzioni tedesche da Francoforte a Bonn*, Milan, 2002; Losano, *Le costituzioni della Germania post-bellica e i diritti fondamentali*, in *Rev.Fac. Derecho*, n.32, Montevideo, Enero-Junio 2021, pp. 225 ff.
131. *See* in an endless literature above all Rosenberg, *Origini della Repubblica di Weimar* (1928), transl. it, Rome 1947, Florence, 1972; Laquer, *La Repubblica di Weimar.Vita e morte di una società permissiva*, Milan, 1977; Gay, *La cultura di Weimar.L'oursider come insider*, Bari, 1978; and above all Wirsching, *Weimar,cent anni dopo*, Rome, 2019.
132. Paggi, *Introduction to Rosnberg, supra*, p. xii ff.
133. *See* in particular Martinelli, *Economia e società*, Milan, 1986.
134. To use Ridola's felicitous expression, *The Constitution of the Weimar Republic as an 'experience' and as a 'paradigm'*, in *AIC Magazine* no. 2/2014, 4.4.2014; at no. 58 *see also* a selection of particularly significant works on the Weimar Republic. *See also* Gordon & McCormick (eds), *Weimar Thought: A Contested Legacy*, Princeton, 2013.
135. Ridola, *supra*, p. 15.
136. These are Ridola's words again, *supra*; Dyzenhaus, *Legal Theory in the Collapse of Weimar: Contemporary Lessons?*, in *The American Political Science Review*, 91(1), March, 1997, p. 121.
     Adams, Weimar Elegies, Reviewed Works: Men in Dark Times by Hannah Arendt; Weimar Culture by Peter Gay; Illuminations by Walter Benjamin, Hannah Arendt, Harry Zohn, in *The Hudson Review* 22(1), Spring, 1969, pp. 165-171.

The connection between fundamental rights and the economic constitution is the instrument intended to catalyse citizens' consensus around the fundamental law and at the same time, the provision of a programme intended to meet the needs of the most disadvantaged social classes over time. This can be deduced from the principles underlying 'economic life': Article 151 states that 'The order of economic life shall correspond to the fundamental norms of justice and tend to guarantee an existence worthy of man for all. Within these limits, the economic freedom of individuals is to be protected.'

The two factors of wealth – (land) ownership and enterprise – are also limited by the needs of the community. According to Article 153, 'Property is guaranteed by the constitution. Its content and limits are fixed by law (...). Property *is obligatory*. Its use, as well as its private use, must be for the common good.' And every citizen is called upon to make his contribution to the preservation and advancement of social harmony: 'Article 163 – Every German, while preserving his personal freedom, has the moral duty to employ his spiritual and bodily energies in such a way as to be useful to the community. Every German must be given the opportunity to be able to provide for his livelihood through productive work. If a suitable occupation cannot be provided for him, he must be provided with whatever is necessary for his livelihood. More detailed regulations will be laid down by Reich law.'

Social peace, preached by the social democratic forces, which set themselves as a unitary and alternative path to the extreme left dominated by Spartacist dominance, and to the extreme right, dominated by conservatives, landowners, large industrialists and national socialists, seems to be guaranteed by the cooperation of the various factors of production: Article 165 states that 'workers and employees must cooperate with entrepreneurs to determine employment and working conditions and for the overall economic development of productive energies. The organisations of the two categories and the contracts concluded by them are legally recognised'.

The relationship between the individual and the community is at the centre of the reflection of the public law scholars of the time, and that debate, in which the reflections of jurists, legal philosophers, political philosophers, sociologists and economists are intertwined, constitutes the foundation of modern constitutional law: the role of the state, the social substratum, the sociality of law are the themes that Weber, Cassirer, Schmitt, Smend, Heller, Neumann and Hensen, among others, measure themselves against.

The enunciation of rights in economic matters constitutes the great novelty of this constitution and subsequent constitutions: but the ambiguity of the dictate lends itself to its adaptation both in constitutions aimed at achieving a new, solid democracy, such as those we find after the Second World War in Italy (1948), in Portugal (1976), in Spain (1978) and in the totalitarian constitutions of Portugal and Spain prior to the Second World War. 'The great dream of the innovative currents', observed Costantino Mortati in 1946, 'was to bring about a new social synthesis, which would be an expression of the Germanic organicist genius and would present itself as a mediation between the two opposing civilisations, the ancient western civilisation and the new one coming from the East'.[137]

The economic system, together with the regulatory system concerning work and welfare, constitute the framework within which the individual-citizen is placed, the framework of the community that now appears alongside the individual. 'The characteristic mark that distinguishes the Weimar Constitution from its predecessors is the overcoming of the individualistic principle and the affirmation of *the priority of the social.*'[138]

Mortati therefore set out three guiding principles: the subordination of socially relevant individual activity to purposes of collective interest; the substitution of the concept of substantial equality for the purely formal; the intervention of the state and other public bodies in the function of production so that it is efficient and so that a just distribution of wealth among the classes is promoted.[139]

An attempt was thus made to create a *mixed economy* system, intermediate between liberal and socialist economics. In other words, Mortati observed, the Weimar Constitution was the embodiment of the bourgeois rule of law: 'the social part of the constitution came to fix that much progress that was achievable in a capitalist regime, while this was left in the meantime in its fundamental structure and in the forces that constituted its support'.[140]

The failure of the Weimar Constitution is therefore to be attributed not so much to its societal project, but to extrinsic causes (the heavy burden of reparations, as well as the world economic crisis of 1929) and intrinsic causes (the lack of support from all social partners and the churches, the emergence of totalitarianism on the right and left).

Costantino Mortati's critical analysis was, however, reflexively directed at the definition of the fundamental lines of the new constitution that was being heralded in Italy: the constitutional programme must be supported by the efficiency of the devices that ensure a social balance; before intervening constitutionally, it is therefore necessary that that balance has already been achieved, otherwise, internal conflicts will reverberate on constitutional stability.

Mortati sinks his criticism even deeper: a constitution that grafts onto a late-liberal body a newly minted economic-social framework, inspired by the protection of the collective interest, cannot have stability. The solidity of the system is nourished by the pervasion of the democratic institutional framework of all economic and social structures.[141]

## §5.03    THE TOTALITARIAN CONSTITUTIONS OF THE 1930S

It is not surprising that – with the exception of Weimar where 'Prussianism' and socialism were combined, according to Osvald Spengler's scornful notation –

---

137. Mortati, *supra*, p. 38.
138. *Ibid.*, p. 39.
139. *Ibid.*, p. 39.
140. *Ibid.*, p. 44.
141. *Ibid.*, p. 55.

communitarian values and an embryo of the welfare state, together with the definition of the roles of the state and private individuals in the management of the economy, appear in the constitutions of totalitarian states. Solidarity, which at the beginning of the twentieth century cements the radical party in France, and is the basis for power management with the socialist party, in the hands of illiberal regimes becomes a weapon to legitimise power.

Significant examples of this are the Portuguese Constitution of 1933, enacted following the *coup d'état* of Antonio Oscar Carmona and Antonio de Oliveira Salazar, and the Spanish Fuero del Lavoro of 1938 signed by Francisco Franco during the civil war, which was to end with the victory of the Falangists a few months after the establishment of a ferocious dictatorship.

The political constitution of the Portuguese Republic, after the enunciation of the rights of citizens, the family, and corporative bodies, provided rules on the 'economic and social order' (Title VIII), whose aim is to 'achieve the maximum production and socially useful wealth', to 'achieve the lowest cost and highest salary compatible with a fair remuneration of the other factors of production, through the improvement of technology, services and credit' (Article 31). Property, capital, labour – the sources of wealth – fulfil 'a social function, in a regime of economic cooperation and *solidarity*, the law being able to establish the conditions of their use or management in accordance with social aims' (Article 35).

For its part, the Fuero del Lavoro is an ideologically very explicit document, presenting itself as the source of the renewal of the Catholic tradition of social justice and as the median way between liberal capitalism and Marxist materialism. It places 'wealth at the service of the Spanish people by submitting the economy to politics'. In these provisions with a strong rhetorical accent, we read that Spanish production 'in the *fraternity of* all its elements' must become 'a unity placed at the service of the strength of the fatherland (...) and the support of the instruments of its power' (Preamble). The protection and guarantee of work, fair pay, rural life are the ways in which this social-political programme is realised, which also deals with enterprise, prescribing that profits 'after satisfying capital with just interest, shall be used in preference to constitute the reserves necessary to ensure the stability of the enterprise and to contribute to the perfection of production and the improvement of the working and living conditions of the workers' (VII); private property is recognised and protected but remains subordinate 'to the supreme interest of the nation, whose interpreter is the State' (XI).

The legal texts thus clearly reflect the political situation that existed at the time the constitutions were approved, they act as their guardians for the future, they express the programmes with which power legitimises itself and obtains consensus: solidarity becomes the shield of these projects, whether they arise from social revolutions or reactionary and conservative regimes.

The Second World War marked a point of discontinuity with the past in all countries, victors and vanquished; not in the totalitarian regimes of Portugal and Spain, which survived the conflict as neutral countries and lasted for more than 30 years after the end of the war.

## §5.04    SOLIDARITY: IN THE CORPORATIST SYSTEM

Between the two world wars, a new movement, later to become a party, established the Fascist dictatorship in Italy. Fascism seized the ganglia of power by exploiting the political weakness of the critical phase following the First World War, in line with the constitutional provisions, a web of very generic rules not yet reinforced by an organic legal culture, and above all fragile because the Statuto albertino (1848) was a flexible constitution, as it could be derogated by ordinary laws.

In the context of Italian private law, in order to understand the meaning of the term 'solidarity', it is necessary to start from the Labour Charter, which was put before the civil code in the original version that came into force on 21 April 1942. As is well-known, the question had arisen in doctrine as to whether it was appropriate to place the enumeration of general principles before the text of the civil code. An important conference had been organised on the subject in Pisa, organised by the local university, in which the masters of the subject had participated. However, Dino Grandi was not in favour of this innovation, fearing that principles, being by their nature, open standards and therefore easily manipulated, would offer the judge-interpreter too wide margins of application. He therefore opted for the placement of the Labour Charter – the document approved in 1927 as a fundamental act of the Regime, therefore as a political act, and then used by the Court of Cassation itself in the field of labour law as a table of values with an interpretative function – as a premise to the Civil Code. In this way, with the promulgation of the third book of the code, and then with the confirmation given by the promulgation of the entire civil code in 1942, the Charter not only became a legal document but also 'the defining content, of a strictly legal nature, of our positive order, as it became following the general renewal of our legislation' (Rel. Min. Guardasigilli, p. 4). It is considered a 'super law' 'inspiring present and future laws and a sure guide in the interpretation and daily application of laws' (*ibid.*). The priority of the supreme authority of the State, the prevalence of the Nation's interest over that of the individual, and the observance of social justice are the pillars of the corporative order 'bringing everywhere that sense of social solidarity that does not oppose one another, but unites and coordinates the various individual interests for the achievement of the Nation's higher ends'.[142] In a few words, the Minister of the Seals illustrates the fundamental characteristics of the new order, which distinguish it from the liberal, individualist model, free from state intervention: individual interests must be subordinated to the aims of superior interest pursued by the state.

In a few lines, the meaning of solidarity is then made clear: it is a feeling, but at the same time, a value, a principle, and therefore a normative command. Individuals are part of society, which, through the division of labour, holds all its components together, and demands that they all cooperate with each other not to realise their own selfish interests but to realise the higher interest of the nation. The collective prevails over the individual, cooperation over conflict: the class struggle is replaced by a homogenised society, flattened on the collective interest.

---

142. *Ibid.*, p. 11.

Already at the outset, Provision II regarded work as a *social duty*.

Provision IV reads: 'In the collective labour agreement, solidarity between the various factors of production finds its concrete expression, through the reconciliation of the opposing interests of employers and workers, and their subordination to the higher interests of production.' And Provision VII: 'The corporative state regards private initiative in the field of production as the most effective and most useful instrument in the interests of the nation. The private organisation of production being a function of national interest, the organiser of the enterprise is responsible for the direction of production before the state. From the collaboration of the productive forces derives reciprocity of rights and duties between them. The worker, whether technician, employee or labourer, is an active collaborator in the economic enterprise, the management of which is the responsibility of the employer.'

Certainly, these are statements that unequivocally mark the subordination of the individual to the state, evoke the image of the Leviathan depicted in Hobbes' edition of the book that assigns all powers to the sovereign, and considers the natural rights of men not pre-existing to the state but granted to them by it. The overcoming of conflict in the name of *social solidarity*, however, warns us that this principle is being bent to the realisation of ends quite different from those that the current Constitution proposes and which it imposes on the legislature-state: there it was a question of introducing social peace mechanisms in which workers could no longer count on their own trade unions, but had to turn to the fascist trade unions, to which employers and employees belonged, and thus found themselves in a state of persistent contractual weakness. Solidarity was objective, not between people, but between the interests of the participants in production.[143]

Here, social solidarity implies the intervention of the state, its action, to bring social classes closer together, to improve the living conditions of disadvantaged groups, to financially support the welfare state, to ensure equal opportunities for all. A very different meaning, much more challenging, and correctly placed in the dialectic of opposing interests.

Again. The Labour Charter outlined the tasks of a very circumscribed welfare state: it provided for remuneration 'in keeping with the needs of the worker and the enterprise' (Declaration XIV), weekly rest (Declaration XV) and paid holidays (Declaration XVI), compensation in the event of non-negligent dismissal (Declaration XVII), preservation of employment in the event of temporary illness (Declaration XVIII), accident insurance and social insurance (Declaration XXVI ff.).

These cornerstones of corporatist law expressed an idyllic vision of labour relations, which did not correspond to the reality of work, where workers were exposed to risks, heavy performance, retaliation and harsh treatment. Legal and political rules bent workers' legitimate claims and expectations with the blackmail of dismissal; political consensus ended up prevailing over individual situations. In short, a facade and nominal solidarity rather than genuine and real values.

---

143. *Ibid.*, p. 83.

In the sphere of private law, the premises of the discourse operated a reformulation of the rules concerning associations, the family, the regulation of property, obligatory relations, compensation for damages, and business activity. Above all, in the regulation of property, the princely institution of bourgeois individualism, one notes the intention to make a break with the past and to redesign the institution with a publicist colouring, and with the declamation of the priority of collective interest over individual interest.[144] The institution of private property, the Report states, must be inspired by *solidarity and collaboration*.[145] The prohibition of emulative acts stands as a principle of solidarity and collaboration between private individuals. And so is the regulation of *immissioni*, in which the interests of property are subordinated to those of the nation, in application of the *principle of sociality*.[146] Certainly, these provisions are striking, compared to those of the liberal codes of the nineteenth century, which centred on the protection of property as the cornerstone of the economic order.[147]

The ownership of the enterprise – agricultural or commercial – is considered in its dynamic, not static dimension (such as the tried and tested one of the simple rentier). Dynamic property is integrated with business activity, to the point that the Minister of the Seals himself outlines an industrialised agricultural property,[148] in which the interests of the parties – the owner, the employees, the recipients of the products and services – are coordinated and balanced with the interest of the state. The call for cooperation in the exercise of enterprise fits into this non-conflictual vision. 'The power of private initiative [is] recognised as a function of the national interests of production; the exercise of every right conceived as a generator of social responsibility; the legal norm conceived as a norm of social justice' (Rel. no. 806). The 'new economic order' advances by incorporating labour into the enterprise, and the labour of the enterprise is far superior to the simple commercial exchange relationship that was envisaged in the nineteenth-century codes. Large and small enterprises, private enterprises and public enterprises are subject to the control and impetus of the state in order to coordinate production and trade with the higher national interest (Rel. no. 838). And the social aspects of the employment relationship are extolled (Rel. no. 845).

With regard to the regulation of the wrongful act, the report recalls the principles of solidarity of the corporate order in three hypotheses, reflected in the wording of the provisions of the code: (i) in the case of the wrongful exercise of a right (Rel. no. 797), but only to say that it does not conform to corporate solidarity, and is sanctioned in contractual matters, for violation of Article 1175, a provision that implies *ex parte creditoris* the consideration of the interest of others and of the superior interests of the community; (ii) in the provision of an equitable indemnity (Article 2047(ii)) in the provision of equitable compensation (Article 2047) for the incapable person, who, while not being liable for the damage caused, must nevertheless comply with the 'duty

144. *Ibid.*, pp. 83 ff.
145. *Report of the Minister of Justice, Dino Grandi, to the King of Italy*, Rome, 1942, No. 406, p. 84 (Relazione al Codice civile).
146. Report No. 412, p. 85.
147. Ferri (G.B.), *Il potere e la parola e altri scritti di diritto civile*, Padua, 2008.
148. Rodotà, *Il terribile diritto*, Bologna, 2012; Irti, *Diritto agrario italiano*, Torino, 1978.

of mutual understanding of members of the community', in observance of the principle of general utility posed by the corporate order, 'which does not isolate the interest of the individual, detaching it from the life of relations (...) but merges all selfishness, to[149] make it a living matter of healthy balance, harmony and coordination for the interests of all' (Rel. no. 799); (iii) in the case of liquidated damages for economic equivalent, in substitution for damages in a specific form, in deference to the corporate consideration of the interests of the parties, so that the compensation is not excessively onerous for the debtor or contrary to the interests of the national economy (Rel. no. 802). Here it is the case to say that corporate solidarity was understood in a very marginal semantic extension: the doctrine, applying the principles of the Constitution and in this case precisely the principles of social solidarity – would have affected the interpretation and application of the rules on the illicit fact much more, drawing nourishment from solidarity for a true and proper refounding of the system. Beyond the techniques for distributing the damage in the most efficient manner,[150] solidarity was placed at the basis of the judgement of liability, thus understanding it as a parameter of conduct, and not only as a criterion for liquidating the damage,[151] and at the basis of the definition of unfair damage, in order to offer protection to physical and moral integrity, subspecies of biological damage,[152] as well as the protection of the person in the various fragments of which his personality is composed, and also for the protection of the environment and consumers.[153]

---

149. Report, No. 412.
150. P. Trimarchi, *Rischio e responsabilità oggettiva*, Milan, 1961.
151. S. Rodotà, *Il problema della responsabilità civile*, Milan, 1964.
152. G. Alpa, *Il danno biologico. Percorso di un idea*, Padua, 1987.
153. G. Alpa, *La responsabilità civile*, Milan, 2018.

CHAPTER 6

# Solidarity in the Second Half of Twentieth-Century Constitutions

## §6.01 THE PREAMBLE TO THE 1946 FRENCH CONSTITUTION

Textual analysis reveals that the principle of solidarity also stands out in contemporary constitutions. Under the same formula, however, they reveal values far removed from those of totalitarian constitutions.

The preamble to the French Constitution of 1946 is significant. The preamble has a history of its own, compared to the overall text, because, due to its political imprint, it will be preserved as the constitutional text that passes from the Fourth Republic to the Fifth as a supplementary text to the subsequent constitution, introduced by De Gaulle in 1958 and currently in force. Note that Title I dedicated to sovereignty states that the motto of the Republic is: *Liberty, Equality, Fraternity*.[154]

The word *solidarity* also appears in the Preamble: 'The Nation proclaims the solidarity and equality of all French people in the face of the burdens of national calamities', albeit limited to exceptional circumstances. But constitutional law scholars emphasise that solidarity is a principle that pervades the entire Constitution and is a qualifying part of the social pact; indeed, it is a value that stands alongside *fraternity*, now placed at a further stage of brotherhood between citizens.

The socioeconomic constitution is all in the preamble because, for the rest, the Charter deals with the structure of the state and the division of powers.

Hence a regression, certainly, even with respect to the Weimar Constitution, and a certain vagueness in the declamation of rights and duties, due to the political moment in which the text is being drafted – we are precisely at the rebirth of the Republic after the defeat of the war and the obscurantist period of Vichy – and also to the need to mediate between the august libertarian tradition deriving from the 1989 Declaration of

---

154. Article 2 c.3.

Rights and the push towards the relativism of rights suggested by a more concrete conception of political relations.[155]

The structural analysis of the text[156] highlights the different components of the constitutional basis: the 'inalienable and sacred' rights proclaimed in the Revolutionary Declaration, the fundamental principles recognised by the laws of the Republic, and the political, economic and social principles enshrined below. These are three bodies of rules-values with different legal qualifications and originating from different experiences: the first, natural law, which today's jurists tend to relativise; the second,

---

155. It is worth quoting the text to savour its rhythm and careful use of words:

> In the aftermath of the victory won by free peoples over regimes that attempted to enslave and degrade the human person, the French people once again proclaim that every human being, without distinction of race, religion or belief, possesses inalienable and sacred rights. It solemnly reaffirms the rights and freedoms of man and citizen consecrated by the Declaration of Rights of 1789 and the fundamental principles recognised by the laws of the Republic.
>
> It also proclaims the following political, economic and social principles as particularly necessary in our time: The law guarantees women equal rights to men in all fields. Every man persecuted for his action in favour of freedom has the right to asylum in the territories of the Republic.
>
> Everyone has the duty to work and the right to obtain employment. No one can be harmed in his or her work or employment because of his or her origins, opinions or beliefs.
>
> Every man can defend his rights and interests through trade union action, and join the trade union of his choice.
>
> The right to strike is exercised within the framework of the laws regulating it.
>
> Every worker participates, through his delegates, in the collective determination of working conditions and in the management of undertakings.
>
> Every good, every enterprise, the use of which has or acquires the character of a national public service or a de facto monopoly, must become the property of the community.
>
> The nation ensures the individual and the family the conditions necessary for their development.
>
> It guarantees everyone, and especially the child, the mother and the elderly worker, health protection, material security, rest and holidays. Every human being who, because of age, physical or mental condition or economic situation, is unable to work, has the right to obtain adequate means of existence from the community.
>
> The Nation proclaims the solidarity and equality of all French people in the face of the burdens of national disasters.
>
> The nation guarantees children and adults equal access to education, vocational training and culture. The organisation of public, free and secular education in all grades is a duty of the state.
>
> The French Republic, true to its traditions, conforms to the rules of international public law. It shall not wage any war with a view to conquest, and shall never use its forces against the freedom of any people. Subject to reciprocity, France allows the limitations of sovereignty necessary for the organisation and defence of peace.
>
> France forms, with the peoples across the sea, a Union founded on equality of rights and duties, without distinction of race or religion.
>
> The French Union is composed of nations and peoples pooling or coordinating their resources and efforts to develop their civilisations, increase their welfare and ensure their security.
>
> Faithful to its traditional mission, France intends to lead the peoples whose care it has assumed to the freedom to administer themselves and to manage their own affairs democratically; rejecting any system of colonisation based on arbitrariness, it guarantees everyone equal access to public functions and the individual and collective exercise of the rights and freedoms that are proclaimed or confirmed hereafter.

156. Chevallier, Essai d'analyse structurale du Preambule, Hal. Archives – ouvertes. Fr./hal – 01728071/ document.

more coruscating, which the Preamble raises to constitutional dignity; the third, more nebulous, contained in the new enunciations provided for by the Preamble itself. The actors are from time to time the People, the Republic, France, the Nation. The beneficiaries also belong to different categories, depending on the rights protected: human beings, the human person, the French, the family, the people.

In addition to the classic freedoms, the Preamble protects the so-called *droits-créances, the* social rights, which presuppose the duties associated with work: the right to employment and remuneration, welfare rights, the right to health care, housing and subsistence, education and so on. Hence the great difference from the '89 Declaration, due not only to the different cultural matrix and the centuries-long distance between the two texts, but also to the fact that the latter brings into play more types of actors – there it was the individual-citizen before the Monarchy – and more sources of law, and not only the law elevated to a sacred source.

The structural reading of the text allows today's jurists to say that this Constitution while recalling the principles of '89, is not subjugated by natural law, because human rights are relativised. The Preamble, by referring to the implementing laws, allows its declamatory utterances to be better contextualised.

But what is most important is the definition of the legal nature of the Preamble. For a long time in France, it was thought that a distinction had to be made between normative texts according to the intensity of the commitment of the public authorities to the individual.

From this perspective, it was easy to argue that the text of the Preamble, as well as that of the '89 Declaration, had an eminently political value, and the public authorities were only bound by the laws that put in place rules implementing constitutional principles. But from the 1970s onwards, especially by the *Conseil constitutionnel*, the immediately binding legal value of the '89 Declaration of Rights and the 1946 Preamble was no longer in doubt.

The texts of constitutional law now accredit the more progressive solution: although when it appeared, the Declaration clearly (and exclusively) had a political significance, its reference in the Preamble of 1946 and then its inclusion in the Preamble of the Constitution of the Fifth Republic inaugurated by De Gaulle and still in force today, make it an *immediately binding* text, as is the 1946 Preamble.

However, as will be discussed in a moment, solidarity is considered a moral rather than a legally binding concept.

For its part, the 1958 Constitution with a very concise preamble recalls the Declaration of '89 and the Preamble of the 1946 Constitution.[157]

Article 2 c.4 repeats the motto of the triad freedom equality fraternity mentioned above.

---

157. 'The French People solemnly proclaim their loyalty to the rights of man and the principles of national sovereignty as defined by the Declaration of 1789, confirmed and supplemented by the preamble to the Constitution of 1946, and to the rights and duties defined in the Charter of the Environment of 2004. On the basis of these principles and that of the free determination of peoples, the Republic offers to the overseas territories that manifest the will to adhere to it new institutions founded on the common ideal of liberty, equality and fraternity and conceived for the purposes of their democratic evolution.'

This has led to the argument – in a research that reconstructs the entire history of the principle of *fraternity*, as linked to that of *solidarity* – that the Preamble gave way to social legislation and an evolutionary interpretation of the Constitutions, in which solidarity stands out, now replacing fraternity, now preparing the ground for its revitalisation.[158]

The French experience is extraordinarily important, rich and significant for us, one could say decisive. Our Constituent Fathers were bound to that experience by many ties, linguistic (until the early years after the Second World War, French was the most widely known foreign language in the world and in Italy), cultural, facilitated by the affinity of the two legal and political systems, given that before the German invasion, many Italian antifascist politicians who were part of the Constituent Assembly had found refuge in France.

There had also been very close cooperation between Italian and French jurists until the mid-1930s. In the sphere of private law, beyond the basic Romanist components, it was enough to consider the affinity of the civil code in force in Italy until 1942 with the Code Napoléon, and the initiative promoted by Vittorio Scialoja for the drafting of a draft Italian-French code of obligations, published in 1928, and the permeability of Italian culture to French legal culture. Hence the relevance not only to the basic choices made by the Constituent Fathers but also to the legal language used in the drafting of the Italian text.

### §6.02    THE THESIS OF THE CONTINUITY OF THE VALUE OF FRATERNITY

As has been documented, in France there is a silence in the constitutional texts that followed from 1789 to 1848, in the sense that fraternity does not appear until 1848, but in the collective imagination (even today) the term is aggregated with those of liberty and equality going back *à rebours* to 1789, as if the revolutionaries themselves had preached its normativity, and as if the two icons of the Revolution, liberty, which was finally guaranteed to all men who were freed from the serfdom of the Ancien Régime, and equality in the formal sense, which made them homologous without differences in legal status (even if differences in de facto status were preserved) could not be considered complete without a third component, brotherhood among men.

To overcome the formal text, some authors have been able to demonstrate that, despite the silence of the texts, the principle was equally felt, concrete and present in the constitutional doctrine of the time. It could be argued that backdating is the result of an anti-historical reinterpretation of the past, of a well-orchestrated anachronism. But the continuity thesis appears more persuasive.

The thesis of continuity is argued in a convincing and skilfully documented manner by Michel Borgetto, in research that takes its starting point from pre-revolutionary French political doctrine in which fraternity is considered the cement of

---

158. Borgetto, *supra*, pp. 230 ff.

society.[159] In revolutionary texts, starting with the Déclaration, fraternity, although not mentioned, is *presupposed*: in his argumentation, Borgetto follows two lines of thought that converge in their results. The first line concerns the idea of fraternity which Borgetto considers underlying liberty and equality because both these principles are connected to the idea of *nation* and *homeland*: therefore, although not mentioned in the general provisions sacredly carved in the Déclaration, it is nevertheless a necessary complement to them. The idea of fraternity, in his view, no longer abandons French public law since the Déclaration, even if in certain phases – the post-revolutionary and Napoleonic periods – the principle remains in the background. With the Second Republic, the principle strengthens and becomes a pillar of constitutional law; it can count on the support of socialist circles and the support of the Church, in the form of *pietas* and Christian *caritas*.[160] From 1848 onwards, fraternity, later changed to *solidarity*, became a constant guideline in the work of the French legislator.[161] In the world of ideas, and from them in the world of law, in the ideals that underpin the entire legal system, fraternity presides over every human consortium.

This line of thought is joined by the second line, which is formed by the legislative choices of state intervention in the economy and private relations. The intensity of its impact on the legal system is felt to a greater or lesser extent depending on the legislator's choices of social duties.[162] This second guideline gradually grew in the twentieth century, first with the foundation of the welfare state, and then after the First World War with the expansion of the welfare state. This alternating but continuous line leads Borgetto to argue that today's solidarity is invigorated by the idea of fraternity.[163]

Borgetto's thesis, while appreciated by many, did not seem convincing to public law doctrine, which emphasises that the mention of solidarity in the Preamble of the 1946 Constitution has a programmatic value, because it cannot be dissociated from its context. The Preamble[164] places obligations on the State, in designing a broad model of social democracy, but it is a programme of a *moral* nature that requires the legislator to take concrete measures to realise it; it is therefore removed from the competence of the *Comité constitutionnel*.[165]

## §6.03    THE REFOUNDING OF THE SOCIAL PACT IN BRITAIN

English legal culture – very permeable to political and philosophical ideas concerning the cohesive forces of the social aggregate, the distribution of power, the relationship between authority and the individual, and the boundaries of social justice – has been the natural *humus of* social rights since the late nineteenth century. There is a continuity between the first claims of trade unions and the principle of equality of

---

159. Borgetto, *La notion de fraternité en droit public français. Le passé, le present et l'avenir de la solidarité*, Paris, 1993.
160. Borgetto, *supra*, pp. 230 ff.
161. *Ibid.*, pp. 356 ff.
162. *Ibid.*, pp. 401 ff., 404 ff.
163. *Ibid.*, pp. 606 ff.
164. Hamon & Troper, *Droit consititutionnel*, 41 ed., 2020-2021, Paris, 2020.
165. *Ibid.*, p. 441.

women's associations, the economic and social struggles following the First World War, and the social re-foundation projects sketched out during the Second World War and then realised with the Beveridge Plan in the early post-war period.

Willian Henry Beveridge published two important works before the war in which he examined the social situation in his country, marked by a deep division between classes, and the supremacy of the landed aristocratic class, aggravated by the economic crisis of 1929: *Unemployment* (1930), in which he delved into the economic and social problems of unemployment, and a historical study on the relationship between prices and wages, from the Middle Ages to the nineteenth century (1939). His idea was that full employment was not sufficient to solve the problems of the economy and social conflict, but that structural state intervention was needed while preserving the liberal framework.[166]

His conception of society, political intervention and economic equilibrium only partly coincided with the theses of John Maynard Keynes. However, Keynes emphasised entrepreneurship, state support only in the commissioning of public works, and market incentives:

> If the state is able to determine the aggregate amount of resources allocated to the increase of the means of production and the basic rate of remuneration of those who possess them, it will have done everything it needs to, he wrote in 1936.[167]

After all, Keynes was an enlightened Conservative, Beveridge wrote the Report commissioned by Parliament in 1942, when Britain had just emerged from the Nazi air siege that had destroyed major cities. He also wanted to give a hope of redemption and gratification to a stricken population that had managed to hold on to its dignity and the strength to resist but also to attack the aggressor. 'Inactivity, ignorance, disease, misery and aspiration' were the 'five giants' against which the Report was based to outline a forward-looking and challenging plan of action. A plan so revolutionary that the government hesitated before publishing it. At the end of the war, Winston Churchill having fallen, Lord Attlee made it his own.

It has been pointed out that the novelty of William Henry Beveridge's plan was that social security was all-inclusive and extended to all: unemployment benefits and pensions, after a transitional period, would be of the same amount, regardless of previous income levels.[168] The Report also envisaged heavy taxation to support subsidies and pensions, which were to be extended to everyone, even those who had not paid contributions. It was, in short, 'the *price of peace*' (1945) that the community, i.e., the state, had to pay in order to legitimise itself and re-found the social pact.

The Plan soon became a model of social doctrine in all western countries, indeed, it is believed to have become more popular abroad than at home. *Freedom from want* had conquered the threshold of normativity and had become one of the cornerstones of the reformers.

---

166. *Full employment in a free society* (1944); transl. it. 1945.
167. Keynes CWK VII: 378, tr. it: 432-3.
168. Beveridge 1942: 9-10.

The Beveridge Plan, as a model of the welfare state, had a great influence also in Italy[169] and is believed to have influenced the discussion and drafting of the economic constitution provisions drawn up by the Constituent Fathers. Social insurance linked with voluntary insurance would have allowed the free market – the size of which was unfamiliar to the Constituents – to operate without deepening the social imbalance, which could be reduced through a shrewd tax system.

## §6.04    THE ITALIAN CONSTITUTION

At the beginning of 1946, when the new democracies were being built on the rubble of the Second World War, in the countries freed from dictatorships, the invigorating air of freedom was breathed, and the hope of a lasting peace was cultivated, the realisation of an economic system capable of providing work for all, the diffusion of culture, in a simple word, the hope of establishing an authentic democracy. A constitutional and social democracy, in which the principle of equality is effective, substantial, and class differences are mitigated through the leverage of taxation, the distribution of uncultivated land, the abolition of privileges handed down by tradition. The creed of the majority is based on the idea that social peace must overcome class hatred and be realised through party and trade union debate, in parliament, in the streets, focusing on cooperation and solidarity.

Palingenesis goes beyond national borders, encompassing the entire continent, and island countries.

Europe must be rethought, its borders entrusted not only to political decisions, the relations between winners and losers, but above all to the cooperation of the peoples. The Ventotene Manifesto (1941) advocates a European federalism in which, in addition to freedoms, economic initiative is protected in order to create a market free of monopolies, of state intrusiveness, of the exorbitant accumulation of private property, of the papier-mâché construction of corporative orders in which, instead of confronting and mediating between opposing interests, the interests of the weak are coercively coerced into submitting to the strong interests. '*Human solidarity* with those who succumb in the economic struggle', reads the paragraph on 'post-war tasks', 'must not, therefore, be manifested in the always demeaning forms of charity that produce the same evils whose consequences they seek to remedy, but in a series of provisions that unconditionally guarantee a decent standard of living to all, whether they can work or not, without reducing the incentive to work and save.[170] In this way, no one will be forced by misery to accept iugatory work contracts any longer'.

In Florence, in May 1946, Pietro Calamandrei wrote the presentation of the second edition of Francesco Ruffini's book on the *Rights of Liberty*, for La Nuova Italia. The first edition had been published in Turin in 1926 by Piero Gobetti with his publishing house. The text, written in Borgofranco d' Ivrea, had been finished by

---

169. Even to the point of influencing the *Lectures on Social Policy*, composed by Luigi Einaudi during his exile in Geneva and later published in 1949 (*see* ref., Milan, 2010).
170. Spinelli & Rossi, *For a Free and United Europe*, Ventotene (reprinted by the Senate of the Republic, Rome, 2017).

Ruffini in September 1925, and Gobetti had wanted to publish it running the risks that the publication of a book considered highly subversive by the fascist regime might have entailed. Despite the climate of illiberty established by Fascism, the author and publisher had taken on a great responsibility in disseminating pages of the highest civil ethics, in which the rights of liberty that the totalitarian regime had long since begun to conculcate were legally reconstructed. Precisely because of the anti-fascism professed by both, the book could only circulate in the bush. Gobetti had manifested his aversion to the dictatorship with *La Rivoluzione liberale* and had already suffered two assaults by squads; having taken refuge in France, he was to die, following the beatings, shortly afterwards, in February 1926; Ruffini, professor of ecclesiastical law at the University of Turin, had signed Benedetto Croce's Manifesto degli intellettuali antifascisti shortly before handing over the manuscript; in 1931, he was to give up his professorship for not taking the oath of loyalty imposed by the regime.

A text, therefore, that evoked the yearning for freedom and that, republished 20 years later, in the Italy liberated from dictatorship and Nazi occupation, indicated the road to follow to rebuild democracy. Calamandrei did not content himself with commenting on those pages, which were, moreover, full of legal wisdom, and accompanied by a collection of the most relevant constitutional texts, from Magna Charta to the fundamental laws of the European countries after the First World War, but he drew up, on the basis of Ruffini's teaching, a fundamental essay entitled *The Future of the Rights of Liberty*. From these pages, which could be considered divinatory, emerge not only essential concepts linking fundamental freedoms to social rights but many formulae that we find in the text of the current Constitution.[171]

Social rights are the conquest of twentieth-century constitutions; and even where the constitution is the result of a customary tradition, as in the English experience, social rights assert themselves as an essential component of democracy: Beveridge's programme becomes a model to be compared with in all European countries.[172] The economic crisis had also provoked a rethinking of the economic system in the United States, and in Roosevelt's New Deal social rights have a positive character – Calamandrei points out in words that will be taken up almost verbatim in the text of the Italian Constitution – 'insofar as they correspond to the state's obligation to remove obstacles of an economic and social nature that stand in the way of the free moral and political expansion of the human person' (p. xxxvi).

Social rights, at the time when Pietro Calamandrei outlines their contents, appear as a revolutionary programme: they are not already fully guaranteed, but mark the path of the new democracy, which is both political and social. Political rights and social rights are 'placed on an equal footing' because the guarantee of rights must not act as a privilege for the few, but must avoid economic inequalities and stand as an obstacle to the participation of all in political life. Justice, equality and dignity are thus the values that underpin modern democracy.

---

171. The text has been republished in a standalone version by Galaad Editions, Giulianova, Teramo, 2018.
172. Ruffini, *supra*, p. 15.

This is the message that Piero Calamandrei entrusts 'to the next Italian constituent assembly' (liii) – carrying out an extraordinary political and cultural operation, making Ruffini's rights of liberty and the 'innovations of the most recent constitutions' (lv). But his thoughts also run to the European and international dimension, because the rights of liberty must be defended 'by an international body that safeguards them *against attacks by the state*' (lv).

In its pages, it paints not only the future of the rights of liberty, but an entire project of constitution and society, in the different experiences realised on a national, European and international level. That project of renewal was only partly realised: in some respects, it expanded and strengthened, in others it proved to be vague.

## §6.05 THE DRAFTING OF ARTICLES 2 AND 3 OF THE ITALIAN CONSTITUTION

In the Italian Constitution, solidarity stands out in the opening norms, where already Article 2 states that the Republic 'requires the fulfilment of the non-derogable duties of political, economic and social solidarity'. The term is used as *if* its meaning were clear and unambiguous, to the point of being considered as expressive of a precept from which obligations are derived for all men. When it is stated that the Republic requires fulfilment, it does not say to whom it is required: but since the first part of the article refers to the protection of individual 'inviolable' rights, which are recognised as guaranteed to *all*, it is reasonable to assume that *everyone is* expected to contribute to taking on the problems of the community, and therefore that all fulfil their duties in solidarity.[173]

Article 3 reads: 'All citizens have equal social dignity and are equal before the law, without distinction of sex, race, language, religion, political opinion, personal and social conditions. It is the duty of the Republic to remove those obstacles of an economic or social nature which constrain the freedom and equality of citizens, thereby impeding the full development of the human person and the effective participation of all workers in the political, economic and social organisation of the country.'[174]

These are words pregnant with meaning and inference. Their enunciation was not easy, the text was debated, written and rewritten many times during the debate that took place first in the Commission of the Seventy-Five and then in the Constituent Assembly. It is understandable that it took some time to unravel the complexity of the text. If the opening provisions were to give the imprint of the new state that was resurgent after the tragedy of the Second World War, the war of liberation and the civil war, with which the country had shaken off dictatorship and monarchy, and had been able to regain its unity, one could not ignore the relationship between the individual and the community, nor guarantee rights to the individual without demanding a contribution of solidarity. A full-bodied contribution, made up of political, economic,

---

173. Pinelli, *Il discorso sui diritti sociali fra Costituzione e diritto europeo*, europeanrights.eu/.
174. Speech of 17 March 1947.

and social aspects: the right-duty to participate in political life, the right-duty to carry out work, whether independent or dependent, manual or intellectual, commercial or cultural, the duty to contribute to taxation. *Individual, Collectivity, State* are thus the pillars on which solidarity is unravelled, understood – precisely because it is contained in a normative text, and deputed to represent a patchwork of rights and duties – as a *normative concept*.

If one reads in the watermark the work of the First Sub-Commission dedicated to drafting the articles on the rights and duties of citizens, one learns that the concept of solidarity was not understood, at least originally, as a normative concept, but rather as – and only – a *political* concept. The difference is not insignificant: a political concept indicates a model for organising the state and social life, which can be implemented in various ways, as a broad directive, without it giving rise to rights and duties on the part of individuals; a legal concept affects the individual legal sphere, creates expectations, imposes behaviour, and, above all, if the precept containing it is violated, implies a sanction. It is therefore endowed with that character of coercibility, which eludes the political concept, always contestable or modifiable, without the need for procedures and deliberations.[175]

Solidarity therefore acquires a more complex dimension than how it was considered in the twentieth-century constitutional texts that preceded the entry into force of the Italian Constitution: there, solidarity was spoken of as the founding bond of human consortium, and as a pillar of the welfare state; its dimension was always individual: the individual vis-à-vis the state, the individual vis-à-vis the community. Here, on the other hand, solidarity is also understood as the founding bond of social formations, the family, associations, the working community – and we could include, of course, parties and trade unions.

The Preamble of the 1946 French Constitution was well in the minds of the Constituent Fathers: but that text cannot be reproduced *sic et simpliciter* in the Italian Constitution because it has a different history. Above all, the Constituent Fathers felt the need to condemn the fascist experience and make the provisions on fundamental rights more analytically usable.

On 24 March 1947, in the afternoon session, the Constituent Assembly approved Article 6 of the draft and relocated it as Article 2 in its final formulation:

> The Republic recognises and guarantees the inviolable rights of man both as an individual and in the social groups where his personality is developed; and requires the fulfilment of the duties of political, economic and social solidarity.

There is therefore a structural difference and a difference in content that make the text much more challenging and implying than the French Constitution: the principle of solidarity is *part of the text* and *not a preamble*, it is also understood as a source of duties as well as rights, and it considers not only the individual in and of itself but also the social formations of which it is part and in which it performs its personality.

---

175. Speech of 17 March 1947.

These three capital differences highlight the fullness of the principle of solidarity as conceived by the Constituent Fathers. Since a Preamble merely constitutes the framework of values in light of which the constitutional text is to be interpreted but does not imply, according to the prevailing orientation, the enunciation of a binding provision in itself, the choice to include the principle of solidarity in a provision – Article 3 (formerly 6) placed at the opening of the constitutional text – implies the intention of the constituent legislator to emphasise the *preceptive nature of solidarity*. The fundamental rights of the individual (not only of the 'citizen') are protected in the individual sphere and in relation to the state. The protection of rights is balanced by the individual's duties towards the community and the State. It follows from the combined provisions of Articles 2 and 3 of the Constitution that the State is responsible for removing obstacles of an economic and social nature so that the principle of equality is also respected in its substantive aspect and to ensure a dignified existence for all. This is why solidarity has been spoken of as a political project.[176]

## §6.06 THE DIMENSION OF DUTY

Solidarity appears in constitutions in the legal form of duty.

In the general theory of law, duty is defined as a passive subjective situation; but there are disagreements about its correlation to law, and about its existence even without the counterpart of law.[177]

A distinction is then made between public duties and private duties, the former being prescriptive of conduct to be performed for the benefit of the State or public administration in general, and the latter in the context of private legal relations. It is clarified that as far as relevant, duties (e.g., duties of solidarity), change their content depending on the era and context in which they are envisaged.

Constitutional duties are the reason for the introduction of the guarantee of rights in the statutes of the early nineteenth century. In other words, as much as citizens are recognised as having rights insofar as they assume duties towards the state; the scope of duties throughout the nineteenth century is not very wide, precisely because the state refrains from interfering in the individual legal sphere. The state demands loyalty, cooperation in the event of war, economic support to finance public expenditure. Since there are no social interests to satisfy, the relief of the sick, the poor, the elderly, widows and orphans is entrusted to the charity and beneficence of private individuals.

As a general category of law, it is significant that the duties appearing in the constitutions of the nineteenth century were considered more political and moral than juridical precisely because of the abstention of the state from any interference in relations between private individuals and hence the free market. This gap was also perpetuated in private law, where the category of duty, associated with that of obligation, had had a dogmatic elaboration that was quite peculiar and distant from

---

176. Carlassarre, *Solidarity: A Political Project*, www.Constitutionalism.it, 2016, no. 1.
177. *See* at length Romano (Santi), *Doveri, obblighi,* in *Frammenti di un dizionario giuridico,* (1947) rit. inalt. Macerata, 2019, p. 127; and now Guastini, *Dovere giuridico,* in *Enc.giur.Treccani,* Roma, 1990, XXI, 4.

that with more rhetorical contours of 'political duties' accredited in public law. In other words, there was 'an unbridgeable gap between legal reality and political imagination'.[178] Although nineteenth-century duties derive from the *pactum subiectionis* and if you like from the *pactum civitatis*, dating back to mediaeval feudal law, in the liberal state duties become the expression of the right of citizenship, with a marked voluntarist connotation.[179] In the post-First World War constitutions, as we have seen, duties with a broader content begin to appear, corresponding to the broader tasks assigned by the state. The criticism of the advocates of authoritarian law, such as Carl Schmitt, focuses precisely on their inconsistency and their inability to have any further legal effect than the limitation in a social sense of the rights of private individuals. But this is precisely where the novelty of those constitutions, starting with the Weimar Constitution, lies: the category of duty/obligation penetrates into the definition of the limits of the subjective right, indeed of the subjective right par excellence, the right to property.

In the post-Second World War constitutions, which open up major social tasks to the state, the duty of solidarity is strengthened. And it is even questioned whether it can be considered as the counterbalance to the recognition and guarantee of fundamental rights because, Giorgio Lombardi emphasises, 'the *proprium of* constitutional duties, as indeed is characteristic of all limiting situations, is that of a series of precepts that the constitution contains to allow their implementation while avoiding the danger of a series of interventions left to the arbitrary will of the legislator'.[180] This does not result in a mere reservation of the law 'but with a mode of implementation of constrained conduct' and therefore the number of duties is constrained and this is found in the provision of Articles 4, 30, 48, and 52-54 of the Constitution. In this sense, constitutional duties are typified and a closed number.[181] The situation of the passive subjective situation of duties/obligations incumbent on private individuals as a result of the creation of subjective rights in their favour by other private individuals is different. Following the implementation – direct or indirect of constitutional principles to relations between private individuals, to each new right, always created within the framework of Article 2 of the Constitution, but freely, correspond duties of abstention and observance on the part of other fellow citizens, and even of cooperation, as will be specified when dealing with solidarity in the sphere of private law.

## §6.07    SOCIAL RIGHTS

Mentioned fleetingly in the constitutions of the nineteenth century, which were more likely to recognise certain fundamental freedoms and to protect the right to property and free enterprise, the rights connected with essential needs began to be recognised at the end of the nineteenth century only in ordinary legislation. The political reason for this recognition is given by the response of the 'mono-class' liberal states to the economic and social demands coming from the poorer classes, often lacking the right

---

178. Lombardi, Do*veri pubblici (dir.cost.)*, entry in the Enc.dir. aggiorn., VI, Milan, 2002, pp. 357 ff.
179. *Ibid.*, p. 358.
180. *Ibid.*, p. 362.
181. *Ibid.*, p. 363.

to vote, certainly unable to contribute to the support of public expenditure with the levy of direct taxes, but nevertheless affected by indirect taxation, as well as by the cost of living. Since they are rights protected not 'en bloc', but from time to time, with different regulatory instruments, and accumulate in a non-systematic manner, their category is defined with blurred contours, and yet they do not deserve marginal consideration. They are considered 'second-generation' rights, alongside the rights of liberty, but they are the rights 'functional to socialisation, to the integration of the individual into society'.[182] They therefore proceed hand in hand with the rights of liberty, once recognised, and their classification may vary, without however affecting their relevance, which is equal to the rights of liberty. They are therefore secondary rights only historically, but not in terms of their rank or nature. They can also be configured as claims addressed to the State, concerning work, housing, standard of living, insurance and social security; rights concerning the family are also included in this category, of course, rights held by family members, not the family as an entity in and of itself, which is a natural social formation without legal personality in the Italian legal system. The rights arising from belonging to a family are to all intents and purposes considered perfect subjective rights, and it is not possible in these pages to make them the subject of a specific analysis.

To return to the category of social rights, their heterogeneous nature, the fact that they are formulated not as negative freedoms – which the person claims from the state (such as the right to life, physical integrity, personal freedom, privacy, etc.) – but as freedoms from something (from hunger, poverty, unemployment, etc.), which therefore imply a cost for the state, and for this reason, they are considered by many as the object of programmes but not of precepts.

This has led to doubts that they can be equated with the rights of liberty, and that like the rights of liberty, they are inviolable, indivisible, inalienable. Authoritative scholars of the Constitution, such as Calamandrei, Giannini, Mazziotti di Celso, and more recently Biscaretti di Ruffia, Zolo, and Guastini, have expressed this view.

But this line of thought is opposed by those who believe that this category of rights is not separable from the rights of liberty, even though it has its own characteristics: Norberto Bobbio has already made it the subject of persuasive arguments, and then Pinelli, Pino, Politi, Baldassarre have argued its immediate protectability.

Their nature as subjective rights of which citizens are holders is confirmed by the Constitutional Court's interpretation of the Constitution, as well as by their protection offered by the legal texts founding the EU: the Treaties and the Charter of Fundamental Rights.

---

182. Pino, *Social Rights: For a Critique of Some Commonplaces*, in *Practical Reason*, no. 2, 2016, pp. 795 ff.

# CHAPTER 7

# Solidarity in Contemporary Constitutions

## §7.01 THE BONN BASIC LAW (1949)

The Bonn Basic Law does not make the principle of solidarity explicit, nor does it provide for an economic construction, but it does make the principle of the dignity of the person cogent.

Unlike the Weimar Constitution, the Basic Law does not contain any provisions concerning labour, with the exception of Article 12.[183] As far as economic relations are concerned, the text takes up the Weimar Constitution on the subject of property.[184] And Article 15 deals with nationalisation.[185]

German doctrine has dealt very expertly with the regulation of the solidarity principle.

Among the most significant contributions are Dieter Grimm's 1973 studies[186] Grimm performs an important cultural operation because he links the principle of solidarity to its cultural foundations linked to French solidarism and preaches its bindingness, and thus its justiciability. His contribution, however concise, is decisive in understanding how the principle was accredited in the German experience. Duguit's

---

183. '1) All Germans have the right to freely choose their profession, place of work and place of training. Professional practice may be regulated by law. 2) No one may be compelled to a certain job, except in the case of a general public obligation to perform a service, which is equal for all. 3) Forced labour is permissible only following a judicially ordered restriction of liberty.' On the embryonic economic constitution of the Basic Law, see Sum, *The Dictatorship of the Spread: Germany, Europe and the Debt Crisis*, Rome, 2014.
184. 'Art. 14: 1) Property and inheritance rights are guaranteed. The content and limits of these shall be determined by law. 2) Property imposes obligations. Its use must also serve the good of the community).'
185. 'Art 15: Land, natural wealth and means of production may, for the purpose of socialisation, be transferred to collective ownership or other forms of collective economy, with a law determining the manner and extent of compensation. The provisions of Article 14, paragraph 3, sentences 3 and 4 shall apply to compensation.'
186. Grimm, *Solidarität als Rechtsprinzip*, Frankfurt a M., 1973.

work is examined in the political and cultural context of late nineteenth-century France, with particular regard to the ideas arising from the spread of the socialist, Marxian and reformist political current. In this line, there is no caesura between public and private law. And the social effects of the industrial revolution postulate the protection of non-selfish interests that require the foundation of a legal system that is not individualist, like the one originating in the French Revolution, but attentive to the relationship between the individual and the community in which he lives and operates. The principle of solidarity becomes the cement for the new social order.

Also noteworthy is the Uwe Volkmann analysis,[187] in which the topic is treated from a philosophical and legal perspective. Volkmann is a professor of constitutional law and philosophy of law, and he conducts his discourse primarily from the perspective of the foundation of human consortium, starting from the assumption that 'the quality of any society is determined not least by how its members relate in solidarity. Wherever the relationship between individual and community, association and disassociation, autonomy and heteronomy, freedom and responsibility is at issue, it is also about the amount of solidarity that people show or owe each other in their private relationships or through society'.

With respect to post-modernity, the principle of solidarity appears to Volkmann as a 'glue' that holds society together despite the vicissitudes of the times that record 'processes of individualisation and alienation in modernity, the worldwide triumph of capitalism over socialism, the consequences of globalisation, neo-liberal demands for social self-regulation, debates on the restructuring or dismantling of the welfare state, the denunciation of the general decline of moral values, and the return to the idea of community in American communitarianism'.

Volkmann emphasises that the terms are welcoming and familiar, but understanding why it is necessary to be in solidarity and that solidarity implies not only an act of will but also duties of behaviour, is not easy. The term is vague and it is difficult to understand how it is transposed into norms for implementation.

The term is also polysense: Volkmann tries to gather its hidden meanings: 'there is spontaneous and lasting solidarity, solidarity between equals and unequals, solidarity based on personal affection, solidarity based on calculation, solidarity in the pursuit of interests and solidarity based on altruism. There is militant solidarity against third parties and solidarity for third parties, solidarity of workers and solidarity of democrats, solidarity of the rich and solidarity of the dispossessed, national and international solidarity'.

Solidarity is also an ambiguous term: it is also found in the monastic brotherhood and in a band of brigands.

If we then look at its effects, solidarity can be directly personal, or manifest within emotional communities such as marriage, family and partnership, within a community of friends, while solidarity with outsiders is manifested in the giving of donations and charitable activities. Group solidarity can also be linked to the interests of a group in

---

187. Volkmann, *Solidarität – Programm und Prinzip der Verfassung*, Tübingen, 1998.

which members work. And finally, solidarity reveals itself as a bond between members: society as a whole is founded on social and political solidarity.

Here the discourse widens because it goes beyond local and national borders, to expand and draw on European ones. This principle is also applied internationally, and, in recent years, also in anticipation of the future, which is expressed through solidarity between generations.

It is therefore a matter of intervention projects in disparate areas, which requires the expenditure of forces and means, and which must be calibrated taking into account the achievable goals, i.e., the *sustainability of* the measures taken and the goals set.

It is precisely on solidarity that the success or failure of the idea of Europe has been measured, and it is precisely on the need to actually implement this principle that bets have been placed to avert its demise.

## §7.02    THE TWO GERMANYS AND THE REUNIFICATION OF THE COUNTRY (1991)

Until 1991, as is well-known, Germany, divided into two countries, had two very different constitutional regimes. The Constitution of the Federal Republic, or Bonn Constitution, of 1949, stands out – it should be noted – for its opening provision, dedicated to the protection of the dignity of the person, a value that cannot be balanced against others, inviolable and intangible. The rules of economic and social relations are entrusted to ordinary legislation. In contrast, the Constitution of the Democratic Republic, also of 1949, provided, alongside the enunciation of freedom rights, a substantial regulation of economic relations.[188] In 1991, following reunification, the

---

188. The constitutional text of the GDR reads: 'Art. 19 – 1) The order of economic life must correspond to the principles of social justice and must ensure a decent existence for all. 2) The economy must serve the collective good of the people and provide for their needs; it must guarantee everyone a proportionate share of total production. 3) Within the framework of these tasks and ends, the economic freedom of everyone shall be guaranteed. Art. 20 – Farmers, merchants, industrialists and artisans are to be encouraged in their private initiative; cooperative mutualism is to be developed. Article 21 – The State establishes the economic plan through its legislative bodies and with the direct participation of its citizens in order to ensure their basic material conditions and increase their well-being. The people's representatives are charged with monitoring its implementation. Article 22 – 1) Property is guaranteed by the Constitution. Its essence and limits are delimited by laws and social duties towards the community. 2) The right of succession shall be guaranteed in accordance with civil law. The State's participation in successions is determined by law. 3) Works of the mind, the rights of authors, inventors and artists shall enjoy the protection, encouragement and material support of the Republic. Art. 23 – Any limitation of property and any expropriation may be carried out only in the general interest and in accordance with the law. They shall be carried out against fair compensation, unless the law decides otherwise. In the event of a dispute over the amount of compensation, the matter will be settled by the ordinary courts unless the law decides otherwise. Art. 24 – 1) All property imposes obligations on its owner. Its use must not be contrary to the public good. 2) Any abuse of the right to property through the establishment of an economic power and to the detriment of the common good shall entail expropriation without compensation and nationalisation of property. 3) Companies of war criminals and active national socialists are seized and become the property of the people. The same happens to private companies that serve a war policy. 4) All private monopolistic organisations, such as cartels, trade unions, complexes (Konzern), trusts and other private organisations aiming at increasing profits by

Bonn Constitution was also extended to the provinces subject to the socialist regime. However, it should be pointed out that each Land has its own constitution, maintaining the cultural and social characteristics handed down by tradition so that provisions concerning the economy and the welfare state can be found in the regional constitutions. By way of example, the 1946 constitution of the Land of Bavaria provides for a detailed regulation of economic relations, which concern market freedoms, labour protection, social insurance, property and agriculture.[189]

---

controlling production, prices and sales will be dissolved and banned. 5) Private landed estates in excess of 100 hectares shall be abolished and subdivided without compensation. 6) After the realisation of this agrarian reform, private land ownership shall be guaranteed to the farmers. Art. 25 – 1) All natural riches of the subsoil, all natural energies that can be economically exploited, as well as mining, steel and iron production enterprises and the electric power necessary for these enterprises, shall be nationalised. (2) In the meantime, their exploitation shall be placed under the control of the Länder or the Republic when it concerns general Germanic interests. Art. 26 – 1) The allocation and exploitation of land shall be placed under control in order to prevent any abuse. Any increase in the value of the land that does not result from the investment of labour and capital in that land shall profit the community. 2) All citizens and their families shall be ensured healthy housing that meets their needs. In this field, the victims of fascism, the severely disabled, the war wounded and refugees shall enjoy the right of priority. 3) The preservation and increase of agricultural productivity through measures for the reclamation and cultivation of the countryside shall also be ensured. Art. 27 – 1) Private economic enterprises susceptible of nationalisation may be nationalised in accordance with the regulations on expropriation. 2) A decisive influence on enterprises or associations may be granted to the Republic, the Länder, the districts or the municipalities, on the basis of a subsequent law, by means of participation in the management or by other measures. 3) Enterprises and economic associations may be connected by law on the basis of an autonomous administration in order to ensure the cooperation of all the productive forces of the people, to make workers and employers share in the management and to regulate the production, manufacture, distribution, utilisation, prices as well as the import and export of economic products in accordance with community principles. 4) Consumer and production cooperatives as well as agricultural cooperatives and their associations shall be incorporated into the community economy taking into account their constitution and nature. Art. 28 – The alienation of landed property, production establishments and shares that are the property of the people, as well as the imposition of encumbrances on such property, shall be subject to the approval of the people's representative body competent for their owners. Such approval may only be granted by two thirds of the legal number of members. Art. 29 – 1) Wealth and income shall be taxed progressively according to social criteria, taking particular account of family burdens. 2) Special criteria shall be used when taxing assets and income from individual employment.'

189. For an in-depth analysis, see Losano, *The Constitutions of Post-War Germany and Fundamental Rights*, in *Revista Fac.Derecho*, Montevideo, 2012, pp. 225 ff.
    It is interesting to read the text of the Constitution of the Land of Bavaria, in which individual rights are balanced against the interests of collectivity:

    Title IV – Economy and Labour – Chapter I – The Economic Order:

    Art. 151 – 1) All economic activity shall be at the service of the common good; it shall serve in particular to guarantee to all an existence of human dignity and to raise progressively the standard of living of all sections of the population.
       2) Within the limits of these purposes, the power to conclude contracts is free, in accordance with the law. Freedom to exercise power, individual decision-making and freedom for the individual to engage in personal activity in economic life are, in principle, recognised. The economic freedom of the individual is limited by respect for

the freedoms of others and respect for the moral requirements of the common interest. Any harmful and immoral legal acts and especially all economic contracts involving exploitation are illegal and void.

Article 152 – The organised production and distribution of economic products intended to ensure the satisfaction of the vital needs of the population shall be directed by the State. It is the responsibility of the State to ensure the supply of energy to the country.

Article 153 – Independent small and middle-class enterprises in agriculture, handicrafts, trade and commerce, industry and trades shall be encouraged by legislation and administration and shall be protected against excessive tax burdens and against absorption. They shall be protected by the state in their efforts to secure economic freedom and independence, as well as in their development through forms of cooperation. The rise of capable elements, who rise from wage labour to an independent existence, shall be encouraged.

Article 154 – The autonomous bodies of the economic sector, democratically elected through the professional associations, shall participate in the tasks of the economic organisation. The details in this respect shall be regulated by a law.

Art. 155 – In order to satisfy the economic needs of all the inhabitants as equally as possible, categories of utilitarian products may be legally constituted, taking into account the vital interests of the independent productive elements, by creating for this purpose public law corporations on a cooperative basis. These associations will enjoy administrative autonomy within the framework of the laws.

Art. 156 – The merger of several undertakings for the purpose of ascertaining economic power and establishing monopolies is prohibited. In particular, cartels, trusts and price agreements whose purpose is the exploitation of the mass of the population or the destruction of independent middle-class enterprises are prohibited.

Art. 157 – 1) The formation of capital is not an end in itself, but a means to develop the public economy.

2) Money and credit serve to create values and satisfy the needs of all inhabitants.

Chapter II Property

Art. 158 – Property creates an obligation towards the entire country. Public abuse of property or property rights is not protected by law.

Art. 159 – No expropriation may be pronounced except in the cases provided for by law and against adequate compensation, which may also be paid in the form of an annuity. In the event of a dispute and as to the amount of the indemnity, legal recourse is permitted before the ordinary courts.

Art. 160 – 1) Natural riches of great importance for the general economy, the most important sources of energy, railways and other means of communication and transport serving the public, canals and enterprises for the supply, of electricity generally belong to corporations or public utility associations.

2) Means of production of vital importance to the community, large credit institutions and insurance companies may be transferred in ownership to the community if the general interest so requires. The transfer will be carried out on a legal basis and against adequate compensation.

3) Enterprises that have become publicly owned may be administered according to the forms of the private economy, if this method serves the economic purpose pursued.

Art. 161 – 1) The distribution and exploitation of land shall be controlled by the State. Any abuse will be repressed.

2) The surplus value of the land, produced without particular expenditure of labour and capital by the owner, is to be placed at the disposal of the community.

Article 162 – Intellectual property, the rights of authors, inventors and artists enjoy the protection and care of the State.

Chapter III Agriculture

Art. 163 – 1) The land is free. The peasant is not bound to serfdom.

2) Land used for agricultural or forestry cultivation on properties of any size is useful to the community.

3) Peasant land ownership is guaranteed.

4) Peasant-owned land shall not be diverted from its purpose. The purchase of cultivated or forested land shall be subject to the demonstration that such land is suitable for judicious exploitation. It shall not constitute a mere capital investment.

5) The expropriation of cultivated or forested land shall not be carried out except for urgent reasons of general interest, and in particular, for colonisation. Expropriation shall take place against appropriate compensation. Model farms and estates shall, however, be preserved.

Art. 164 – 1) Through the application of technical advances, improvements in vocational education, the practice of agricultural cooperation and the boost given to production and sales, the rural population will be assured a decent and humane existence on its hereditary homeland.

2) Adequate agricultural income will be guaranteed by means of price and wage regulations in line with the general economic situation, as well as market regulations. These will take place on the basis of agreements between producer, distributor and consumer organisations.

Art. 165 – Over-indebtedness of farms shall be prevented by law as far as possible.

Chapter IV The Work

Article 166 – 1) Labour is the source of the people's prosperity and is placed under the special protection of the State.

2) Everyone has the right to create a comfortable life for himself through his work.

3) Everyone has the right and the duty to choose a job in accordance with his or her aptitudes and education and useful to the community, within the terms provided by law.

Art. 167 – 1) Human labour constitutes the most valuable asset of a people and as such is protected against exploitation, against labour accidents and against anything that may be harmful to health.

2) Any exploitation that results in harm to health constitutes an offence of assault and battery.

3) Any infringement of provisions whose purpose is to protect against health hazards and damage in companies will be prosecuted.

Art. 168 – 1) All kinds of honest work are of equal worth and entitle to adequate remuneration. For the same work, men and women shall receive equal pay.

2) Income earned without work by persons able to work will be subject to special taxes by law.

3) All inhabitants of Bavaria are entitled to assistance when they are unable to work or have been unable to find work.

Art. 169 – 1) Minimum wages may be set for each profession that allow the worker a minimum living wage for him and his family and that correspond to the cultural situation of each person.

2) Collective labour agreements between workers' and employers' trade unions shall be binding on the members of such trade unions and, when the general interest so requires, may be declared mandatory. Art. 170 – 1) The right of coalition in defence and for the improvement of working conditions and economic conditions is guaranteed to all and for all professions.

2) All agreements and measures intended to restrict or hinder the right of coalition are illegal and null and void.

Art. 171 – Everyone has the right to be protected against the vicissitudes of life by social insurance within the framework of the law.

Art. 172 – The rights and duties of workers and employers shall be regulated by special law. Art. 173 – Provisions concerning maximum weekly working time shall be the subject of a law.

Art. 174 – Every worker is entitled to a rest period. This is guaranteed in principle through weekend leave and paid annual leave. Special conditions specific to certain professions shall be the subject of a law. Loss of wages resulting from statutory holidays will have to be compensated.

Article 175 – In all economic enterprises, workers have the right to participate in the discussion of all matters that concern them. In major undertakings, they have the right to exercise direct influence on the management and administration of these. To

In the constitutions of the Laender, there are expressions referring to solidarity, sometimes connected to human dignity[190] or the tasks of the state. There are also formulas that are difficult to apply, such as those requiring everyone to cooperate in the event of accidents, catastrophes or particular crises Article 46 of the Brandenburg Constitution).

German doctrine has long discussed – as has North American doctrine – the difference and dialectical relationship between *community* and *society*. In the end, the two terms ended up overlapping, but this outcome is justified by the evolution of society, which, from a class society, becomes a multi-class society, and then a single-class society. It is clear that the 'community' represents an environment in which people are closer and in which differences are less emphasised or exploited as in a society divided into groups or worse between a majority some and minorities. The principle of solidarity requires not only the avoidance of cruelty, the avoidance of torture, and therefore respect for the physical integrity of persons,[191] but also respect for self-determination, freedom of communication, and the dignity of the person in all situations in which they may find themselves.[192] This leads to the paradox of seeing solidarity and freedom in opposition: the former imposes a duty to contribute to the needs of others, the latter allows each person to behave freely as long as his or her behaviour complies with the law. To avoid this conflict, Denninger emphasises, the legislator typifies the duties of solidarity.

At the time of the drafting of the acts relating to the unification of the two Germanies, it was discussed whether to include a provision in the Basic Law of Bonn implying an obligation of solidarity imposed on every citizen. But the idea was discarded, given the vagueness of the term and the difficulty in defining its boundaries. It was noted, however, that the lack of a formal provision on the subject would not have prevented a *social* norm of solidarity from being derived by interpretation.[193] In this sense, solidarity has also been spoken of as a synonym for *citizenship*,[194] a term used by Thomas Humphrey Marshall to designate the legal position of the individual within modern societies that recognise not only fundamental rights but also social

---

this end, they will form works councils in accordance with the terms of a special law. This law will also contain provisions concerning the participation of works councils in the recruitment and dismissal of workers.

Art. 176 – The workers, being equal members of the economic organisation, shall take part in the work of economic organisation together with all those who exercise their activity in economic life.

Article 177 – 1) Labour disputes shall be settled by labour courts composed of an equal number of workers and employers and an independent president.

2) Arbitration decisions in labour disputes may, in accordance with applicable laws, be declared by the government to be mandatory for all.'

190. Denninger, *Constitutional Law and Solidarity*, in *Solidarity*, edited by K. Bayertz, Dordrecht, 1999, pp. 225 ff.
191. According to Rorty, *Contingency, Irony and Solidarity*, Cambridge, 1989.
192. Denninger, *supra*, p. 234 (but *see also Rechtsperson und Solidaritaet*, Frankfurt am Mein, 1967).
193. Baurmann, *Solidarity as a Social Norm and as a Constitutional Norm*, in *Solidarity, supra*, pp. 243 ff.
194. Lukes, *Solidarity and Citizenship*, in *Solidarity, supra*, pp. 273 ff.

rights, 'a form of fundamental human equality connected with the concept of full membership of a community'.[195]

## §7.03    THE CONSTITUTIONS OF THE SCANDINAVIAN AND BENELUX COUNTRIES

The constitutions of the Scandinavian countries are of little interest, either because they are outdated – such as the Constitution of Norway, of 1814 – or because they are insignificant, such as the Constitution of Sweden, or that of Denmark (of 1953) in that they do not provide for anything other than the right to work; the welfare state has been solidly realised in those countries through ordinary laws.

An exception is the Constitution of Finland, which, in addition to the usual fundamental rights, contains three important provisions, concerning the right to work and freedom of enterprise, the right to social security, and liability for environmental damage.[196]

Even in the Benelux, the constitutional texts do not carry significant provisions. In Belgium, the 1994 Constitution (derived from the original text of 1831) also lists

---

195. T.H. Marshall, *Citizenship and Social Class, and Other Essays*, Cambridge, 1950 (tr. it.: *Cittadinanza e classe sociale*, edited by S. Mezzadra, Roma-Bari: Laterza, 2002). On this point *see* Costa, *Cittadinanza*, voce dell'Enciclopedia del Novecento, III Appendice, Roma, 2004.
196. 'Article 18 – Right to work and freedom of enterprise

(1) Everyone has the right to earn his livelihood through employment, profession or trade of his choice, as provided by law. Public authorities have the task of protecting the labour force.
(2) Public authorities promote employment and work in order to guarantee everyone the right to work. The law lays down rules on the right to receive vocational training.
(3) No one may be dismissed without lawful cause.

Art. 19 – Right to social security

(1) Those who are unable to provide themselves with the necessary means for a dignified life have the right to receive what is indispensable for subsistence and assistance.
(2) The law guarantees each and every person the right to subsistence in the event of unemployment, sickness and disability, and in old age, as well as in the event of the birth of a child or the loss of a child's caregiver.
(3) Public authorities guarantee adequate social, health and medical services to everyone, as specifically provided by law; they promote the health of the population. Furthermore, public authorities support families and those responsible for children, so that they can ensure their well-being and personal development.
(4) Public authorities promote everyone's right to housing, as well as the possibility of providing one's own housing.

Article 20 – Environmental Responsibility

(1) Nature and biodiversity, the environment and national heritage are the responsibility of each and every one.
(2) Public authorities do all they can to ensure that everyone has the right to a healthy environment and the opportunity to participate in decisions that affect the environment in which they live.'

among the fundamental rights a provision that alludes to an embryonic welfare state.[197]

The Dutch Constitution of 2002 provides for the protection of the right to work (Article 19) and livelihood (Article 20) and the protection of the environment (Article 21).

Luxembourg's Constitution, originally dating back to 1868, was reformed in 1999, with the introduction of Articles 9-31 on fundamental freedoms, but does not contain any rules concerning the economy and labour.

## §7.04    THE PORTUGUESE CONSTITUTION (1976)

In the years between the Second World War and the present, two constitutions the Portuguese Constitution of 1976 and the Spanish Constitution of 1978 – offer different models for considering solidarity. Both are models that represent a clear break with previous, totalitarian experiences and thus express in their lexical emphasis a yearning for the freedoms and dignity of the human condition unimaginable in the previous era and are projected into a more dignified future.

The Portuguese model conforms in vocabulary to the Italian Constitution and the German Basic Law.

The Spanish model implements solidaristic principles by outlining a broader scenario of political and social action.

The Portuguese Constitution is more detailed in the definition of individual provisions. The Spanish Constitution, for its part, has been the subject of a very extensive literature, the expression of a culturally organised public law. The examination of the two texts, within the limits of the usefulness of the discourse, cannot be delved into further, as, moreover, they deserve to be.

Simplifying the discourse, the Portuguese Constitution, which came into being following the socialist and libertarian proclamation that removed the country from Salazar's fascist yoke, is based on the value of human dignity (Article 1), establishes among the State's tasks the protection of the well-being and quality of life of the people, to whom it recognises economic, social, and cultural rights, guarantees the dignity of the person, and also the right to genetic identity, within the limits in which cryopreservation and genetic techniques are allowed. It devotes an entire chapter to workers' rights, freedoms and guarantees. As far as the economic constitution is concerned, Article 56 provides for the policy of full employment, consumer protection (Article 60)

---

197. 'Article 23 Everyone has the right to lead a life in conformity with human dignity. To this end, the law, decree or regulatory measure referred to in Article 134 shall guarantee, taking into account the corresponding duties, economic, social and cultural rights and define the conditions for their exercise. In particular, these rights include: 1st the right to work and to the free choice of an occupation, within the framework of a general employment policy aimed, *inter alia*, at ensuring the most stable and highest possible levels of employment, the right to fair working conditions and remuneration, as well as the right to information, consultation and collective bargaining; 2nd the right to social security, health protection and social, health and legal assistance; 3rd the right to decent housing; 4th the right to the protection of a healthy environment; 5th the right to cultural and social development.'

and cooperation (Article 61); solidarity is placed among the pillars of the welfare state (Articles 63 ff.); the right to housing, environmental health, quality of life, and protection of the weak (Articles 71 and 72) is stated. Particularly important are the provisions that in economic matters promote sustainable development: social justice is ensured with the necessary correctives to overcome inequalities also through fiscal policy; social cohesion is promoted; economic inequalities between regions are corrected; cooperation is promoted.

The Constitution was revised in 1997.

Social rights include social security (Article 36), health (Article 64), housing (Article 65), the environment (Article 66), and the rights of the disabled, as well as 'cultural' rights. A robust welfare state realisation programme is also envisaged.

The doctrine has emphasised the community value of solidarity and its foundation on the dignity of the human person.[198] Particular attention is paid to the person, preaching the anteriority of legal relevance to recognition by the state. This principle is substantiated and coloured in the democratic state under the rule of law.[199] Social life imposes a correlation between all members of society, based on responsibility: it is the fulfilment of social duties that makes it possible to protect the person, health, the environment; the search for and defence of the common good imposes a common feeling of collective conscience, which implies social responsibility, including intergenerational responsibility.[200]

## §7.05    THE SPANISH CONSTITUTION (1978)

Unlike the Federal Constitution of the Portuguese Republic, the Constitution of the Kingdom of Spain entrusts to a 'preamble' the task of identifying the founding values of the new democracy: 'The Spanish nation, wishing to establish *justice, freedom, and security* and to promote the good of all those who make it up, in the use of its sovereignty, proclaims its will to Guarantee democratic coexistence within the framework of the Constitution and laws in accordance with a just economic and social order; Consolidate a rule of law that ensures the supremacy of the law as the expression of the will of the people; Protect all Spaniards and peoples of Spain in the exercise of human rights, their cultures and traditions, languages and institutions; To promote the advancement of culture and the economy in such a way as to ensure a dignified quality of life for all; To realise an advanced democratic society and to collaborate in the strengthening of peaceful relations and effective collaboration between all the peoples of the earth.'

It is the 'superior' values – the supreme principles, we would say, taking into account the wording of the provisions on the law in general that precede our civil code that govern the entire constitutional system. Very soon the doctrine, alongside the

---

198. Fernandes Mendonça, *Rev.de Derecho*, 2018, no. 18, pp. 91 ff.
199. Barroso, *A dignidade da pessoa humana no direito constitucional contemporaneo*, Belo Horizonte, 2014, p. 62.
200. Fernandes Mendonça, *supra*, pp. 109 f.

values mentioned, constructed others, deriving them from the text, from its interpretation, as well as from legal tradition, such as legal certainty and solidarity.[201] In addition, solidarity is seen as the cement of human consortium and the basis of fundamental rights.[202]

Reconstructing the normative fabric in which these values are placed, we note Article 9:

(2) according to which 'It is the duty of the public authorities to create the conditions for freedom and equality of the individual and of the groups to which he belongs to be real and effective, and to eliminate obstacles that prevent or hinder their full enjoyment and to facilitate the participation of all citizens in political, economic, cultural and social life'; Art. 10 (1) 'The dignity of the person, the inviolable rights inherent to that dignity, the free development of the personality, respect for the law and for the rights of others are the foundation of political order and social peace'; and, in particular, the rights that form the basis of the welfare state: on labour, Art. 35. '(1) All Spaniards have the duty to work and the right to work and to the free choice of a profession or trade, to promotion through work and to a remuneration sufficient to meet their needs and those of their family, without there being any discrimination on the basis of sex'; art. 40 '(1)The public authorities shall promote favourable conditions for social and economic progress, as well as a fairer distribution of regional and personal incomes, within the framework of a policy of economic stability. A policy of full employment shall be implemented with special effort.

(2) Similarly, the public authorities shall promote a policy that ensures vocational training and retraining, supervise the conditions of safety and hygiene at work and guarantee the necessary rest by limiting the working day, by providing periodic paid holidays and by creating appropriate centres for this purpose'. Art. 41 '(1) The public authorities shall ensure a public social security system for all citizens, guaranteeing adequate assistance and social benefits in situations of need, especially in the event of unemployment. Assistance and supplementary benefits shall be free'; Art. 149 refers to the directives of social security.

In addition to the pillars of the welfare state, the Spanish Constitution deals with the environment (Article 45), housing (Article 47), young people, the handicapped and the elderly (Articles 48 ff.).

The principle of solidarity, so widespread in the constitutional fabric, has prompted a vast literature, in Spain,[203] as well as in the countries of Latin America, which refer to the Spanish experience as a modern constitutional model. Historical aspects are combined with political, economic and legal aspects.

---

201. Peces-Barba, *Securitad judica y solidaridad como valores de la Constitucion espanola, Funciones y fines del derecho; estudios en homenaje al profesor Mariano Hurtado Bautista*, 992, ISBN 84-7684-326-7, pp. 247-272; Fernandez Segado, *La solidaridad como principio constitucional*, in *Rev. Theoria y Realidad Constitucional*, 2012, no. 30, pp. 142 ff.
202. Vidal Gil, *Solidaridad y derechos humanos, Diccionario critico de los derechos humanos*, Sevilla, 2000, pp. 121 ff.
203. *See* in particular Cabo Martin, *Teoria constitucional de la solidaridad*, Madrid, 2006 and therein extensive bibliography.

As in Italy, solidarity has been examined in all its semantic profiles, and its polysemy has been investigated from philosophical and ethical, economic, social, international, and even legal perspectives:[204]

> The fundamental nature of the principle, as well as its expansive tendency, its transformation from duty to right, has been argued in all its declinations, in a singular affinity with Italian culture.[205]

## §7.06    THE CONSTITUTIONS OF THE FORMER SOCIALIST COUNTRIES OF THE EU

A quick glance at the constitutions of the former socialist countries that have joined the EU shows us that the process of constitutionalisation of rights has moved on, recovering the focus on social rights from previous systems. Following the achievement of political freedom, it recognised fundamental rights for citizens.

The Czech Republic has a preamble and only a few provisions concerning fundamental rights in its 1993 Constitution.

It is the shortest constitution among those in force today.

The text of the Slovak Republic introduced in 2015 is much more detailed, providing for the protection of fundamental rights and freedoms (Article 12), enumerating the obligations incumbent on citizens (Article 13), protecting the dignity of the person (Article 19), protecting private property, which entails obligations (Article 20), and in a special section devoted to economic, social and cultural rights, guaranteeing freedom in the choice of work and profession (Article 35), protecting health (Article 40) and the environment (Article 41).

Slovenia defines in the Constitution of 1991 a social state under the rule of law, in which human rights and fundamental freedoms are protected (Article 5), listed in detail in Articles 14 ff., and, as far as other personal rights are concerned, private property is protected (Article 33), personal dignity and security (Article 34), freedom of employment (Article 49), the right to social security (Article 50) and medical care (Article 51) is guaranteed. In a special section on social and economic relations, it guarantees employment (Article 66), ensures property has a social function (Article 67), protects the environment (Article 72), free economic initiative (Article 74), trade union freedom and the right to strike (Article 76).

---

204. Duràn, *Los limites de la solidaridad*, Digital Csic, 2003. Herrera, *El concepto de solidaridad y sus problemas politico-consitucionales. Una perspectiva iusfilosofica*, Rev. Est.soc., 2013, no. 46, p. 63 For the Colombian legal system *see* Canon Ortegon, *La solidaridad como fundamento del Estado social de derecho, de la seguridad social y la protecciòn social en Colombia*, in *Paginas de Solidaridad social*, 2017, 1, pp. 5 ff.; for the Peruvian system Valdivieso Lòpez, *Solidridad y deber juridico.Aportes para la fundamentaciòn juridica de la responsabilidad social corporativa*, Ius, 2020-12-31, pp. 1 ss.

205. In this sense, and for the Argentine legal system, Cordoba, *La solidaridad como un principio general del derecho in Argentina, Seminario permanente sobre investigaciòn del derecho de la persona humana, familia y sucesiones*, 29 May 2019; Garcia Ramìrez, *La solidaridad como deber*, Buenos Aires, 2011.

Bulgaria gave itself a constitution in 1991, which has since been amended several times. After a brief preamble, the text regulates the protection of the environment (Article 15), labour (Article 16), private property (Article 17), public goods (Article 18), economic enterprise (Article 19) including cooperatives. Fundamental rights and duties are enumerated in Articles 25 ff. with regard to labour (Article 48), social security (Article 51), health (Article 52), environment (Article 55).

Romania also gave itself a constitution in 1991, later revised several times, even in 2003. Articles 15 ff. enumerates the fundamental rights and then provides for the protection of health (Article 34), the environment (Article 35), work and social protection (Article 41), private property (Article 44), economic freedom (Article 45), and guarantees a dignified standard of living (Article 47); an ad hoc provision provides for the fundamental duties, concerning loyalty to the State, defence, tax obligations (Article 54) and the exercise of one's rights.

With regard to the Baltic Republics, the most extensive is the Constitution of Lithuania, of 1991, in which the second chapter is dedicated to the relations between the individual and the State, personal freedoms, property (Article 23) and the principle of equality (Article 29); the third chapter, dedicated to relations between society and the State, protects the family and religious associations; the fourth chapter is dedicated to the economy and work, protecting private property and economic freedom as long as they are useful to the community (Article 46), the right to work (Article 8), health (Article 53) and the environment (Article 54).

The 1991 Constitution of Latvia, after an extensive preamble, devotes a chapter – the eighth – to 'fundamental human rights', and protects personal freedoms (Article 105), freedom to choose work (Article 106) and social security (Article 109).

The Estonian Constitution of 1992, briefly, after a short preamble ensuring the protection of national values also for future generations, enunciates the principle of equality and personal freedoms (Article 12), protects welfare-related rights (Article 28), the freedom to choose work (Article 29) and the conduct of economic activities (Article 31).

Obviously, it is not enough to just read the texts; it is necessary to verify their implementation by national legislators and their interpretation by courts and doctrine. However, it is at least significant that all the 'new' constitutions contain a section devoted to social rights, and some of them also emphatically spell out *constitutional duties*. Even where an ad hoc section provides for the regulation of economic relations, it neither limits nor provides for state intervention in the economy.

# CHAPTER 8

# The New Social Doctrine of the Catholic Church

Since the Second World War, with the renewal of the Church, the Church's stance on the social question has multiplied. The demand for justice grows ever stronger, as do the trade unions and parties. Militant Catholics are divided and many militate in secular parties and trade unions to obtain better conditions for workers.[206] Here the problem is different, it is not so much the economic condition that worries the Church, but the spread of new social practices, from consumerism to communications, that distance the faithful from the divine word.

Two encyclicals are relevant: *Gaudium et spes*, 1966, and *Populorum progressio*, 1967, both attributable to Paul VI, issued in consonance with the results of the (Second Vatican) Council.

Social conditions are also relevant. First and foremost, the principle of human dignity is emphasised: 'excessive economic and social inequalities between members and between peoples of the one human family cause scandal and are contrary to social justice, equity, the dignity of the human person, and social and international peace'. As for social justice, the stance appears sharper than in the past:

Justice and equity similarly require that mobility, which is absolutely necessary in a developing economy, be regulated in such a way as to prevent the lives of individuals and their families from becoming uncertain and precarious. With regard to workers who, coming from other nations or regions, contribute with their labour to the economic development of a people or an area, any discrimination in remuneration or working conditions must be carefully eliminated. Furthermore, all, and first and foremost the public authorities, must treat them as persons, and not simply as mere instruments of production; they must help them so that they can take in their families and provide themselves with decent housing, and

---

206. For a reconstruction of the post-Second World War historical-political framework, *see* Cau, *La via maestra alla giustizia sociale. Alcide De Gasperi tra solidarismo e corporativismo*, in *Scienza e politica*, 2010.

encourage their integration into the social life of the people or region that receives them. As far as possible, however, jobs should be created in the regions of origin themselves.

In addition to reaffirming the right to sufficient and dignified remuneration, and the right of association, with which to peacefully confront and conflict with counterparts, the encyclical legitimises the strike (which the Quadragesimo anno had declared illegitimate) and invites states to introduce a network of institutions for welfare and social security that preserves citizens' sense of participation and responsibility. Property is also no longer considered a natural right, but an asset that must be used to realise the interests of others as well, and the latifundium is opposed. Even more determined is the encyclical *Populorum progressio* (1967), which redefines the starting points of the Church's social theory. Property is no longer an intangible natural right, and 'does not constitute for anyone an unconditional and absolute right'. The economy is at the service of man. Political programmes must 'reduce inequalities, combat discrimination, liberate man from his bondage, make him capable of becoming the actor responsible for his material improvement, his moral progress, the full unfolding of his spiritual destiny'.

And here, finally, is the explicit mention of the principle of solidarity: the second chapter, entitled 'Towards the development in solidarity of mankind' states the principle of the *fraternity of peoples*:

> 43. The integral development of man cannot take place without the united development of humanity. As we said in Bombay: 'Man must meet man, nations must meet as brothers and sisters, as the children of God. In this mutual understanding and friendship, in this sacred communion, we must likewise begin to work together to build the common future of humanity.' And we also suggested the search for concrete and practical means of organisation and cooperation, in order to pool available resources and thus achieve true communion among all nations.

Solidarity is considered a *duty*, and liberal capitalism a model that must be corrected. The final appeal is for collective solidarity:

> We are all in solidarity on this journey. We therefore wanted to remind everyone of the magnitude of the drama and the urgency of the work to be done. The hour of action has already sounded: the survival of so many innocent children, the access of so many unfortunate families to a human condition, the peace of the world, the future of civilisation are at stake. It is up to all men and all peoples to assume their responsibilities.

With the Encyclical *Octogesima adveniens* (1971) 80 years after *Rerum novarum*, Paul VI updated his thinking with regard to the new pitfalls of the modern world, from ideologies to the media, unemployment, emigration, and returned to the criticism of Marxism, considered incompatible with Christian doctrine both for its incitement to class hatred, its totalitarian spirit, and its scientific aspirations to interpret history. The just aspirations of social justice are here drowned in an exquisitely political discourse.

The fundamentals of the Church's social doctrine are again formulated in John Paul II's 1981 encyclical *Laborem exercens*. The discourse is all about work, which cannot be treated as a commodity, nor man as an instrument of production. The principles of solidarity and dignity of the person must guide the resolution of conflicting interests. The Pope condemns economism and materialism, reaffirms the right to private ownership also of the means of production (as already emphasised in the encyclical *Mater et magistra*) and places labour within the sphere of fundamental rights, which implies correctives to 'rigid capitalism'. Solidarity is the central theme of the 1988 encyclical *Sollicitudo rei socialis*.

The exercise of solidarity within any society is valid when its members recognise each other as persons. Those who count the most, having a larger portion of common goods and services, feel responsible for the weakest and are willing to share what they possess. The weakest, for their part, in the same line of solidarity, do not adopt a purely passive or destructive attitude towards the social fabric, but, while claiming their legitimate rights, do what they are entitled to for the good of all. Intermediary groups, in turn, do not selfishly insist on their own particular interests, but respect the interests of others. Positive signs in the contemporary world are the growing awareness of the solidarity of the poor among themselves, their interventions of mutual support, their public demonstrations in the social scene, without resorting to violence, but by presenting their needs and rights in the face of the inefficiency or corruption of the public powers. By virtue of its evangelical commitment, the Church feels called to stand by the poor crowds, to discern the justice of their demands, to help satisfy them, without losing sight of the good of the groups within the framework of the common good. The same criterion applies, by analogy, in international relations. Interdependence must be transformed into solidarity, based on the principle that the goods of creation are meant for all: what human industry produces through the processing of raw materials, through the contribution of labour, must equally serve the good of all.

In the theological interpretation of social problems, solidarity is undoubtedly a Christian virtue. Already in the previous exposition, it was possible to glimpse numerous points of contact between it and charity, which is the hallmark of Christ's disciples (*Jn* 13:35). In light of faith, solidarity tends to go beyond itself, to take on the specifically Christian dimensions of total gratuity, forgiveness and reconciliation. Then the neighbour is not only a human being with his rights and fundamental equality before all but becomes the living image of God the Father, redeemed by the blood of Jesus Christ and placed under the permanent action of the Holy Spirit.

A century after the promulgation of the encyclical *Rerum novarum*, John Paul II returns to the principles of social doctrine. Once again, he corrects his aim, but from a very different vantage point: a globalised world economy in which the capitalist model is now victorious in every region, pending the 'fall of the wall', and the fall of real socialism in which the pontiff himself had collaborated.

The Church recognises the proper *function of profit* as an indicator of good company performance: when a company makes a profit, it means that the factors of production have been properly employed and the corresponding human needs duly met. However, profit is not the only indicator of the company's condition. It is possible for the profit and loss accounts to be in order and at the same time for the men, who are the company's most valuable asset, to be humiliated and their dignity offended. In addition to being morally inadmissible, this cannot fail to have negative repercussions for the economic efficiency of the company. Indeed, the purpose of the company is not simply the production of profit, but the very existence of the company as a *community of men* who, in different ways, pursue the satisfaction of their fundamental needs and constitute a particular group at the service of society as a whole. Profit is a regulator of the life of the enterprise, but it is not the only one; to it must be added the consideration of *other human and moral factors* that, in the long run, are at least equally essential to the life of the enterprise.

The criticism of Charles Marx, carried out in a straightforward manner, is clear-cut; at the same time, however, the Pope raises the problem of the exploitation of man and the legitimisation of capitalism.

The Church has no models to propose. Real and truly effective models can only come about within the framework of different historical situations, thanks to the efforts of all those responsible for addressing concrete problems in all their intertwined social, economic, political and cultural aspects. To this commitment, the Church offers, as an *indispensable ideal orientation,* her own social doctrine, which – as we have said – recognises the positivity of the market and enterprise, but indicates, at the same time, the need for these to be oriented towards the common good. It also recognises the legitimacy of workers' efforts to achieve full respect for their dignity and greater spaces for participation in the life of the company, so that, while working together with others and under the direction of others, they can, in a certain sense, 'work on their own' exercising their intelligence and freedom.

The integral development of the human person at work does not contradict but rather favours the greater productivity and effectiveness of work itself, even if this may weaken established power structures. The company cannot be considered only as a 'corporation of capital'; it is, at the same time, a 'corporation of persons', in which those who provide the capital necessary for its activity, as well as those who collaborate in it with their work, are part of it in different ways and with specific responsibilities. In order to achieve these ends, a *large associated workers' movement is* still needed, whose goal is the integral liberation and promotion of the person.

The *solidarity* called by Leo XIII by the term *friendship*, seen by Pius XI as *social charity*, by Paul VI as the *civilisation of love*, acquires an even more pregnant meaning with John Paul II: the capitalist economy corrected by the values of *social justice*.

Today, the cornerstones of the social doctrine are solidarity between workers, the meaning of work as an instrument for the moral elevation of the individual, its combination with globalisation and digitalisation, the sharing of wealth, the appreciation of private enterprise and initiative and the free market, which must not lead to alienation or consumerism, and the protection of the environment.

The market that has become global has stimulated first and foremost, on the part of rich countries, the search for areas where they can relocate low-cost production in order to reduce the prices of many goods, increase purchasing power and thus accelerate the rate of development centred on increased consumption for their domestic market. Consequently, the market stimulated new forms of competition between states in order to attract production centres of foreign companies through various means, including favourable taxation and deregulation of the labour market. These processes have led to the *reduction of social safety nets* in exchange for the pursuit of greater competitive advantages in the global market, with serious danger to workers' rights, fundamental human rights and the solidarity implemented in the traditional forms of the welfare state.

The market is subject to the principles of so-called *commutative justice,* which regulates precisely the relations of giving and receiving between equal subjects. But the Church's social doctrine has never ceased to emphasise the importance of *distributive justice* and *social justice* for the market economy itself, not only because it is embedded in the meshes of a broader social and political context but also because of the web of relationships in which it takes place. Indeed, the market, left solely to the principle of equivalence of value of exchanged goods, fails to produce the social cohesion it needs to function well. Without internal forms of solidarity and mutual trust, the market cannot fully fulfil its economic function. And today it is this trust that is lacking, and the loss of trust is a serious loss.

Universal solidarity, which is a fact and for us a benefit, is also a duty.

The principle of subsidiarity must be kept closely connected to the principle of solidarity and vice versa because if subsidiarity without solidarity falls into social particularism, it is equally true that solidarity without subsidiarity falls into welfarism that humiliates the bearer of need.

*Laudato si'*, on the care of the common home is the encyclical with which Pope Francis places the principle of solidarity within the framework of the problems of today's world: Francis (24 May 2015) Pollution, planetary inequality, integral ecology, ecological conversion. And it is concerned with solidarity between generations.

The discourse is taken up in the encyclical *Fratelli tutti* of 3 October 2020:

> Fraternity is not only the result of conditions of respect for individual freedoms, nor even of a certain regulated equity. Although these are conditions of possibility, they are not sufficient for it to arise as a necessary result. Fraternity has something positive to offer freedom and equality. What happens without consciously cultivated fraternity, without a political will for fraternity, translated into an education for fraternity, dialogue, the discovery of reciprocity and mutual enrichment as values? What happens is that freedom shrinks, resulting rather in a condition of solitude, of pure autonomy to belong to someone or something, or only to possess and enjoy. This by no means exhausts the richness of freedom, which is oriented above all to love.

# CHAPTER 9

# Solidarity in European Law

The history of the idea of solidarity in the modern sense shows that this value took root in Western Europe in the nineteenth century, was constitutionalised, became a founding principle of many legal systems, and was already a common value/principle well before European Constitutions referred to it.

Re-reading the texts of the founding treaties of the EU now, starting with the 1957 Treaty, in light of this narrow history, the term solidarity can be given a more solid content. Admittedly, it is a polysense term. It is used many times, in different contexts.

The preamble to the Economic Community Treaty states that the signatory states: 'DESIRING to intensify solidarity between their peoples while respecting their history, culture and traditions, ....'

And then 'DETERMINED to promote the economic and social progress of their peoples, taking into account the principle of sustainable development in the context of the realisation of the internal market and the strengthening of cohesion and environmental protection, and to implement policies to ensure that progress in economic integration is matched by parallel progress in other areas.'

And again:

Article 2 The Union is founded on the values of respect for human dignity, freedom, democracy, equality, the rule of law and respect for human rights, including the rights of persons belonging to minorities. These values are common to the Member States in a society characterised by pluralism, non-discrimination, tolerance, justice, solidarity and equality between women and men.

While some are *common values*, the others are characteristics of today's society. Solidarity would therefore not be a value but a principle.

One should not overemphasise the use of terms, especially when they are placed in provisions of broad, somewhat vague meaning. Here the sophistication lies in the distinction between values and principles. But the Union texts often equate *principles* with *values*, as, e.g., Article 6: fundamental rights are equated with principles (c. 3: fundamental rights, as guaranteed by the European Convention for the Protection of Human Rights and Fundamental Freedoms and as they result from the constitutional traditions common to the Member States, are part of Union law as general principles).

The rights, freedoms and principles of the Charter shall be interpreted in accordance with the general provisions of Title VII of the Charter governing its interpretation and application and with due regard to the explanations referred to in the Charter, which indicate the sources of these provisions.

## §9.01    THE DISCUSSION ON THE SOLIDARITY PRINCIPLE

Despite the fact that solidarity is a well-proven principle and explicitly and even literally enshrined in most European Constitutions, as briefly documented above, its legal relevance and accreditation within the European legal system is still a matter of debate. Yet, the principle has been woven into the constitutional system for more than two centuries, if one goes back to the French Revolution. Being incorporated in constitutional texts, it has aspects that jurists cannot underestimate because: (i) it is a term/concept/notion of a legal nature; (ii) it has the value of a principle; (iii) it is a principle *common* to the Member States of the Union; (iv) it is a principle mentioned in many *primary sources of* the Union.

All these characteristics must be examined in detail.

In the legal text, as enunciated by the constitutions, the terms used, and the words that compose it, are not written at random. Each term has its own meaning, taken in isolation, coloured by the overall meaning of the proposition in which it is set. In other words, 'language makes law'.[207] The jurist not only 'does things with words',[208] but, by means of words, does things with rules.[209] In our literature, this aspect of the machinery of law is well present[210] and constitutes one of the cornerstones of legal hermeneutics.[211] Now having decided – in a process of approval of a constitutional text by an elected body – to include a certain term in a legal proposition

---

207. Sabatini, *Il linguaggio normativo come uso prototipico della lingua*, in *Le parole giuste*, Atti del convegno organizzato dal Senato della Repubblica with University of Pavia, Rome, 2017.
208. According to John Austin's famous phrase used in the lectures he delivered at Harvard in 1955, now translated for Marietti, *Come fare cose con le parole*, Genoa, 2019.
209. Thus taking up the motto of Austin, Twining & Miers, How to Do Things with Rules, Cambridge, 2012; *ibid.*, *The Use of Words Always Has an Ideological Bent, as Foucault Teaches in the Words and Things*, Milan, 2016.
210. Among the many, *see*, in particular, Caretti, *Discutere del linguaggio dei giuristi per riflettere sul loro ruolo oggi: qualche considerazione a conclusione del convegno 'la lingua dei giuristi'*, in *Osservatorio sulle fonti*, no. 3/2015, pp. 1 ff. where a critical review of the studies on the subject, in particular by Nencioni, *Idealismo e realismo nella scienza del linguaggio*, La Nuova Italia, Firenze 1946; Fiorelli, *Storia giuridica e storia linguistica*, Giuffrè, Milano, 1957; Piovani, *Mobilità, sistematicità, istituzionalità della lingua e del diritto*, Giuffrè, Milano, 1962; P. Grossi, *Un dialogo con i comparatisti su lingua e diritto*, in *Riv. int. fil. dir*, 2014, pp. 412 ff. 3 S: N. Bobbio, *Scienza del diritto e analisi del linguaggio*, in *Riv. trim. dir. proc. civ.*, 1950, pp. 342 ff.; Scarpelli, *Filosofia analitica e giurisprudenza*, Nuvoletti, Milano, 1953; Orestano, *Realtà, parole, valori nella scienza del diritto*, in *Riv. dir. civ.*, 1985, pp. 461 ff.; Pugliatti, *Grammatica e diritto*, Giuffrè, Milan, 1978. 4 Cf. Sacco, *Lingua e diritto*, in *Ars interpretandi*, 2000, pp. 117 ff. The works of Paolo Grossi are illuminating in this regard: *see* among the many references in particular *L'invenzione del diritto*, Roma-Bari, 2017; Grossi, *Ritorno al diritto*, Roma-Bari, 2015; *ibid.*, Introduzione al Novecento giuridico, Roma-Bari, 2012.
211. *See* in particular, the studies by Riccardo Guastini, *L'interpretazione dei documenti normativi*, Milano, 2004, and by Francesco Viola and Giuseppe Zaccaria, *Diritto e interpretazione. Lineamenti di teoria ermeneutica del diritto*, Roma-Bari, 1999.

is not a politically (and legally) irrelevant fact: if the reason why that term has been chosen to make up a legal text is already significant, the fact that that term has been elected to make up a constitutional text is even more significant. The constitutional value implies that that term is not only *cogent* but also rises to the role of *guiding principle*.

Moreover, since it was constantly taken up by the constitutions of the Member States, it was to be considered a *common principle*, a value in the proper sense, and thus had already been recognised before it was literally mentioned in the Charter of Rights of the Union and before it was part as a pillar of the table of values on which it is based.

Therefore, the objections that are still made to the principle of solidarity today, trying to undermine its role, appear misleading: it is doubted that it has a legal value[212] and it is believed that the principle summarises third-generation rights, hence not political rights, nor social rights in the strict sense, but rights relating to consumer protection, the environment, and subjective legal positions that can be claimed against public authorities.[213] And therefore the term would be too broad, and, having such a composite content, also equivocal.

It may therefore seem curious that analyses of the sources of the EU legal system do not include solidarity among the fundamental principles applied. Takis Tridimas, for instance, identifies equality, proportionality, legal certainty, protection of reasonable expectations, fundamental rights, the right of defence and damages as general principles of constitutional rank.

Solidarity is not even mentioned in the index of terms used[214] without adding that in his opinion, the principles have an interpretative rather than a directly applicative value.[215] Norbert Reich, although attentive to the social aspects of European law, when describing the general principles of EU civil law, instead of referring to solidarity prefers to deal with the principle of protection of the weaker party,[216] along with autonomy, non-discrimination, effectiveness, balancing of interests, proportionality, good faith and, with some doubt, the prohibition of abuse of rights. The principle of solidarity is not even given an entry (except for that in the solidarity of obligations) in the Encyclopaedia of European law edited by Marx Planck of Hamburg.[217]

On the contrary, Juergen Basedow expounds extensively on the resources of the principle and its application in various areas of the European legal order;[218] significant components of this area are the principle of equality and non-discrimination, the principle of good faith, the protection of the weaker party, and the protection of the employee.

---

212. Peraldi Leneuf, *Solidarité(s): perspectives juridiques* – Actes de colloques de l'IFR n°6 sous la direction de Maryvonne Hecquard-Théron le 22 juillet 2009.
213. *Ibid.*
214. Tridimas, *The General Principles of EC Law*, Oxford, 1999.
215. *Ibid.*, p. 33.
216. Reich, *General Principles of EU Civil Law*, Cambridge-Antwerpen-Portland, pp. 37 ff.
217. Planck, *Encyclopedia of European Private Law*, Oxford University Press, 2012.
218. Basedow, *EU Private Law: Anatomy of a Growing Legal Order*, Cambridge-Antwerpen-Chicago, 2021, pp. 451 ff.

As we can see, the content of the principle can be varied, extending from its essential and original core – the sphere of social rights – to all the applications of the values of the person used as a limit to the free market and the autonomy of private individuals, including fundamental rights, the protection of the weaker party (such as the consumer, the saver, the worker) and the principles of civil law, so to speak classic, such as good faith and fairness, which can be understood in an individual dimension or in a collective dimension. It is evident that a broad notion of solidarity entails the inclusion in its semantic value of declinations that can also be examined outside it: the balancing of rights, the prohibition of the abuse of rights, the conduct of good faith can be understood both as factors of social cohesion and as techniques for controlling the conduct of private individuals pursuing their interests.

### §9.02    THE LISBON TREATY AND THE CHARTER OF FUNDAMENTAL RIGHTS

The *discrimen between the* past and the present is given, also with regard to the introduction and application of the solidarity principle by the Lisbon Treaty approved in 2007. This treaty, which partly amended the previous treaties, also gave legally binding force to the Charter of Fundamental Rights, the political document decided by the Union in Nice in 2002. Its legal effects take effect in 2009, but, as will be discussed, the Court of Justice of the European Union started applying the Charter immediately after its approval.

The Charter constitutes, if not a true constitution, an instrument equated to the Treaties and balanced with them. There are other significant innovations in the Lisbon Treaty: competition is no longer considered a fundamental objective of the EU, as it was in the 1957 founding treaty, but is mentioned in Additional Protocol No. 25; an essential factor, energy, is introduced in the solidarity clause in which the Member States undertake to support each other in case of need; and the need to combat climate change is specified in international agreements.

The Lisbon Treaty has fundamentally changed the structure of the Union, made it more compact, and strengthened the ties between the Member States and between the peoples. In other words, despite having a lower rank than a 'constitution', the Charter is seen as a para-constitutional document: having emphasised the personalist principle, the Charter has altered the set of political principles on which the Union rested, corrected the very idea of a free market, and imposed supportive duties aimed at bringing states in difficulty closer together.

To the analysis of the political meaning of the Lisbon Treaty, and thus, the analysis of the political meaning of solidarity, we need to add the *binding legal dimension*, which has, by its very nature and effects, an equally political, reinforcing, and not merely symbolic or rhetorical meaning.

This is why the most widespread analyses of the concept of solidarity from the European perspective – such as Rainer Zoll's historical analysis or Steinar Stjerno's political analysis – must be corrected in light of the *binding nature* assumed by the Charter of Rights essentially in 2002 and formally in 2009.

It is clear that the principle takes on different colours depending on the context in which it is placed and the goals the interpreter wants to achieve. But this does not mean that it should be ignored or even opposed.

Solidarity thus becomes the cement of human consortium, operating as a cohesion mechanism, as a dialectical element between individual and collectivity, as a factor of unity. Solidarity implies obligations (it is therefore seen as a duty): obligations between individuals and the group. But it will be seen that in the context of relations between individuals, the principle of solidarity also creates obligations between individuals and not only between the individual and the group.[219]

It is current therefore to use the technique of distinguishing to clarify (sometimes also to 'strip away') the meaning of solidarity: one distinguishes social solidarity from welfare solidarity from a conflict perspective, moving from the Aristotelian notion of 'friendship' to the social contract of Russovian memory, from Durkheim's concept of mechanical/organic solidarity to Parsons' concept of obligation solidarity.

In examining the way solidarity operates in the EU, the difference between the proclamation of the principle by Union instruments and its de facto application was highlighted.

Robert Schuman had already spoken, at the outset, in anticipation of the conclusion of agreements to establish European bodies, of a process of integration that could be initiated through de facto solidarity: 'Europe will not be able to be built all at once, nor will it be built all at once; it will arise from concrete realisations that first create de facto solidarity. The union of nations demands the elimination of the age-old contrast between France and Germany: the action taken must concern France and Germany first and foremost.'[220] And now, rediscovering that formulation, a de facto solidarity has been theorised to emerge when balancing economic and social measures.

This is the process of 'socialisation' of the EU described by Andrea Biondi, Eglè Dagilytè and Esin Kuçuk:[221] a process that unravels through the regulation of citizenship, health protection, education, the environment, immigration, welfare and territorial cohesion. Each of these areas reconciles the reasons of the market with those of citizens, thus giving rise to an application of solidarity that is measured in turn by freedoms, wealth distribution, justice and economic efficiency. These balancing efforts can be measured by two limits placed on the one hand at the lowest level of solidarity, as emerges from the *Pringle* case, and on the other hand at the highest, as emerges from the *Halaf* case.

## §9.03     THE JURISPRUDENCE OF THE COURT OF JUSTICE

The Court of Justice plays a major role not only in resolving cases of internal conflicts within the Community administrative organisation but also in defining conflicts between Community bodies and private individuals, in protecting fundamental rights,

---

219. Borger, *The Currency of Solidarity*, Cambridge, 2020.
220. Declaration of 9 May 1950.
221. *Solidarity in EU Law: Legal Principle in the Making*, Cheltenham, 2018.

and in dictating the interpretative rules that shape the meaning of the sources of Union law.

This was also the case for the definition of the meanings of solidarity. Some decided cases have become milestones in the jurisprudential construction of the meaning of solidarity.

In order to follow the articulation inherent in Community bodies, one case concerns solidarity between states, and the other case solidarity of a state with non-EU citizens, although this classification does not exclude that, in fact, solidarity also operates simultaneously at other levels, e.g., between private individuals, even if they do not have the same nationality.

In the *Pringle* case,[222] some Member States had legitimately signed a treaty parallel to the founding treaties of the Union concerning the European Stability Mechanism (ESM), which did not extend to all the States of the Union; the Court held that the agreement did not constitute a violation of the rules of the Treaty and that the decision of the Commission that had endorsed it was legitimate. In the second (Case C-528/11) that states can freely give access to immigrants without using the corridors established by the Dublin Treaty.[223]

The most discussed interventions concerned the legitimacy of the bail-in in the Greek financial affair.

---

222. Case C-370/12, Judgment of the Court (Full Court) 27 November 2012. The operative part states that (1) Examination of the first question has disclosed no factor of such a kind as to affect the validity of European Council Decision 2011/199/EU of 25 March 2011 amending Article 136 of the Treaty on the Functioning of the European Union with regard to a stability mechanism for Member States whose currency is the euro.

    Articles 4(3) TEU, 13 TEU, 2(3) TFEU, 3(1)(c) and (2) TFEU, 119 TFEU, 123 TFEU and 125-127 TFEU and the general principle of effective judicial protection do not preclude the conclusion between the Member States whose currency is the euro of an agreement such as the Treaty establishing the European Stability Mechanism between the Kingdom of Belgium, the Federal Republic of Germany the Republic of Estonia, Ireland, the Hellenic Republic, the Kingdom of Spain, the French Republic, the Italian Republic, the Republic of Cyprus, the Grand Duchy of Luxembourg, Malta, the Kingdom of the Netherlands, the Republic of Austria, the Portuguese Republic, the Republic of Slovenia, the Slovak Republic and the Republic of Finland, concluded in Brussels on 2 February 2012, nor the ratification thereof by those Member States.

223. Judgment of the Court (Fourth Chamber) of 30 May 2013:

    (1) Article 3(2) of Council Regulation (EC) No. 343/2003 of 18 February 2003 establishing the criteria and mechanisms for determining the Member State responsible for examining an asylum application lodged in one of the Member States by a third-country national is to be interpreted as allowing a Member State, which is not the one identified as the State responsible on the basis of the criteria set out in Chapter III of that regulation, to examine an asylum application even in the absence of the circumstances making the humanitarian clause in Article 15 of that regulation applicable. That possibility does not depend on the fact that the Member State responsible under those criteria did not reply to a request to take back the asylum seeker concerned.

    (2) The Member State in which the asylum seeker is present shall not be obliged, in the course of the procedure for determining the Member State responsible, to seek the opinion of the United Nations High Commissioner for Refugees where the records of that Office show that the Member State identified as the State responsible on the basis of the criteria set out in Chapter III of Regulation No. 343/2003 is in breach of the rules of Union law on asylum.

In *Ledra Advertising*[224] (Joined Cases C-8/15 P to C-10/15 P), the Court held that 'Financial services play a central role in the EU economy. Banks and credit institutions are an essential source of financing for companies active in different markets. Moreover, banks are often interconnected and many of them conduct their business internationally. It is for this reason that serious difficulties in one or more banks risk spreading rapidly to other banks, either in the Member State concerned or in other Member States. This in turn risks producing negative spillover effects in other sectors of the economy' (judgment of 19 July 2016, *Kotnik and Others*, C-526/14, EU:C:2016:570, paragraph 50).

In the present case, the measures set out in the contested paragraphs provide in particular for the Bank of Cyprus to take over the secured deposits of the Cyprus Popular Bank, and for 37.5% of the unsecured deposits of the Bank of Cyprus to be converted into shares, with full voting and dividend rights, as well as the temporary freezing of another part of these unsecured deposits, with the clarification that, should the Bank of Cyprus be over-capitalised vis-à-vis the target minimum capital level of 9% in a crisis, a share buy-back will be conducted in order to reimburse the unsecured depositors the amount corresponding to the over-capitalisation.

In view of the objective of ensuring the stability of the banking system in the euro area, and in light of the imminent risk of financial losses to which depositors at the two banks concerned would have been exposed in the event of their failure, such measures do not constitute a disproportionate and impermissible intervention affecting the very substance of the applicants' right to property. They cannot, therefore, be regarded as unjustified restrictions of that right.[225]

In light of these elements, it cannot be considered that, in permitting the adoption of the contested points, the Commission contributed to an infringement of the applicants' right to property guaranteed by Article 17(1) of the Charter.

It follows that the first condition for invoking the non-contractual liability of the Union is not satisfied in the present case so the claims for damages brought by the applicants must be dismissed as unfounded in law.

It is clear that the Court always employs a certain amount of discretion in deciding questions. And that the observance of the principle varies depending on the sectors and the relationship between national and European regulation. Hence the need to distinguish between solidarity in the market, solidarity with redistributive purposes, solidarity with constitutive purposes, solidarity with administrative purposes.

Solidarity is also seen as an efficient integration factor.

In this sense, Andreas Grimmel's research explains that beyond textual statements, solidarity is composed of three factors: *voluntariness, self-denial,* and

---

224. Judgment of the Court (Grand Chamber) 20 September 2016.
225. By analogy, Judgment of 10 July 2003, Booker Aquaculture and Hydro Seafood, C-20/00 and C-64/00, EU:C:2003:397, paras 79 to 86.

*identification.*[226] Voluntariness in truth only captures one aspect of the theme, because solidarity is a social duty, as made clear by examining modern constitutions. But Grimmel believes that acts of solidarity must be performed freely on the basis of an uncoerced choice and that this choice depends on the desire to set aside one's own self-interest and behave generously towards others, working together with others, in a group, in an association, in a party.

Within the European Union, solidarity has been put in check by the use of *cost-benefit analysis.* And it is clear that when economic parameters prevail over social ones, solidarity evaporates. Grimmel, however, is thinking of *horizontal solidarity,* whereas the concept, as repeatedly emphasised, is complex, and also encompasses the *vertical* perspective.

On the contrary, in the European perspective, the vertical perspective *prevails.*

An analysis of the Treaties gives us a strong idea of solidarity, given the numerous occasions on which this principle is evoked.

As Marc Blanquet observes, despite the fact that the Union has a strong economic characterisation in its origins, the constant reference to the value-principle of solidarity shows that the founding ideas of the origins have been gradually corrected over time and have become attenuated and that solidarity operates within the Union as the driving force behind initiatives aimed at making not only economic but also political and social integration more efficient. This is the project of action confirmed by the Commission in 2002,[227] in anticipation of the enlargement – even doubling – of the Union with the entry of other European countries, whose values are summed up in the words *Peace, Freedom, Solidarity.*

Hence several areas in which the principle of solidarity operates: (i) between the Union and the Member States, (ii) the peoples of the Member States, (iii) between the Member States, (iv) between Europe and the countries beyond the sea, and (v) between generations.

The Court of Justice has applied this principle in an impressive number of cases. A search on the Court's website shows, at the beginning of 2022, as many as 13,059 judgments that used the term 'solidarity', 11,271 that used the term 'social solidarity', and 8,065 that used the term 'human solidarity'.

Beyond the frequency of the use of this term and beyond the application of this principle, research on the subject has revealed five different meanings of solidarity:

    (i)  solidarity as a modern representation of the charity of tradition;
    (ii)  solidarity as mutual support;
    (iii)  solidarity as a tempering of economic risks;
    (iv)  solidarity as a limitation of the individual exercise of fundamental rights; and
    (v)  solidarity as a limitation of economic freedoms and competition.

---

226. *Le Grand absent européen:solidarity in the politics of European integration,* in *Acta Politica,* 10 June 2020, online; but *see also* Grimmel & My Giang (eds), *Solidarity in the European Union,* Berlin, 2017.
227. Communication of 4 December 2002, No. 728 (final), Pour l' Union européenne. Paix, Liberté, Solidarité.

These different meanings indicate that the division into three groups according to whether one refers to solidarity between individuals, between states and citizens, or between the Union and states is rather artificial and does not fully express the potential of such a relevant value.

This is why new interpreters point out that the Court could have been more generous in its use of the principle, taking into account the needs of citizens.[228]

Neither are these needs met by organisations that do their utmost to support vulnerable groups, as shown by other recent research.[229]

It is, however, a fact that the principle of solidarity goes beyond the context of the welfare state, to which, however, it is appropriate to make a reference, albeit a brief one, because it constitutes the chosen ground from the perspective of the application of the Union's rules.

## §9.04 THE EUROPEAN PILLAR OF SOCIAL RIGHTS

Apart from the export and customs regulation issues, which take into account the numerous conventions concluded by the EU with non-EU countries, in which fundamental rights, social relations and the environment are protected (so-called Generalised Scheme of Preferences and Generalised Scheme of Preferences Plus), the main topic concerning the social aspects of European policy and legislation focuses on the establishment of a European pillar of social rights.

In 2017, the Commission approved a Communication (2017.250 final) in which it highlighted the goal of achieving a fair, pan-European labour market. The pillar therefore concerns labour law, in which the principle of solidarity for the weakest category of actors, i.e., employees, is expressed.

These are values recognised internationally by the United Nations, the International Labour Organisation and the Council of Europe. The social acquis has been supplemented by the Charter of Fundamental Rights.

The Communication states that the rights included in the pillar must be balanced against the principles of subsidiarity and proportionality, 'which state that action at EU level should only take place where the objectives can be better achieved at Union level and that action should be limited to what is necessary to achieve the objectives of the Treaties. These principles ensure that decisions are taken as close as possible to the citizens of the Union and that measures proposed at EU level are based on proven added value. This corresponds to what citizens expect and is the most effective and efficient approach'.

These are rights that are already recognised and that the Commission wants to make effective, such as adequate preparation for employment, equal opportunities in accessing the labour market, gender equality, combating discrimination on the grounds

---

228. Schiek, *Solidarity in the Case Law of the European Court of Justice-Opportunities Missed?*, in *Transnational Solidarity Concept: Challenges and Opportunities*, ed. Krunke, Petersen & Manner, Cambridge and a literature search there.
229. Lahusen & Grasso, *Solidarity in EuropeL Citizens' Response in Time of Crisis*, St Philip Press, 2020.

of identity, fair working conditions, sufficient pay to lead a decent life, safety at work, full information in the event of dismissal, protection of personal data, treatment of children and their education, social protection in the event of unemployment, and so on.

The pillar is therefore the subject of a very demanding action plan of the European Union, and precisely for this reason, it has provoked a vast debate, due to its dense content, not only social but also political. It is evident that it cannot be appreciated by sovereignist countries, and, for those who are oriented in a democratic and progressive sense, it may also appear unrealistic, given the differentiation of rules within national systems.

It was also pointed out that the pillar is unclear in its assertion of rights ownership: the enumeration of rights mentioned above concerns individual active subjective positions; they would be weakened if they were only recognised collectively. It was also noted that there is a need for more coherence in the Union's policies, because on the one hand, the Member States are obliged to reduce debt, and on the other hand the pillar implies increased costs for the public sector.

The discussion on the social pillar was ongoing when the pandemic hit Europe, perhaps even more virulently than in other continents. In addition to the serious damage to life, health, social and economic relations, the pandemic changed people's living habits, aggravated unemployment, alienated employees from work, and depressed the economy.

The summit of the European Council of Ministers held in Porto on 8 May 2021 concerning social Europe had to take these circumstances into account to dictate the Union's social agenda. Once again there is talk of solidarity, of course between the Member States and the Union towards the Member States, but it is clear that the principle of solidarity is manifested towards the weak and thus directly affects workers and their families.

It reads in the declaration made at the end of the work:

1. We stress the importance of European unity and solidarity in the fight against the COVID-19 pandemic. These values have defined the response of European citizens to the crisis and are also at the core of our common project and our distinctive social model. Now more than ever, Europe must be the continent of social cohesion and prosperity. We reaffirm our commitment to work for a social Europe.

2. Since the start of the COVID-19 pandemic, rapid, critical and comprehensive action at EU and national level has protected millions of lives, jobs and businesses.

3. The same spirit of unity and solidarity inspired our historic July 2020 agreement on the Multiannual Financial Framework and the specific recovery effort under Next Generation EU. As we accelerate the green and digital transitions, this massive European investment and associated reforms will enable the Union and its Member States to resolutely embark on the reform path towards a fair, sustainable and resilient recovery. A collective, inclusive, timely and cohesive recovery will strengthen Europe's competitiveness, resilience, social dimension and role on the global stage.

The summit took into account the priorities that guide the Union's political and socioeconomic action today:

8. We will put education and skills at the centre of our political action. The green and digital transitions will offer huge opportunities for European citizens, but will also bring with them many challenges, which will require more invest- ment in education, vocational training, lifelong learning as well as skills upgrading and retraining, so as to stimulate employment transitions to sectors with increasing labour demand. At the same time, changes related to digitisa- tion, artificial intelligence, teleworking and the platform economy will require special attention in order to strengthen workers' rights, social security systems and occupational health and safety.

Together with the other pillar objectives, these address the sectors that could cooperate more than others for recovery.

The Community Charter of the Fundamental Social Rights of Workers sets out the general principles on which the European labour law model is based. It applies to the following areas: free movement of workers, employment and wages, improvement of working conditions, social protection, freedom of association and collective bargain- ing, vocational training, equal treatment for men and women, information, consulta- tion and participation of workers, protection of safety and security at the workplace, protection of children, adolescents, the elderly and disabled persons.

These social rights represent a basis of minimum principles, common to all Member States of the EU. The provisions of the Charter were taken over by the Treaty of Lisbon (Article 151 of the Treaty on the Functioning of the EU) and the EU Charter of Fundamental Rights.

The Charter was adopted in accordance with the preamble of the Treaty establishing the European Economic Community, which recognises the need to work for the constant improvement of the living and employment conditions of European citizens.

It was not adopted by the United Kingdom until 1998 when the principles of the Charter were incorporated into the Treaty of Amsterdam.

In the Charter, the social rights of workers are set out in 26 provisions, but their content is expanded to include the rights of children, the elderly and the disabled.

The Maastricht Treaty included *the principle of solidarity between the Member States in* Article 2 of the founding text of the Community.

It is clear from this regulatory change that the principle of solidarity goes beyond the area of labour law and social security, and extends to other areas, including the area of relations with states outside the Union.

Solidarity is a guiding principle of the Union's foreign policy (Common Foreign and Security Policy (CFSP)). It is stated in Union documents that 'The Amsterdam Treaty of 1997 established a more efficient decision-making process including con- structive abstention and qualified majority voting (QMV). In December 1999, the European Council established the role of the High Representative for CFSP.'

The 2003 Treaty of Nice introduced further changes to simplify the decision- making process and mandated the Political and Security Committee (PSC), established by a Council decision in January 2011, to exercise political control and strategic direction of crisis management operations.

The Treaty of Lisbon (2007), which entered into force on 1 January 2009, provided the Union with a legal personality and an institutional structure for its external service, as well as eliminating the pillar structure introduced by the TEU in 1993. The Treaty created the European External Action Service (EEAS) and updated the European Security and Defence Policy (ESDP), which is an integral part of the Common Foreign and Security Policy (CFSP).

The legal basis of the CFSP was defined in the TEU and revised in the Lisbon Treaty. Articles 21 to 46 of Title V TEU lay down the 'General Provisions on the Union's External Action and Specific Provisions on the Common Foreign and Security Policy'. Articles 205 to 222 of Part Five of the TFEU deal with the Union's external action. Finally, Articles 346 and 347 of Part Seven also apply.

This legislation also affects border protection policy, asylum and immigration policy, and funding for these humanitarian activities:

> Article 101 of the Treaty on the Functioning of the Union stipulates that the Council, acting on a proposal from the Commission, and in a spirit of solidarity, shall take the necessary measures to remedy the economic situation and the supply of certain products (in particular related to natural energies). And it introduced the *solidarity clause* in case of terrorist attacks, natural or human disasters.

But in spite of these actions, there is a widespread conviction that there is an asymmetry between the integrated market discipline, which is very incisive in the national legal systems of the Member States, and the Community rules concerning social relations, with the fear that the former will end up prevailing over the latter.[230]

Obviously, the question invests in a diachronic perspective, the period of the economic crisis that began in 2008, on which a very large bibliography has been compiled, and then the crisis caused by the COVID-19 pandemic.

Article 152 TFEU in fact promotes the social partners in the management of socioeconomic relations, but it preserves the autonomy of national legal systems and thus slows down the unification of discipline that could raise the level of social protection in Europe.

The problem directly affects the formula of the *social market economy*, which should be considered prevalent over the other, now relegated to the margins of the European legal system, of the *open market economy in free competition*.[231] But it is clear that the rules emerging from the Treaties and the Charter are one thing, their interpretation and application by the Court of Justice, with the weight it has on the decisions of national judges who must apply the Union's rules, is quite another. When

---

230. Scharpf, *The Asymmetry of European Integration*, Working Paper, Freie Universitaet Berlin, 2009, n.6: Joerges, *Will the Welfare State Survive the European Integration?*, in E.J. Soc. Law, 2011, n.1, pp. 4 ff. Sciarra, *The European and Labour: Solidarietà e conflitto in tempo di crisi*, Roma-Bari, 013.

231. On this point, *see* Giubboni, *I diritti sociali nell' Unione europea dopo il Trattato di Lisbona. Paradossi, rischi e opportunità*, in *Persona e mercato*, 2011, pp. 3 ss. Sorrentino, *I diritti fondamentali dopo Lisbona*, in *Corriere giur.*, 2010, n.2, 145 ss.

economic freedom prevails at the expense of social rights, the principle of solidarity is weakened, if not cancelled. So much so that a few years ago there was talk of 'decomposed solidarity' and of European citizenship in trouble.[232] Indeed, it is necessary to take into account not only the guarantee of social rights in constitutional texts but also access to justice. The pivot therefore of social rights in Europe is the Court of Justice.[233] This is why Hans Micklitz has spoken of *judicial activism on the part of* the Court, which, in his opinion, has constructed a model of a welfare state that is not fully developed, in which access to justice rather than social justice prevails; but he has also argued that the Court tends to let the European model prevail over those of the national countries.[234]

The two visions of the situation are clear: on the one hand, it is argued that the European social model, emerging from the legal texts, has reached the highest level of protection of rights (fundamental and social as a whole), and the Court is criticised for decisions that drag the welfare state into the economic market; on the other hand, the Court is criticised for being too active in the construction of the social system, but for operating on the side of access to justice rather than on the side of administering fairer justice.

In this sense, solidarity – in the matter of social rights – would be diminished, because it would be degraded to individual (and horizontal) solidarity – undermining the very substance of European citizenship. Hence the call for the issues to be referred to *politics*, i.e., to the bodies of the Union, rather than to EU *justice*.

The jurisprudence of the Court of Human Rights in Strasbourg must also be taken into account when shaping the European social system, given the relevance of the European Convention to domestic law, always within the perimeter of the counter-limits constituted by the fundamental principles of our Constitution.[235]

## §9.05 THE JURISPRUDENCE OF THE EUROPEAN COURT OF HUMAN RIGHTS

The Strasbourg Court applies the European Social Charter, introduced in 1961 and subsequently amended in 1990 and 1994. Although referred to in the Single Act of 1986, the Social Charter does not completely overlap with the social law standards that can be derived from the Treaties and the Nice Charter. What is more, with the Court of Justice having blocked the EU's accession to the Convention on Human Rights in its second opinion in 2014, this disassociation, this, so to speak, squinting view of social rights in Strasbourg, Brussels and Luxembourg, ends up weakening the social system in Europe and diminishing the consistency of European citizenship.[236]

---

232. Somek, *Soldarity Decomposed*, E.L. Rev., 6, 2007, 787 ff.
233. Giubboni, *I diritti sociali, supra*, pp. 40 ff.
234. Micklitz, *Judical Activism of the European Court of Justice and the Development of the European: Social Mode in Anti-Discrimination and Consumer Law*, in EUI Law, 2009, 19.
235. Cantisani, *Il volto sociale dell'Europa la compenetrazione tra le carte dei diritti e il ruolo delle corte e dei giudici nazionali*, in *Dir.amm.* 2022, n.1.
236. Ciancio, *At the Origins of the European Union's Interest in Social Rights*, in Federalismi.it, 14.9.2018.

The overall picture of the ECHR's work can be seen from the Report of the European Committee for Social Rights, which indicated the areas in which violations of the Convention have been recorded: health and safety, especially in work related to the digital market; accidents at work and occupational diseases; life expectancy, which varies according to gender, regions, urban and rural areas, income and level of culture; infant mortality; the situation of the elderly; the general health situation; social security. The collection of cases is significant: it involves Italy mainly in the treatment of Roma.

## §9.06 SOLIDARITY BETWEEN MEMBER STATES

The EU is a 'community of solidarity'.

And the Court of Justice itself has taken this into account in resolving some relevant cases.

Among the most recent is case T-883/16 of 10 September 2019 in which, in a tariff dispute between the Republic of Germany and the Republic of Poland concerning the use of the OPAL pipeline, the Court of Justice, at first instance, condemned Germany for failing to observe the principle of energy solidarity. Article 194(1) TFEU had to be applied in this case, which reads:

> Within the framework of the establishment or functioning of the internal market and taking into account the need to preserve and improve the environment, Union policy on energy shall aim, in a spirit of solidarity between Member States, to:
>
> a) ensure the functioning of the energy market,
> b) ensure the security of energy supply in the Union,
> c) promote energy saving, energy efficiency and the development of new and renewable energies,
> d) promote the interconnection of energy networks.

In the text, the court argues by explaining the origin of the provision, and the obligations arising from the principle of energy solidarity:

> The application of the principle of energy solidarity does not mean (…) that the Union's energy policy must under no circumstances have a negative impact on the particular energy interests of a Member State. However, the institutions of the Union and the Member States are obliged to take into account, when implementing that policy, the interests of both the Union and the various Member States and to balance those interests in the event of conflict.

The Court therefore legitimised the action of the Commission, which was responsible for assessing whether the amendment of the OPAL pipeline exploitation regime proposed by the German regulator could affect the energy interests of other Member States and, if so, balance those interests against the interest of the Federal Republic of Germany and, if appropriate, the Union.

The Court of Justice, to which the German Republic had appealed, upheld the decision (Case C-848/19 P, 15 July 2021).

The problem of solidarity between States becomes particularly relevant when the principle becomes an instrument for controlling decisions taken by a Member State that are contrary to Union directives. With regard to the right to reside and work of European citizens within the Union, the Court ruled in Grzelczyk C-184/99 of 20 September 2001 that '1. The status of citizen of the Union is intended to be the fundamental status of nationals of the Member States, enabling those who find themselves in the same situation to obtain, irrespective of their nationality and subject to the exceptions expressly provided for in that regard, the same treatment in law. A citizen of the European Union who resides lawfully in the territory of the host Member State may rely on Article 6 of the Treaty (now, after amendment, Article 12 EC) in all situations falling within the scope *ratione materiae of* Community law.'

It is stated in the grounds of the judgment that:

> 2. Article 1 of Directive 93/96 on the right of residence for students does not require – as one of the conditions for obtaining the right of residence – the possession of economic resources of a certain amount or that their existence must be proven by specific documents. The rule simply speaks of a declaration or any other means, at least equivalent, enabling the student to assure the competent national authority that he has sufficient resources for himself and, possibly, his spouse and dependent children to prevent him and those family members from becoming a burden on the social assistance system of the host Member State during their stay.

That interpretation does not, however, preclude the host Member State from considering that a student who has had recourse to social assistance no longer satisfies the conditions to which his right of residence is subject and, in compliance with the limits in that regard imposed by Community law, from taking measures to have that national's residence authorisation terminated or that authorisation no longer renewed. However, such measures may in no circumstances become the automatic consequence of recourse to the social assistance of the host Member State by a national of another Member State.

In fact, Directive 93/96, like Directives 90/364 on the right of residence and 90/365 on the right of residence for employed and self-employed persons who have ceased their occupational activity, allows for a degree of financial solidarity of nationals of that State with those of the other Member States, especially when the difficulties encountered by the beneficiary of the right of residence are of a temporary nature. Moreover, a student's financial situation may change over time for reasons beyond his control. The veracity of his declaration can therefore only be assessed at the time when it is made.

Certainly, the Court has contributed through its case law to making the principle of solidarity constitutionally sound in the constitutional apparatus of the Union. Even if this apparatus has not been translated into an actual constitution, it can nevertheless be derived from the preambles and principles of the Treaties and the precepts of the Charter of Fundamental Rights.

However, the expectations of many were more advanced and courageous: one wonders whether the Court missed the opportunity to make this principle even more visible and operational.

## §9.07    SOLIDARITY BETWEEN EUROPEAN INSTITUTIONS AND MEMBER STATES

The operation of the principle between the Union's institutions and the Member States is plastically represented by the case that pitted Slovakia and Hungary against the Council of the Union, the Commission and the Parliament, which had regulated with various provisions the reactions to the emergency situation created by the migratory flows, especially in the Mediterranean countries, mainly in Italy and Greece.

This is Case C-643 /15 decided by the Court on 6 September 2017.

There are several general principles to be found in the Treaties that the two countries had invoked. However, the Court balances the principles and dismisses the appeal against the Council's decision endorsed by the Commission to distribute the masses of migrants who landed in the two Mediterranean countries among the countries of the Union.

For their own benefit, the plaintiff states had invoked the principle of proportionality, but the Court had a good game in rejecting these arguments in order to justify the Council's decision:

> he Council, faced with the emergency situation in which the Hellenic Republic and the Italian Republic found themselves as a result of an unprecedented influx of migrants during the months of July and August 2015, had to adopt measures that could be rapidly implemented and produce concrete effects in order to help those Member States to control the significant migratory flows on their territory.
>
> In addition, in light of the considerations and statistical data set out, *inter alia*, in recitals 12 to 16 in the preamble to the contested decision, it cannot validly be maintained that the Council committed a manifest error of assessment in considering that that situation required the adoption of a temporary relocation measure of a binding nature.
>
> Indeed, it is apparent, first, from recital 15 in the preamble to the contested decision that the Council had noted that numerous measures had already been taken to come to the assistance of the Hellenic Republic and the Italian Republic in the context of migration and asylum policy, and, second, from recital 16 in the preamble to that decision that, since the significant and growing pressure on the Greek and Italian asylum systems was likely to persist, the Council had considered it essential to show solidarity with those two Member States and to supplement the measures adopted up to that point by providing for the temporary measures provided for by that decision.
>
> In that regard, in adopting the contested decision, the Council was indeed required, as is, moreover, apparent from recital 2 in the preamble to that decision, to give effect to the principle of solidarity and fair sharing of responsibility between the Member States, including in financial terms, compliance with which is required, under Article 80 TFEU, in the context of the implementation of the common policy of the Union on asylum.

Advocate General Bot had insisted precisely on the principle of solidarity to request the dismissal of the appeals.

In short, it is a long-standing principle that the Court applies when reminding Member States that they must observe the principles of the Union and comply with the obligations they entered into when initially joining the EEC, which later became the EC and then the EU.

In a case (C-32/72, decided on 7 February 1973) in which Italy had taken measures to temper the obligation imposed by Community measures to reduce slaughtering and milk production, the Court had clarified that '24 In allowing Member States to benefit from the Community, the Treaty imposes on them an obligation to comply with its rules. The fact that a State, in view of its national interests, unilaterally upsets the balance between the advantages and the burdens arising from its membership of the Community, undermines the equality of the Member States before Community law and leads to discrimination against their nationals, first and foremost those of the State which infringes Community rules. 25 This failure to fulfil the duties of solidarity accepted by the Member States on their accession to the Community *shakes the Community legal order to its foundations.*'

## §9.08   SOLIDARITY BETWEEN THE UNION AND ITS CITIZENS

In addition to solidarity between states, the Union considers the application of solidarity in relations with citizens. But if citizens can rely on national solidarity, the principle of subsidiarity prevails. This is the theorem used in the *Hurd* case (C-44/84 decided on 16 January 1986).

Following the establishment of the European Communities, schools were founded for the employees of the Communities in the different Member States. Teachers enjoyed the privilege of receiving a supplementary fraction of salary as employees of the Communities, compared to the treatment of national teachers.

In fact, the principle of solidarity had been invoked by the plaintiff in order to enjoy the privileged treatment in taxation reserved for nationals of other nationalities working as teachers in European Schools; however, as a British citizen, he had to be subject to the taxation of his country and could not be treated as if he were a national of another Member State. The Court ruled out that teachers who are employed by the Communities but who are nationals of the host State could also claim tax equality:

> The financial burden of this mechanism falls entirely on the Community budget, since, (…) the latter makes up the difference between, on the one hand, the sum of the income paid by the School and the national salaries of the teachers and, on the other hand, the overall amount of the budget of the European School. All the additional payments made by the School under Article 24(2) of the Staff Regulations are therefore charged directly to the Community budget. 43 In order to assess the harm which arises to the Community from such a practice on the part of a Member State, it is not sufficient to consider only the case of the Hurd or the British teachers at the European School in Culham, but it is also necessary to take account of the situation which might result from the application of similar practices in other Member States. 44 The generalisation of conduct such as that of the British

authorities in the case of the Hurd would lead to a real transfer of funds from the Community budget to the national budget and, from a financial point of view, would have directly detrimental consequences for the Community. A Member State could thus unilaterally undermine the system of financing the Community and sharing the financial burden among the Member States. Such consequences cannot be accepted. The conduct giving rise to them infringes the duty of sincere cooperation and assistance incumbent on the Member States vis-à-vis the Community, which finds its expression in the obligation, laid down in Article 5 of the EEC Treaty, to facilitate the Community in the performance of its tasks and not to jeopardise the attainment of the objectives of the Treaty.

It is up to each Member State concerned to decide for itself how it intends to prevent its taxation practice in respect of the teachers of the European Schools from having a detrimental effect on the system of financing the Community and sharing the financial burden among the Member States.

The principle of solidarity is seen here in two respects: as a subsidy of the worker – but without it being at odds with the national tax system – and as participation of the individual in the community through the tax levy.

In St Prix (C-507/12 decided on 19 June 2014), the Court clarifies the meaning of the term 'worker' for the purposes of freedom of movement and establishment:

In the context of Article 45 TFEU, a person who provides, for a certain period of time, services for and under the direction of another, in return for which he receives remuneration, is to be regarded as a worker. Once the employment relationship has ended, the person concerned loses, in principle, the status of worker, it being understood, however, that, on the one hand, that status may produce certain effects after the termination of the employment relationship and that, on the other hand, a person who is genuinely seeking employment must also be classified as a worker (Caves Krier Frères, C-379/11, EU:C:2012:798, paragraph 26 and the case-law cited there).

Consequently, and for the purposes of the present case, it must be emphasised that the free movement of workers implies the right for nationals of the Member States to move freely within the territory of the other Member States and to reside there in order to seek work (see, in particular, Case C-292/89 Antonissen v. Commission (EU:C:1991:80), paragraph 13).

It follows that the status of worker within the meaning of Article 45 TFEU, as well as the rights arising from such a status, do not necessarily depend on the existence or actual continuation of an employment relationship (see, to that effect, Lair, 39/86, EU:C:1988:322, paragraphs 31 and 36).

On this basis, the interpretation of Article TFEU was resolved to the effect that a woman who stops working or seeking employment because of physical limitations related to the last stages of pregnancy and the period after childbirth retains the status of 'worker' within the meaning of that article, provided that she resumes her work or finds other employment within a reasonable period of time after the birth of her child.

Advocate General Nils Wahl had raised the question of differential treatment of the female worker, as opposed to the male worker, which would have violated the principle of equality, and the question of inferior treatment of the foreign female worker, even if Community, which would have implied a violation of the principle of non-discrimination. Hence, also by virtue of the principle of solidarity, the proposed solution to the questions was accepted by the Court.

The role of the Court of Justice is therefore essential in affirming the principle of solidarity. But its work does not satisfy all interpreters.

It has recently been pointed out that the Court is not always straightforward. The argument that the Court's judgments are reasoned on the basis of the special circumstances of the case submitted to them does not overcome the criticism of its work.

However, the rights guaranteed by the European Social Charter and the Charter of Fundamental Rights provide at constitutional level a range of subjective positions that appears unique in the world, far superior to the legal conditions offered by other systems of advanced capitalist countries. The jurisprudence of the Court of Human Rights can also confirm this exceptionality of the European model.[237]

Solidarity, combined with European citizenship,[238] with the principle of dignity and equality, proves to be an operational tool to achieve a more promising social justice.

In order to assess the relevance of the principle of solidarity, understood as a normative concept, in a comprehensive manner, it is necessary to examine not only the welfare state, where it also plays an essential role, even if used reductively,[239] but also other areas: the *economic crisis of* 2008, the situation of migrants and migration policies, and the *COVID-19* crisis.

These are the three epoch-making events that cast doubt on the consistency of the Court's interpretation of primary sources.

The first emergency has opened a wide-ranging debate,[240] with different evaluations of its critical impact on the Union down to its foundations: in particular, two penetrating and discouraging analyses have been reported, one by Ulrich Beck[241] and the other by Juergen Habermas.[242] And scenarios for a relaunch of the Union in a federalist sense have been outlined,[243] in contrast to failed budgets that date back to the very origins of the federalist movement.[244]

237. Jimena Quesada, *Social Rights in the Case Law of the Court of Justice of the European Union: The Opening to the Turin Process*, Conference on Social Rights in Today's Europe, Nicosia, 24 February 2017.
238. Somek, *Solidarity Decomposed: Being and time in European Citizenship*, U. of Iowa College of Law, Legal Studies Research Papers, No. 07-13, May 2007.
239. Sciarra, *supra*.
240. *See* the bibliography in Grimmel (ed.), *The Crisis of the European Union*, London and New York, 2018; Federico & Lahusen, *Solidarity as a Public Virtue? Law and Public Policies in the European Union*, London and Turin, 2018.
241. *The Crisis of Europe*, Bologna, 2012.
242. *This Europe is in Crisis*, Roma-Bari, 2012.
243. Cozzolino, Forte, Palazzi, *Europa:che fare?*, Naples, 2019.
244. Somma, *Against Ventotene*, Rome, 2021.

# CHAPTER 10

# Doubts about the Effectiveness of the Solidarity Principle

## §10.01 EUROSCEPTICISM

For almost 30 years, there has been a debate, on the part of Eurosceptics, but also on the part of Europhiles, as to whether the EU has betrayed its original ideals and has turned into a concentration of states dedicated above all to the formation of an integrated market and the building of a liberal economy tempered by certain social policies, rather than a sui generis model tending towards a federation, with a firm basis of values and an economy based on solidarity.

The fact that the project of a European *Constitution* and a European *civil code* has disappeared[245] does not seem to me to be a particularly strong and persuasive argument: the constitution proper has been replaced by the Charter of Fundamental Rights, which is indeed on a par with the Treaties but is also a legally binding text that the Court of Justice uses to affirm the values of the individual; for its part, the demise of the project for a European civil code was not a failure because, on the one hand, it was possible to ascertain the existence of an already consolidated European private law, even if not systematised by an organic codification, and on the other hand, the proposed models (e.g., Draft Common Frame of Reference (DCFR)) were used for the reform of some civil codes – the European civil code was not a failure because it was not a failure. On the other hand, the models proposed (e.g., the Draft Common Frame of Reference) have been used for the reform of some civil codes – e.g., in Germany and France – and have served to construct a new branch of legal science, namely European private law, which consists of three strands: the general principles of European private

---

245. Micklitz, *The Visible Hand of European Private Law in Regulatory Matters*, in EUI Waking Papers, Florence, 2010; *Il fascismo del diritto privato europeo*, in *Contr. Impr. Europa*, 2021, p. 103; Sangiovanni, *Solidarity in the European Union*, in Oxford J. Leg Stud., 33(2), 2013, pp. 213 ff.

law, current European private law, and the areas of national law of European derivation.

Rather, it is worth verifying, from the point of view of the principle of solidarity, how it has been applied at certain particularly significant moments. Establishment of the euro, control of migration, resolution of the economic crisis, control of the pandemic, and reactions to the war in Ukraine are all litmus tests for understanding, beyond the formal facts, how the principle of solidarity has been applied.

### (i) The introduction of the euro

Since 1 January 1999, 11 EU countries have introduced the euro as their new common currency. Today, the euro is the currency adopted by 19 EU countries and more than 340 million European citizens.[246]

Other states outside the Union have also adopted the euro on the basis of specific agreements or unilaterally: the Vatican, San Marino, Monaco, and Andorra.

The euro did not actually start circulating in the 12 countries of the Union until 1 January 2002.

With the Maastricht Treaty in 1992, the conditions were set for the creation of the Economic and Monetary Union. Member States could only adopt the new currency if they had a deficit of 3% of Gross Domestic Product or less and a debt ratio of less than 60%.

On 1 June 1988, the European Central Bank was established.

The exchange rates of the currencies of the first 11 Member States participating in the Monetary Union were set and the gradual transition to the single currency took place.

The economics and finance ministers of the EU Member States that are part of the euro area are responsible for compliance with the Stability Pact and monitor budgetary and public finance policies. European documents specify that:

> The principles on which the Maastricht Treaty is based derive from two important documents produced respectively in April 1989 and October 1990 by the European Commission, namely: the *Delors* Report and the one called *One market one money*. The former, which was based on the principle of vertical subsidiarity, attributed to the European Community functions that concerned the plurality of the member states while it left to the individual countries competences aimed at satisfying the needs of the individual peoples in order to realise their welfare. It also set as a prerequisite for the adoption of the single currency the maximum homogeneity of the individual national economic systems.[247] The second outlined the benefits and costs of an economic and monetary union.

---

246. The euro is the official currency adopted by the 19 states that are currently part of the European Economic and Monetary Union (EMU), i.e., Austria, Belgium, Cyprus, Estonia, Finland, France, Germany, Greece, Ireland, Italy, Latvia, Lithuania, Luxembourg, Malta, the Netherlands, Portugal, Slovenia and Spain: the collection of these nations is frequently referred to as the 'Eurozone'.
247. Szaza, *The Road to European Monetary Union*, Palgrave Macmillan, March 1999, p. 54. 95 Olivo and Santaniello, *Storia dell'Integrazione europea*, Bologna 2015 p. 48. 96 Rizzuto, *supra*, p. 138. 44.

Price stability is the mainstay of the system, according to the ordoliberal direction.[248]

Our country, which was characterised by high public debt, took steps to abruptly reach the 3% deficit/GDP benchmark through the imposition of a heavy Eurotax instead of applying the *opting-out* clause.

Giuseppe Guarino argued that the introduction of the euro was done by regulation, and therefore with a regulatory instrument that was not adequate for the importance of economic change. A currency based on the immutable primacy of short-term budgetary rigour, on a constraint imposed on economically and socially non-homogeneous realities, on stability elevated to dogma.

But the organisation of the system had been prepared for years, it was debated in Parliament, and it is difficult to think of a democratic deficit. If anything, the economic effects were worse than expected because, as is well-known, prices doubled and all citizens – at least in Italy – became poorer. It is difficult to say whether the economic situation without the euro would have been better because the favourable counterbalance has been the stabilisation of the currency, the containment of inflation, the enlargement of the market thanks to the easier comparability of prices.

It was pointed out that the merits of monetary reform are manifold: the ease with which prices can be compared between countries, which stimulates competition between companies, benefiting consumers; price stability; the common currency making it easier, cheaper and safer for companies to buy and sell in the euro area and to trade with the rest of the world; greater economic stability and growth; better integrated and thus more efficient financial markets; greater influence on the global economy; a tangible sign of European identity.

This is not the place to discuss the problems of the euro, but it is useful to recall what the Court of Justice has ruled in certain cases that put the principle of solidarity at stake.

The system of financial support is conditional on the maintenance of the rule of law. In fact, in two interrelated judgments, the European Court of Justice rejected the appeals lodged by Poland and Hungary against support refusals that were determined by the violation of the rule of law in those countries.

The rule of law is based on principles of legality, according to which the legislative process must be: transparent, accountable, democratic and pluralistic; of legal certainty; of prohibition of arbitrariness of executive power; of effective judicial protection, including access to justice, by independent and impartial courts, including with regard to fundamental rights; of separation of powers; of non-discrimination and equality before the law.

Precisely in view of the current situation in Poland and Hungary, following the measures that have restricted the independence of judges and implemented the principles of the Charter of Fundamental Rights in those countries, the European Commission has decided to apply the sanctions provided for in Regulation 2020/2092

---

248. Calandri, Guasconi, Ranieri, *Storia politica e economica dell'integrazione europea: dal 1945 ad oggi*, Milan, 2015, p. 304; Blanchard, *supra*, p. 548.

of the European Parliament and of the Council of 16 December 2020 on a general system of conditionality for the protection of the Union's budget. The Regulation allows for the suspension of financial measures in the event of a breach of the principles of the rule of law by a Member State, which seriously and directly undermines or threatens to undermine the sound financial management of the budget or the protection of the Union's financial interests. This resulted in a court case before the Court of Justice (C-156/21) opened by Hungary against the Parliament and the Council, and a parallel case (C-157/21) opened by Poland.

Advocate General Manuel Campos Sánchez Bordona stated in his conclusions that the purpose of the regulation is to create a specific mechanism to ensure the proper implementation of the Union budget where a Member State commits a breach of the principles of the rule of law which jeopardises the sound management of Union funds or its financial interests. The regulation aims to protect the rule of law by using a sanction mechanism different from that of Article 7 TEU (which allows for the suspension of certain rights of Member States that have violated the rule of law); to this end, it establishes an instrument of financial conditionality.

**(ii) Economic Crisis**

The global economic crisis of 2008 also hit Europe and stability was maintained at the cost of great sacrifices. The question arose as to whether the principle of solidarity could have better withstood the consequences of the crisis, without driving Greece into bankruptcy. The Union bodies distinguished between financial solidarity provided by the Union to states in difficulty and financial solidarity between Member States, which is not regulated by the Union but is left to inter-state agreements.

However, these initiatives are limited in subject matter and subject to the occurrence of exceptional circumstances. Article 122 TFEU provides that:

1. Without prejudice to any other procedures provided for by the Treaties, the Council, acting on a proposal from the Commission, may decide, in a spirit of solidarity between Member States, upon the measures appropriate to the economic situation, in particular if severe difficulties arise in the supply of certain products, notably in the energy sector.
2. Where a Member State is in difficulties or is seriously threatened with severe difficulties caused by natural disasters or exceptional circumstances beyond its control, the Council, on a proposal from the Commission, may grant Union financial assistance to the Member State concerned under certain conditions. The President of the Council shall inform the European Parliament of the decision taken.

Decisions are subject to the rules of the Stability Mechanism (ESM). Now, as the obligations undertaken by states can be very demanding, the Court of Justice specified, in the *Pringle* case,[249] how the stability principle should be applied.[250] An Irish citizen

---

249. *See* overleaf.
250. Case C-370/12 of 27 November 2012.
    The reference for a preliminary ruling concerns, first, the validity of European Council Decision 2011/199/EU of 25 March 2011 amending Article 136 of the Treaty on the Functioning of the European Union with regard to a stability mechanism for Member States whose currency

(Pringle) had argued that Decision 2011/199, insofar as it amended Article 136 TFEU by adding a paragraph 3, which provided that '[t]he Member States whose currency is the euro may establish a stability mechanism', ended up granting Member States a competence in the area of monetary policy with regard to Member States whose currency is the euro, which was not allowed. This was in order to oppose its state, Ireland, becoming subject to the ESM and thus entering into overly burdensome commitments.

The Court clarified that Articles 123 TFEU and 125 TFU are preventive in nature, as they are aimed at reducing the risk of sovereign debt crises as much as possible, the establishment of the stability mechanism aims at managing financial crises that might occur despite any preventive action taken:

> (...) the activities of the ESM do not fall under the monetary policy covered by the aforementioned provisions of the TFEU.
> 96 In fact, according to Articles 3 and 12(1) of the ESM Treaty, the ESM does not have the objective of maintaining price stability but is aimed at meeting the financing needs of ESM members, i.e., Member States whose currency is the euro, which are already experiencing, or are threatened with, serious financial problems, if indispensable to safeguard the financial stability of the euro area as a whole and that of its Member States. To this end, the ESM is neither entitled to set official interest rates for the euro area nor to issue euros, since the financial assistance it grants must be fully financed, in accordance with Article 123(1) TFEU, by paid-in capital or by issuing financial instruments, as provided for in Article 3 of the ESM Treaty.
> 97 As is apparent from paragraph 56 of this judgment, the possible effect of the activities of the ESM on price stability is not such as to undermine that finding. Indeed, even supposing that the ESM's activities could affect the level of inflation, that effect would only be the indirect consequence of the economic policy measures adopted.

Much more relevant was the *Anagnostakis case* in which it was discussed whether it was possible for a State in difficulty (in that case, Greece) to escape its obligation to repay the onerous debt due to the occurrence of a state of necessity; the appellant had launched a public subscription to this effect under the banner 'One

---

is the euro (OJ 2011 L 91, p. 1), and, second, the interpretation of Articles 2 TEU, 3 TEU, 4(3) TEU, 13 TEU, 2(3) TFEU, 3(1)(c) TFEU and 3(1)(c) TFEU. 1), and, second, on the interpretation of Articles 2 TEU, 3 TEU, 4(3) TEU, 13 TEU, 2(3) TFEU, 3(1)(c) and (2) TFEU, 119 TFEU to 123 TFEU and 125 TFEU to 127 TFEU and of the general principles of effective judicial protection and legal certainty.

The application was made in the context of an appeal from a judgment of the High Court (Ireland) brought by Mr. Pringle, an Irish Member of Parliament, against the Government of Ireland, Ireland and the Attorney General and seeking a declaration, first, that the amendment of Article 136 TFEU by Article 1 of Decision 2011/199 constitutes an unlawful amendment of the TFEU and, second, that by ratifying, approving or accepting the Treaty establishing the European Stability Mechanism between the Kingdom of Belgium the Federal Republic of Germany, the Republic of Estonia, Ireland, the Hellenic Republic, the Kingdom of Spain, the French Republic, the Italian Republic, the Republic of Cyprus, the Grand Duchy of Luxembourg, Malta, the Kingdom of the Netherlands, the Republic of Austria, the Portuguese Republic, the Republic of Slovenia, the Slovak Republic and the Republic of Finland, concluded in Brussels on 2 February 2012 (hereinafter 'the ESM Treaty') the 'ESM Treaty'), Ireland would undertake obligations incompatible with the Treaties on which the European Union is founded.

million signatures for a Europe of solidarity'. The General Court[251] ruled out that the current rules allow for the annulment of the obligation for state of necessity and dismissed the appeal and the judgment was upheld on 12 September 2017 (C-589/15 P), by the Court on appeal.

### (iii) Migration flows

The regulation of immigration would also require an in-depth study that is beyond the scope of this work. However, it is worth recalling the Dublin Regulation, the third act that the Union has given itself to regulate this matter. Here the principle of solidarity operates in a twofold manner: towards immigrants, who request entry into a Union state to flee death or deprivation inflicted in Third World countries; towards the states of first reception and those of final destination which is currently being revised, which sets out the modalities for rescuing immigrants in the country of first reception and then the distribution by quotas among all Member States.

Here too, the Court of Justice has supplemented the discipline with its interpretations. It should be noted that the TFEU provides for this:

> The Union shall develop a common immigration policy aimed at ensuring, at all stages, the efficient management of migration flows, fair treatment of third-country nationals residing legally in Member States and the prevention of, and enhanced measures to combat, illegal immigration and trafficking in human beings.
>
> Article 80 The policies of the Union referred to in this Chapter and their implementation shall be governed by the principle of *solidarity* and fair sharing of responsibility, including its financial implications, between Member States. Whenever necessary, the acts of the Union adopted pursuant to this Chapter shall contain appropriate measures to give effect to this principle.
>
> On the basis of these principles, and in particular the principle of *solidarity*, several regulations have been adopted. The most recent, which has not yet been amended to take account of the situation that has arisen in recent years, is Regulation (EU) No 604/2013.

This regulation establishes the *criteria and mechanisms for determining the Member State responsible for examining an application for international protection lodged in one of the Member States by a third-country national or a stateless person.* Responsibility for examining the asylum application lies with the State which has played the most significant role in the applicant's entry into the territory of the EU, i.e., the Member State where the applicant's family reunification can best take place (Article 8-11); the Member State which issued the applicant with a valid residence permit or entry visa (Article 12); the Member State whose border was crossed illegally by the applicant, also known as the first illegal entry criterion (Article 13). The latter is the criterion most frequently applied, probably due to the difficulty of proving the conditions required by the previous criteria.

---

251. Case T-450/12 of 30 September 2015.

In this way, the outermost countries – in particular Greece, Italy, and then Spain for maritime immigration, and the Eastern countries for land-based immigration – were affected.

The interpretation of the principle of solidarity in this area is very problematic, and has met with much criticism from legal experts: it has been said, correctly, that it is a dimidiated solidarity;[252] that it is a solidarity with different degrees of relevance, depending on whether it is understood as an act of spontaneous charity, as a mutual obligation, or as risk mitigation[253] or a solidarity with different directions.[254]

In any case, the Court of Justice ruled that the principle enshrined in Article 80 TFEU is not a mere policy directive but a principle of law that imposes an obligation on Member States to comply with it. The contrary argument had been put forward by Slovakia and Hungary (joined cases 643 and 647/15) who did not want the relocation of immigrants who had entered from other Member States, but the Court had a good game in refuting this argument, although it preferred to limit solidarity to immigration policies[255] and reaffirmed this principle in its judgment of 2 April 2020 *European Commission v. Republic of Poland, Hungary and Czech Republic* (joined cases C-715/17, C-718/17 and C-719/17).[256]

Considering the various events summarised above, it emerges that the 'Europa system' would require a rethink. The structures are pachydermic, the offices over-crowded and unproductive, the legislation gigantic, and the spirit of solidarity is not particularly deep-rooted. From this point of view, the idea that arises from the overall analysis is that it takes time for the 'pachyderm' to move before solidarity measures are taken, and the initiatives do not always appear satisfactory. It is clear that the migration policy has penalised the states exposed in the front row on the external borders, that the competition between states to hoard quantities of vaccine in conflict with each other has penalised the slowest and poorest, that the economic sanctions imposed on Russia for the wicked Ukrainian war clash with the trade balances that individual states have with that country, on the availability of raw materials that each state can count on, and on many other factors that differentiate and distance Member States from each other.

---

252. Ross in Prebil, *Promoting Solidarity in the European Union*, Oxford, 2010; and Giubboni, *A Certain Degree of Solidarity? Free Movement of Persona and Access to Social Protection in the Case of Law of the European Court of Justice.*
253. Schiek, *Solidarity in the Case Law of the European Court of Justice-Opportunities Missed?*, in *Transnational Solidarity*, Cambridge, 2019.
254. Obradovic, *Cases C-643 and C-647/15: Enforcing Solidarity in EU Migration Policy*, european-lawblog, 2 October 2017.
255. Rizza, *Obligation of Solidarity and Loss of Values, in Law, Immigration and Citizenship*, 2018, no. 2 and therein extensive references of doctrine and case law.
256. Dirri, *The Court of Justice returns to the migrant relocation mechanism between identity claims and the upholding of the founding values of the European Union*, in AIC, 2020 no. 5; Lang, *Obligations Are Met: Notes Around the Judgment of the Court of Justice of the European Union of 2 April 2020*, Joined Cases C-715/17, C-718/17 and C-719/17, *Commission v. Poland, Hungary and Czech Republic*, in AIC, 2020, no. 6.

CHAPTER 11

# The Economic Foundations of the European Solidarity

Reference has been made several times in these pages to the European economic model. A model, sui generis, certainly based on the market and its freedoms, but not a model insensitive to social needs, precisely because it recognises the internal connection, the co-essentiality, of fundamental rights and social rights, the limits to private autonomy and the social tasks of the European institutions.

In the programme dedicated to the EU, one can read the statements that form the basis of the European economic and social model, the principles by which the EU is guided by the so-called *social market economy*: 'People and businesses in the EU can only grow if the economy works for them. The EU's social market economy, which is unique in the world, enables economies to grow and reduce poverty and inequality. With a Europe that rests on stable foundations, the economy can fully meet the needs of EU citizens. That is why it is essential to strengthen small and medium-sized enterprises, the backbone of the EU economy. Just as it is essential to complete the Capital Markets Union and deepen Economic and Monetary Union.'

These statements are imbued with ideological and programmatic meaning: on the one hand, they are based on the assumption that the only permissible form of economic system is the free market, on the other hand, they entrust the system with tasks that imply correctives to the 'failure' of the market, i.e., the fight against poverty and the reduction of inequality. The market, considered in isolation, can only reward strong contractors, tolerate exploitation, promote wealth, and for this, it must be corrected with (political and) social goals. In order to achieve these goals, it was necessary to create an integrated market, strengthen small- and medium-sized enterprises, achieve free trade in people, services, goods and capital, and, if possible, create economic and monetary union. The goals of this ambitious programme were only partially achieved. Even without taking into account the two crises that slowed down its development – the economic crisis of 2008 and the health crisis of 2020 – monetary union for the whole of Europe has not been achieved; as of the 27 Member States, only 19 have introduced the single currency (Austria, Belgium, Cyprus, Estonia, Finland, France, Germany, Greece, Ireland, Italy, Latvia, Lithuania, Luxembourg, Malta, the Netherlands, Portugal, Slovakia, Slovenia, Spain), banking union has not been realised, nor has fiscal union.

The Union's official documents also trace the historical roots of this sui generis economic model back to the nineteenth century, in particular to the solidaristic initiatives that opposed the pure capitalist economy.

The Ciriec report prepared by the Economic and Social Committee in 2012 tends to emphasise cooperation as an antidote to unbridled capitalism, and sensitive to social needs, in connection with the programmes of economists who had developed correctives to the market economy.[257]

In this period, therefore, the theorists of social economics did not elaborate or promote any alternative or complementary vision to that of capitalism, but instead developed a theoretical approach to society and the 'social', seeking a reconciliation between ethics and economics through the moralisation of individual behaviour, as in the model of F. Le Play,[258] for whom the goal to be pursued by economists is neither welfare nor wealth but social peace.[259] In the second half of the nineteenth century, two great economists, John Stuart Mill and Léon Walras, exerted a profound influence on the theories of social economy, to which they gave a new orientation. Mill paid particular attention to the economic associationism of workers in the form of both cooperatives and mutual societies. In his major work, the *Principles of Political Economy*, he examined in detail the advantages and disadvantages of workers' cooperatives and called for the promotion of the creation of this type of society in view of the resulting economic and moral benefits. In the wake of Mill, Léon Walras was convinced that cooperatives could play an important role in resolving social conflicts, fulfilling an essential 'economic function, not by eliminating capital but by making the world less capitalist, as well as a no less fundamental moral function, consisting of introducing democracy into the mechanisms of the production process'.[260]

Walras's work *Études d'Économie Sociale: théorie de la répartition de la richesse sociale* (Studies in Social Economy: Theory of the Distribution of Social Wealth), published in Lausanne in 1896, marks a substantial discontinuity from the original theory of social economy traceable to the model proposed by F. Le Play. With Walras, the social economy becomes both a field of study of economic science and a sector of economic activity full of cooperatives, mutuals and associations as we know them today. It is at the end of the nineteenth century that the main features of the modern concept of social economy, inspired by the values of democratic associationism, mutual movement and cooperativism, take shape.

Official EU sources also specify the current boundaries of this economic model.

The new social economy is taking shape in the EU as a pole of social utility embedded in a pluralist economic system, comprising also a public and a market

---

257. Ciriec, *The Social Economy in the European Union*, Brussels, 2012, Chapters 1 and 2.
258. Azam, 2003.
259. de Carbon, 1972.
260. Monzón, 1989.

economy sector. The challenge facing the social economy is to overcome the risk of the flattening of its distinctive features, which are what give it its specific social utility. To this end, social economy actors need to deepen their understanding of the values that make up their common core and use all social and cultural levers in line with those values to assert an autonomous institutional profile and achieve a multiplying effect of their economic and social potential. The challenges and trends described above constitute, rather than an exhaustive decalogue, a proposal open to debate, a starting point for reflection in the new phase that has opened in Europe with the recent enlargements of the Union. In this new phase and in this new social economy, the prominent place and the responsibility for defining the specific profile and strategic objectives that the social economy should adopt in order to play a leading role in the construction of Europe legitimately lie with the social economy actors themselves.[261]

In concrete terms, the objectives of the model are based on the prevalence of the individual and the social objective over capital; on voluntary and open membership; on an open organisation of the structure of economic actors; on the reconciliation of the interests of entrepreneurs and users with the general interest; on the defence and application of the principles of solidarity and responsibility; on the autonomy of management and independence from public authorities; on the allocation of the majority of the operating surplus to the achievement of sustainable development objectives, to services of interest to members or to services of general interest.

This last profile, which constitutes a novelty in the evolution of the model, conforms, as we shall see, to the principles of sustainability developed in the UN for more than 20 years. But the Union's official adherence to these goals is once again one of the aspects of the system's exceptionality, compared to others pursued in the West.

A distinction must, however, be made between two meanings of social market economy: a more circumscribed one, which focuses on the Third Sector, i.e., on social enterprises and entities that are not dedicated to the pursuit of profit but carry out cultural and social activities also organised in economic forms but reinvest their profits in the activity,[262] and a broader one, which concerns the correctives to the pure market economy.

The first meaning concerns only a segment of the whole system, and can therefore also be considered adequately represented by the Union's official websites that refer to Stuart Mill and Walras, without however offering a complete historical picture that should take into account not only the emergence of cooperativism but also the foundations of socialism through the parties and trade unions of the late nineteenth century.

The second meaning, which is then the one universally used to describe the Union's policy choices, deserves special attention because this direction, espoused by the Union at the turn of the 1980s and more widely since the 1990s, lies at the centre of the two existing alignments, one informed by the free market economy, prevalent in North America, and the other by the state economy, not collectivist as in the twentieth

---

261. CIRIEC, *Recent Developments in the Social Economy in the European Union*, Brussels, 2016.
262. European Union, *Social Economy and Social Entrepreneurship*, Brussels, 2014.

century but focused on the state-directed market as in Russia and China, informed by 'state capitalism'.

## §11.01  'ORDOLIBERALS' AND SOCIAL ECONOMISTS

The cultural foundations of the Union's economic system can thus be found in two currents that merged in the second half of the twentieth century: the 'ordoliberal' current and the social business economy current. The former goes back to Walter Eucken and Fritz Bohm (Freiburg School), the latter to Alfred Mueller-Armack and Ludwig Erhard (Cologne School and Frankfurt School). It is barely worth mentioning that 'ordo' is a term derived from the journal Ordo published by the School of Freiburg. But it is a significant term; it alludes to an essential aspect of the model, which is based precisely on the interpenetration of law and economics. This is because the market cannot function without an order dictated by legal rules,[263] without competition, stable money and a balanced budget; the legal order must also ensure a democratic constitutional order, which is interdependent on the economic process. It is a direction that is based on supply policy, 'based on savings that translates into investment, on work that is remunerated in relation to its efficiency and the improvement of human capital, on risk and technological progress'.[264] The Cologne School is also based on the interpenetration of law with the social sciences and combines economics with sociology. Of the various systems that can be elaborated from this perspective, the favoured one is based on private autonomy, on the social contract whereby the individual gives up part of his freedom to allow the freedoms of others, and the collectivity, to pursue its collective interests. The competition model is integrated with the welfare state: state interventions are aimed at guaranteeing individual free initiative and reducing inequalities. It is an irenic conception that reconciles Catholic social doctrine, evangelical social ethics,[265] and socialism with liberalism.

Bohm, as a jurist, interprets the new order as a set of rules that emancipates individuals from the petrified social structures of the Ancièn Régime, makes them market actors and frees them to carry out their transactions in pursuit of their profits. It thus elects private law as the rule of the market: private law guarantees individuals freedom of action, and only needs the state to make sanctions binding, but not to allow the market to function. A society based on the rules of private law eliminates the inequalities established by a status-based order.[266]

To tell the truth, this is not a great novelty since the overthrow of statuses and the liberation of business activities in a market free of privileges and privations has always

---

263. On this point, see Forte, Felice, C. Forte (cur.), *L'economia sociale di mercato e i suoi nemici*, Soveria Mannelli, 2012.
264. *Ibid.*, p. 15.
265. *Ibid.*, p. 17.
266. Bohm, *La società di diritto privato e l' economia di mercato*, in F. Forte, Felice, C. Forte, *supra*, pp. 67 ff. Bohm's theses, first expounded in a work in 1937, aroused much interest even outside Germany; see Gueli, in *Riv. Dir. Comm.*, 1937, II. In those years, when National Socialism had just taken power, his theses were not considered subversive of the totalitarian model.

been considered one of the most important aspects of the French Revolution.[267] And the transition from status to contract[268] had marked, according to Henry Sumner Maine's happy insight, the freedom of individuals not only in the social sphere but also in the economic sphere.

More. It is debated whether, in the medieval period, one could speak of a 'market' in the proper sense insofar as exchanges were not part of the 'pure' game of supply and demand, subject as they were to the weight of moral, social or religious imperatives, or due to the intervention of political powers. The conclusion was self-evident: the ancient economy clearly could not be defined as a market economy since exchanges did not obey the 'free' game alone.[269] Only in fairs could one freely bargain, and for this reason, a set of rules autonomous from the state – the *lex mercatoria* – was formed, which only with the Napoleonic codification was brought under state control.[270]

Moreover, the boundaries of the market were geographical and very narrow. The circulation of money and credit was entrusted to the instruments of private law.

However, bringing the rules of the economy back into the realm of private law has the merit of rescuing the system from collectivist escapes or overly restrictive interventions by the state. In addition to this, the indication of the free market as a necessary source of the 'economic constitution' advocated by Eucken in 1939 – in a totalitarian context such as that of the Nazis – had the merit of claiming spaces of freedom and market efficiency at the same time.[271] In other words, the state must maintain the free economic order without altering the interplay of market factors.

Eucken and Bohm are to be credited with coordinating the rules of the market with those of the organisation of politics and society: out of their connection comes the winning economic model. If one preaches, as many liberalists do, market freedom without bothering to know the legal status of operators, without freeing operators of constraints or without supporting operators in their social position, one risks pandering to the inequalities produced by a free but uncontrolled game. The 'economic constitution' is composed of the rules governing property, the family, the law of obligations, administrative law, etc. *Laissez-faire*, per se, is not the optimal model because it does not prevent cartels, restrictions on competition, oligopolies and monopolies: only the preservation of competition, with targeted state intervention, can ensure market efficiency. Unleashed market forces do not lead to a situation of freedom for all, nor can they ensure an efficient market.[272] In this sense, Eucken's seminal book already explains in its subtitle, why it is necessary to consider economics in connection with

---

267. F. Braudel, *Civilisation matérielle, économie et capitalisme*, 3 vols., Paris, 1967-19.
268. Maine, *Ancient Law: Its Connection with the Early History of Society and Its Relation to Modern Ideas*, London, 1861.
269. Rosenthal, *The Fruits of Revolution: Property Rights, Litigation and French Agriculture (1770-1860)*, Cambridge, 1992.
270. Galgano, *Lex mercatoria: Storia del diritto commerciale*, Bologna, 1993; Angelici, Caravale, Moscati, *Negozianti e imprenditori: 200 anni dal Code de commerce*, Milno, 2008.
271. Thus Eucken in his seminal work *Die Grundlagen der Nationaloeconomie*, Berlin, 1939 (viii ed, 1989).
272. Vanberg, *The Freiburg School*, in *The Social Market Economy*, supra, p. 143; Goldschmidt, Alfred Müller-Armack and Ludwig Erhard: *Social Market Liberalism*, Freiburg Discussion Papers on Constitutional Economics 04/12, 2004.

law, in particular, *private law: it refers to* the social market economy as *adhering to reality.*

Therefore, free competition, basic to this economic order, must be aimed at protecting consumers.[273]

The market economy must therefore be geared towards détente and peace among the citizens. On the social aspects of the market economy insists Muller-Armack,[274] who believes that the liberal economy can better guarantee social security than a centralised economy.[275] The market as an open system in which economic rules are intertwined with those that protect personal freedoms and place consumers on an equal footing with producers becomes a guarantee for development.[276]

273. Gerber, *Law and Competition in Twentieth Century Europe: Protecting Prometheus*, Oxford, 1998; Köhler & Nientiedt, *The Muthesius Controversy: A Tale of Two Liberalisms*, Freiburg, 2015.
274. In *The Social Market Economy, supra*, pp. 339 ff.
275. *Ibid.*, pp. 345 ff.
276. *Ibid.*, pp. 352-353.

# CHAPTER 12

# Solidarity in Private Law: The Italian Experience

## §12.01 FOREWORD

The principle of solidarity in private law plays just as important a role as it does in public law. It has already been emphasised that the great public/private partition is no longer relevant and that there are many aspects of the direct incidence of public law in relations between private individuals, such as the incidence of private forms in the realisation of public programmes.[277] The regulation of property is also informed by this contamination, both from the point of view of the conclusion of private law transactions on public property and from the point of view of the public use of private property.[278] The invention of the category of *common goods* is another symptomatic example of the permeability of the boundary between the two sectors. Now, among private individuals, solidarity is coloured by different experiences: from charity to altruism, from charity to social activity, from non-profit economic initiatives to economic activity that allocates part of its profit to the realisation of social aims. In Italy, these purposes have been brought together in the discipline of the so-called Third Sector, in which non-profit organisations, and social enterprises, stand alongside 'responsible' enterprises that allocate a portion of their profits to social initiatives.[279]

For a long time, solidarity between private individuals relied on *voluntariness*. In the free market in which each, as a self-referential monad, pursues its own interest,

---

277. Alpa, *Dal diritto pubblico al diritto privato*, Modena, 2017; Sordi, *Diritto pubblico e diritto privato. Una genealogia storica*, Bologna, 2020.
278. On this point, *see* now Cerulli Irelli, *Diritto pubblico della proprietà e dei 'beni'*, Turin, 2022.
279. On the category of the commons, *see* Rodotà, *I beni comuni. L'inaspettata rinascita degli usi collettivi*, Bologna, 2018; *Il terribile diritto. Studi sulla proprietà privata e i beni comuni*, Bologna, 2013; Mattei, Reviglio, Rodotà, *I beni pubblici: dal governo democratico dell'economia alla riforma del codice civile*, Roma, 2010; Marella (cur.), *Oltre il pubblico e il privato. Per un diritto dei beni comuni*, 2012.

without having to care about others except for the fact that it has to live with them, deal with them, negotiate or conflict with them, there is no place for coercive solidarity. There are, of course, associations, brotherhoods, and cooperatives that have at their basic principles of mutuality; there are societies in which members cooperate for the achievement of a common purpose. But private interest is the driving force behind every initiative.

On the contrary, in a corporate society, private interest must be reconciled with public interest, and the relationship between private individuals is coercively entrusted to solidarity.

## §12.02   SOLIDARITY IN CONTRACTUAL RELATIONS

The entire paragraph devoted to Article 1175, according to which creditor and debtor must behave fairly, in observance of the principles of corporate solidarity, deserves to be read carefully.[280]

Here, of course, it is not a question of solidarity as a bond of patrimonial liability, but as a principle to which the conduct of the parties must adhere from the moment of the commencement of negotiations to the termination of the relationship, and to the sentence of ultra-activity (the so-called post-contract), if any.

The indications of the Report are clear, and on several occasions, Minister Guardasigilli has made this principle explicit, which he defines as *immanent*: a principle 'that imposes in every field the corporate consideration of the interests of the parties in conflict and of the pre-eminent interests of the community' (Rel. no. 802). First of all, it is clarified that the new code has not accepted the principle of *favor debitoris* (Rel. no. 555). It is reiterated that the defence of credit is the defence of savings, thereby emphasising – without the need for explication – that the individual economic operation must be seen in the overall context of the activities exercised, which are not indifferent to the State, but contribute to the realisation of the public interest. The intermingling of private and public interests is thus the *leitmotif of the* Guardasigilli's interpretation of the rules of the civil code.

With the fall of the Regime and the abrogation of the corporative order and with it the provisions or parts of provisions that referred to it, either by directly referring to it or by adding the qualifying adjective *corporative* to the terms used, the question of the solidarity of private interests and its pertinence to the parties to an obligatory relationship remained open. It was intertwined with the interpretation and application of the good faith (or fairness) clause.

The doctrine was divided between those who, after the fall of the corporative order, considered that the interventionist rules in the economy had been replaced by a free market discipline, intolerant of any authoritative initiative, and those who instead wanted to save the principle of solidarity no longer understood in the corporative meaning but in line with the constitutional provisions. The difference in perspectives

---

280. Rodotà, *Il principio di correttezza e la vigenza dell'art. 1175 c.c.*, in *Banca borsa tit. cred.*, 1965, I, pp. 9 ff.

does not only concern the role of open clauses, but more generally, the concept of cause, the system for checking the merits of the interests involved, the extension of constitutional principles to negotiation operations concluded by private individuals, and, in an even more general perspective, the creative function of judicial interpretation and the constitutionalisation of private law.

Two opposing conceptions, therefore, to which the opposition between a *liberalist* and a *communitarian* vision of private law, so to speak, is ill-suited. But alongside the authors' views of the sapiential format of law, the jurisprudential format must be considered. Here we find curious contradictions in both the synchronic and diachronic dimensions.

### §12.03 CONSTITUTIONAL SOLIDARITY IN RELATIONS BETWEEN PRIVATE INDIVIDUALS

By way of example, up to the 1970s, jurisprudence embraced the conception of the cause of the contract as an *economic-social function*, which Emilio Betti had theorised in 1943 when he had printed his prodigious volume on the general theory of the legal transaction, and then consolidated and preserved for subsequent editions.[281] This theory was perfectly in line with the arguments of the Minister of the Seals but was considered plausible and suited to the system even after the fall of the corporate system. And jurisprudence applied it for many decades, and even today it is still eyed among the maxims of the Court of Cassation.[282] And in the contraposition between Emilio Betti and Giuseppe Stolfi – who in turn proclaimed the theory of the will as an expression of natural law as historically coessential to human activity – the doctrine was divided, tending however to prevail anti-dogmatic, anti-voluntaristic, functional

---

281. The last one, *Teoria generale del negozio giuridico*, published by Utet, dates from 1960, now reprinted by ESI Napoli, 2002.
282. *See, e.g.,* Court of Cassation no. 2196 of 30 January 2020, according to which 'The refusal by the promissory purchaser to enter into the final sale of a property without the certificates of habitability or habitability and conformity with the building permit, even if the failure to issue them depends on the inertia of the Municipality – against which, moreover, the promising seller is obliged to take action – is justified, even if it is a matter of an event occurring prior to the entry into force of law no. 47 of 1985, since the aforesaid certificates are essential, since the purchaser has an interest in obtaining ownership of a property suitable for performing the function economic social and meeting the needs of the purchaser. no. 47 of 1985, since the aforesaid certificates are essential, since the purchaser has an interest in obtaining ownership of a property suitable to fulfil the function economic social as well as to satisfy the needs that lead to the purchase and, that is, the usability and marketability of the property'; Cass. 8 November 2016, n.22626, in the mind of which, 'the judge, where the exception "inadimplenti non est adimplendum" is raised by the party, must proceed to a comparative assessment of the opposing breaches also having regard to their proportionality with respect to the economic – social function of the contract and to their respective impact on the balance of the contractual relationship, the positions of the parties and their interests, so that if it is found that the non-performance of the party against whom the objection is raised is not serious or of minor importance in relation to the interest of the other party under Art. 1455 of the Civil Code, it must be held that the latter's refusal to perform its obligation is not in good faith and therefore not justified under Art. 1460(2) of the Civil Code'.

reactions attentive to the concrete function of the contract.[283] The 'legal transaction', an abstract category considered too ideologically connoted and historically outdated, was now consigned to the annals of the past.

It was in the 1960s, with Stefano Rodotà, that the erosion of the subjective and voluntarist theory of the contract began, and the *favour for* general clauses, in particular for good faith and fairness, was nurtured.[284] Ugo Natoli[285] considers good faith as a criterion for evaluating the behaviour of the parties in the performance of the obligation; others, such as Adolfo Di Majo, consider it an *ex lege* obligation, an integrative source of the negotiation regulation, and therefore destined to operate not at the level subsequent to the origin of the obligation, but at the very moment of its coming into being.[286]

The Court of Cassation endorses this interpretation:[287] the solidaristic commitment finds its primary limit solely in the subject's own interest, bound, therefore, to the performance of all legal and/or material acts that are necessary to safeguard the other party's interest *but, nevertheless, to the* extent that they do not entail an appreciable sacrifice to the other party'.[288] Good faith is the governing rule of contractual discretionality: this is the title of a contribution delivered to Corriere Giuridico by Vincenzo Carbone in 1994, who a few years later was to become President of the Court.[289] And the Court with a now univocal orientation has emphasised the role of the principle of good faith also in the integration of the contract, as proposed in past years by Stefano Rodotà.[290] Again recently, a thematic report prepared by the Office of the Supreme Court of Cassation states that 'constitutional principles, and in particular those of social solidarity, expressed in Article 2 of the Constitution, require that private autonomy no longer be considered as a value in itself, but as an instrument for the pursuit of interests that conform to the fundamental values that inspire the system. In fact, the principles of fairness and good faith understood in a constitutionally oriented sense allow the judge to intervene more and more incisively in the governance of the contract, by reviewing the structure of interests defined by the contracting parties'. The judge's review is intended to ensure the 'fair balance of interests'.[291]

---

283. For an acute reflection on the matter *see* now Brutti, *La storicizzazione del diritto contrattuale*, in *Liber amicorum Guido Alpa*, Rome, 2019, pp. 17 ff. Brutti, *Vittorio Scialoja, Emilio Betti. Two Versions of Civil Law*, Turin, 2013.
284. Rodota, Il principio di correttezza e la vigenza dell'art. 1175 cod. civ., in Banca, borsa, tit. cred., 1965, I, 149 ss.
285. Natoli, L'attuazione del rapporto obbligatorio, I, Trattato di diritto civile e commerciale, directed by A. Cicu and F. Messineo, XVI, 1974, 159 ff.
286. L. Di Majo, Delle obbligazioni in generale, in Comm. Scialoja-Branca (art. 1173-1176), Bologna-Rome, 1988, 335.
287. Cass.17 June 1974, n.1781 in Foro it., 1974, I, c.122; cass, 3 November 1999, n.12310, in Foro pad., 2000, p. 348; Civil cassation, section II, 29 August 2011, no. 17716 *supra*; Civil cassation, section I, 22 January 2009, no. 1618; Civil cassation, section I, 25 November 2008, no. 28056; Civil cassation, section I, 6 August 2008, no. 21250; Civil cassation, section I, 27 October 2006, no. 23273).
288. Cass. civ., s. III, 30 July 2004, no. 14605.
289. Prof. Vincenzo Carbone was First President from July 2007 to July 2010.
290. Rodotà, *Le fonti di integrazione del contratto*, Milan, 1969.
291. Court of Cassation, Ufficio del Massimario, Rel. no. 116.

It can then be seen how good faith, from being an interpretative criterion pursuant to Article 1366 of the Civil Code to an evaluative criterion of conduct, pursuant to Articles 1337 and 1375 of the Civil Code, and from being a source of obligations to cooperate, pursuant to Article 1175 of the Civil Code, also becomes a source of integration of the contract and a corrective criterion of its balance. The literature on the subject is vast.[292]

The direction taken in the 1970s[293] was immediately accepted by the courts but was consolidated in the following decades. The *Fiuggi* case is emblematic: it concerned the leasing of thermal waters and mineral water production plants where the rent to be paid to the municipality of Fiuggi was commensurate with the production price freely fixed by the lessee. Faced with the increase in prices due to the normal inflationary process, the municipality had not adjusted the selling price at the time of production in order to limit the level of the fees but had increased it at the product distribution stage. Hence the damage suffered by the municipality. Following a complex judicial affair with alternating fortunes for the litigants, the Court of Cassation upheld the Municipality's arguments with a judgment that summarised as follows:

> The clause, inserted in the contracts 'for the management and operation of the concessions of mineral water springs' and 'for the leasing of the thermal establishments' concluded by the Municipality of Fiuggi with a private individual, which, by giving it 'complete freedom' to determine the factory price of the bottles, enables that same private individual to lock in that price despite monetary devaluation, preventing the same municipality from also obtaining the adjustment of the rent correlated to the repeated price, is contrary to the principle of good faith which, by its cogent value, contributes to forming the *regula iuris* of the concrete case, determining, integrally, the content and effects of contracts and guiding, at the same time, their interpretation and execution.[294]

Of particular interest, in the body of the explanatory statement, is the justification given for the use of the good faith clause as a means of implementing the constitutional principle of solidarity:

> assuming that the contractual law did indeed attribute to Ente Fiuggi 'complete freedom' in determining the factory price of the bottles, it could not, however, be held to be free from the duty of fairness (Article 1175 of the Civil Code.), which in the system acts as an internal limit of every subjective legal situation, whether active or passive, contractually attributed, thus contributing to the relative conformation in an amplifying or restrictive sense with respect to the apparent physiognomy, so that compliance with formal legality does not translate into a sacrifice of substantial justice and the (mandatory) duty of solidarity, now constitutionalised (Article 2 of the Constitution), is not disregarded. 2 of the Constitution), which, when applied to contracts, integratively determines their content or effects (art. 1374 of the Civil Code) and must, at the same time, guide

---

292. *See Court of Cassation*, Rel. no. 116, Good faith as a source of integration of the negotiation statute: The role of the judge in the governance of the contract, 2010 and therein extensive quotations.

293. Macario, *Ideologia e dogmatica nella civilistica degli anni Settanta: il dibattito su autonomia privata e libertà contrattuale*, in *Studi in on.di N.Lipari*, Milano, 2008, pp. 1491 ss.

294. Cass. 20 March 1994, no. 3775, in *Foro it.*, 1995, I, c. 1296.

their interpretation (art. 1366 of the Civil Code) and execution (art. 1375), in compliance with the well-known principle according to which each of the contracting parties is bound to safeguard the interest of the other, if this does not entail an appreciable sacrifice of its own interest. If this is the role of good faith (in the objective sense) and if it, therefore, contributes to the creation of the *regula iuris of* the concrete case, by virtue of the cogent value that the cited norms assign to it and that, as a 'cardinal principle' of the system, inductively extractable from the system, it must be, in general, recognised, it appears surprising, to say the least, to relegate to the 'meta-legal' (as the reported sentence did, under the influence, evident, of persistent mistrust towards the principle in question, even though denounced by doctrine with particular vigour from the early 1960s onwards and in part removed by more recent case law) the municipality's expectation of a price increase merely because it is left to the other party's allegedly discretionary choices, ignoring, in addition to everything else, that fairness constitutes the very rule governing discretionary power and therefore prohibits its abuse.

The use of the good faith clause for corrective purposes in connection with the principle of abuse of rights shows how the legislator's intent was reversed in a literal sense: the drafting of the Civil Code had avoided the inclusion of a rule on the abuse of rights to prevent judges from having indiscriminate power that would have given rise to legal uncertainty as well as an exercise of functions permitted only to the legislature; here, on the other hand, it is precisely the combination of good faith and solidarity that legitimises the judge to apply the general clause in an implementation function of the constitutional principle, leading to results of equity and social justice.

Emblematic cases of the application of the principle of solidarity, according to the meaning given to the Italian Constitution, are judgments of the Court of Cassation concerning the termination ad nutum of contracts and the liability for breach, the judicial reduction of excessive penalty clauses, the application of the German institute of Verwinkung (not codified by the Italian legislator), the selection of void clauses in banking contracts, the compensation of moral damages in breach of contract, and so on.[295]

---

295. *See* Alpa & Andenas, *European Private Law*, Milan, 2022.

# CHAPTER 13
# Social Justice and Contract Law

## §13.01    THE CONTRACT AND SOCIAL JUSTICE

It has been said that the principle of social solidarity operates in the sphere of relations between private individuals with regard to the family, and thus to relations between spouses and in the treatment of children,[296] to associations[297] and companies, in particular cooperatives and mutual societies, in the definition of corporate social responsibility and sustainability programmes (which will be discussed in a moment), and in many other areas. What appears particularly significant to the jurist is the way in which the principle of (social) solidarity has been accredited in the way of conceiving the role of the contract, which has always been considered one of the instruments used by private individuals to realise their selfish interests. Hence the problem of whether the legal organisation – the legislative rules, their interpretation and application, the techniques of negotiation and conciliation – can govern the transaction by affecting it, or should it leave the contracting parties to their fate.

In a free market, the state refrains from intervening, there are no spaces other than those occupied by private individuals, and private individuals carve out their own destiny with their own hands, i.e., with their own skill, their economic power, their social position. Mirroring this way of putting things is the story of the discipline of the contract that unfolds throughout the nineteenth and early twentieth centuries. Suffice it to recall the fate of the subordinate employment contract, in the nineteenth-century codes placed within the type of lease (*locatio operarum*) and in the common law experience placed in the meanderings of personal liberties. In the legal systems,

---

296. Sesta (ed.), *Codice dell'unione civile e delle convivenze*, Milan, 2017; D'Agostino, *Una filosofia della famiglia*, 2nd ed., Milan, 2003; Tondi della Mura, *Famiglia e sussidiarietà, ovvero: dei diritti (sociali) della famiglia*, in *Modelli familiari tra diritti e servizi*, edited by M. Gorgoni, Naples, 2005; Caferra, *Famiglia e assistenza. Il diritto della famiglia nel sistema della sicurezza sociale*, 3rd ed., Bologna, 2003: Lenti, Manfredi, Morozzo Della Rocca, Olivero, Stradini, *Doveri di solidarietà e prestazioni di pubblica assistenza*, Napoli, 2013.
297. Dei, *Cultures and practices of gift and solidarity*, Enc, Treccani online, 2015.

although founded on different cultural, economic and social structures and traditions, there are singular uniformities. When it had to be decided whether restrictions on bakers' working hours were legitimate and in conformity with the Constitution, the Supreme Court judges answered in the negative (*Lochner v. New York, 1905* (198 U.S. 45).[298] Precisely in the same years in Italy and France, a debate developed among jurists, sensitive to the social implications of the regulation of legal institutions, from property to contracts and liability. Obviously, the debate was opened by exponents of legal socialism, who wondered whether the discipline of civil law was suitable, as it had been devised in 1865 (and even earlier, given that its model was the Napoleonic Code of 1804) to regulate relations between private individuals in an economic and social context that had changed a great deal since those times.

The aim was to see whether legal rules could be used to correct the economic operation, i.e., to temper the employer's prevarications, improve the conditions of work performance, ensure that the risk was not borne entirely by the weaker party in the relationship.

There is, however, an important difference between the conception of civilists open to the relevance of the social aspects of private law and the conception of the role of law in modern times: in that case, one thought of the legislative format as the corrective to be made to the legally and economically unbalanced relationship of private individuals; in our case, in addition to the legislative format, one also aims at the jurisprudential format, i.e., the intervention of the judge through the instruments placed at his disposal by the legal system, i.e., general principles, general clauses, the prohibition of abuse of rights, the *exceptio doli* and so on.

The issue is illustrated with exemplary clarity and simplicity by Emanuele Gianturco in the prolusion to the Corso di diritto civile read at the University of Naples in 1891.[299] Gianturco starts from the premise that in modern codes, contract law exalts the will and freedom, and the legislator 'disregards the unfairness that the alleged equality of rights of the contracting parties may in fact give rise to'. Of course, the legislator cannot and must not be the universal guardian. Thus individualism triumphs in the name of the freedom of the contracting parties. But the state, Gianturco observes, 'cannot be indifferent to serious social injustices, cannot abdicate its social duties, since the pretended economic harmonies often result in the most bitter disagreements'. Codes of *private law* must be transformed into *codes of private social law*. 'The social question is almost all in the civil code': at the end of the nineteenth century, the examples Gianturco cites to prove his point are dazzling. First and foremost, the work lease, mentioned above; then the treatment of agrarian contracts, whose freedom of content may require the farmer to bear the risks arising from chance, and the renunciation of indemnity for investments made; and again the measure of mortgage interest that may border on usury.

---

298. Most recently *see* Ridolfi, *A Re-reading of Lochner v. New York More Lhan a Century Later*, in *Diritticomparati*, 2005; Pinelli, *The Debate on the Legitimacy of the Supreme Court*, associazi-onedeicostituzionalisti, 2010.
299. *Opere giuridiche*, Rome, 1947, vol. II.

Gianturco's pages can be brought up to date. They show us that social justice can also be achieved by using the rules of common law, and thus also with the rules intended to govern contracts in general. As we have seen, it is precisely good faith, which gives entry to the principle of solidarity, that is a suitable instrument.

It is not just a matter of rebalancing individual relationships: when we speak of social justice, we are referring to entire categories of relationships, between employers and employees, between entrepreneurs and consumers, savers or users, and even between large and small or medium-sized enterprises. In other words, reference is made to a new conception of law that acts as the bearer of the interests of the weak, not merely refraining from intervening, or acting as the referee of a game played by the parties on their own strength.

This is the meaning of the manifesto that scholars from several European universities, in bringing their contribution to the realisation of a European civil code, advocated by invoking the social justice of the contract.[300]

And we speak first of all of the contract in general, i.e., of rules intended to govern all contracts, not just categories of contracts operating in the market in which *market failures are* to be corrected.

In this regard, it has been referred to as *proactive* solidarism,[301] which differs from *corrective* or *defensive* solidarism and from social solidarism that operates in the relationship established by the individual with the community but rather aims at conforming to the contractual relationship so that it does not lend itself to exploitative purposes but rather realises equitable social relations. This thesis has been put forward in a peculiar context, the analysis of the remedies offered by the rules of the civil code to the pandemic, but it has been said that it also applies to the economic development of a society in crisis due to the ecological transition, the shortage of energy resources, and the exacerbation of inequalities.

Social justice also means giving full value to human rights and fundamental rights in contract law, again, considering contract rules in general.

### §13.02    CONTRACT AND FUNDAMENTAL AND HUMAN RIGHTS

The area in which the principle of solidarity manifests itself most eloquently is that of the protection of fundamental rights. Following different trajectories, such as originally offered by administrative justice, as in France, offered by civil justice, as in Italy and Germany, offered by Parliament with reference to the ECHR, as in England, European models have accredited the idea that also in private law, and within the framework of contract law, it is possible to give extensive protection to fundamental rights. The 2009 draft of a European civil code also records this conclusion.

---

300. AA.VV., *Social Justice in European Contract Law: A Manifesto*, in *E.L. Journal*, 10(6), 2004, pp. 653 ff.
301. Mattei & Quarta, *Three Types of Solidarity: Beyond the Crisis in Contract Law*, in *Giust.civ.com*, 2020, n.5.

It is not possible here to carry out a full analysis of the subject; please refer to the copious literature.[302]

## §13.03    FUNDAMENTAL RIGHTS, GENERAL PRINCIPLES, CONTRACT LAW

Over the last few decades, there has been a very interesting phenomenon, the increasingly frequent (but less and less perceived) use of the term 'principle'. The use is recorded in national experiences, in EU acts as well as in European law harmonisation projects. In national experiences, one can speak of a 'constant discussion' in which principles are accredited by a long-standing tradition. This is the case with the legal culture that was formed in Italy,[303] Germany[304] and Austria.[305] Here, first the study and application of Roman law, and thus of the *regulae iuris* (listed in Book L of the Justinian Digest), which constituted one of the epiphanies of general principles, formulated in the form of *brocardi*,[306] then the study of natural law in its opposition to positive law. Then again, the construction of the legal system in 'geometric' form, according to principles of rationality. So much so that even in the texts where interpretative rules were regulated by law (the special laws and civil codes) the general principles corresponded (and for some experiences still correspond) to *analogia legis*.

For English legal culture, one must rather speak of a 'rediscovery': after Jeremy Bentham's *Principles of Morals and Legislation,* this terminology migrated into the studies of logic and philosophy. For American legal culture, one can speak of a 'complex' relationship because recently, the issue has mainly taken place within the analytical legal philosophy of Ronald Dworkin, who explained how principles should be taken seriously, perhaps recalling the desecrating hints of the founders of legal realism.[307] For French civil law, one can speak of a 'discovery' because – with the exception of the work of François Gény,[308] always regarded with suspicion by the formalists, and much appreciated instead in Italy – civil law has been overtaken by administrative law in the use of expression and its practical application.

In this panoply of references, the expression 'principle' takes on multiple meanings, which multiply even more when one considers the contexts in which the

---

302. Alpa & Conte, *Fundamental Rights and Freedoms in Contractual Relations,* Turin, 2018; AA.VV., *Le libertà fondamentali dell'Unione europea e il diritto privato,* edited by F. Mezzanotte, *Introduction by A. Zoppini,* Rome, 2016; Navarretta, *Il contratto democratico e la giustizia contrattuale,* in *Riv. Dir.civ.,* 2016, p. 1262 ff.; Mak (Ch.), *Fundamental Rights in European Contract Law,* Kluwer Law International, 2008.
303. For the historical reconstruction of the formula 'general principle' and homologous expressions, *see* Alpa, *I principi generali,* Milano, 1993 (2d ed. 2006); Guastini, *Le fonti del diritto e l'interpretazione,* Milano, 1993.
304. In the extensive literature, *see* Alexy, *Theorie der juristischen Argumentation,* 1978, translated in Italian, *Teoria dell'argomentazione giuridica,* edited by M.La Torre, Milan, 1998.
305. Bydlinsky, *Juristische Methodenlehere und Rechtsbegriff,* Munich, 1991.
306. Stein, *Regulae juris. From juristic rules to legal maxims,* Edinburgh, 1966.
307. Dworkin, *Taking Rights Seriously,* 1977, transl. *I diritti presi sul serio,* translated by F. Oriana and G. Rebuffa, Bologna, 1982; Benditt, *Law as Rule and Principle,* Stanford, 1976.
308. Gény, *Méthode d'interprétation et sources de droit privé positif,* Paris, 1899.

word is used in projects of harmonisation, standardisation, codification of European private law.

Here are a few examples: in Ole Lando and Hugh Beale's 'Principles' (Principles of European Contract Law (PECL)), the expression indicates the 'general rules of contract law' (Article 1:101(1)) and likewise for the Unidroit Principles (Preamble, paragraph 1).

In the Draft Common Frame of Reference, the expression from time to time includes rules that do not have the force of law, definitions, or general rules.[309] What is important, however, is the stance taken in the introduction: the fundamental principles, underlying the rules, express conflicting values, are not prioritised, and are mentioned only as examples. In a first inventory, they are mentioned as:

> justice, liberty, *protection of human rights*, development of the internal market, solidarity and social responsibility, freedom, security and justice, protection of consumers and others in need of protection, preservation of cultural and linguistic pluralism, rationality, legal certainty, predictability, efficiency, reasonable reliance, and proper allocation of responsibility for the creation of risks.

Apart from the specific mention in some rules of human rights – which will be discussed below – even if the principles are not placed on a hierarchical scale, it should not be thought that in the intention of the drafters of the Draft, human rights constitute a group of interests that conflict with other interests within a text intended to give a systematic regulation to the subject matter of contracts, without playing a prominent role. On the contrary, Article 1-1:102(2) provides that the rules collected in the Draft 'have to be read in the light of any applicable instruments guaranteeing human rights and fundamental freedoms and any applicable constitutional laws'.

The Principes *directeurs of the* Association Henri Capitant and the Société de Législation comparée (of 2008) distinguish the Principes *directeurs* from the other principles, which they regard as general rules shared by the EU Member States. The collection then corrects the PECLs that also bring innovations among the rules suggested as contractual models to be imitated, from which to draw inspiration or in which to find the tools to resolve issues. Here, among the guiding principles are: (i) freedom of contract, (ii) legal certainty and (iii) fairness, a term that is translated in the commentary of the draft with a tripartite meaning of 'good faith, fair dealing and cooperation'.[310]

There is no mention of fundamental rights.

Fundamental rights are also lost along the way in the later developments of the harmonisation of the rules of contract, which relies on simplified, concise, partial texts.

The transitional text between the regulation of contracts in general of the Draft (Book II) and the Draft Regulation on the sale, called Feasibility Study for a Future

---

309. Principles, *Definitions and Model Rules of European Private Law: Draft Common Frame of Reference*, Outline edition, edited by C. von Bar, Clive, Schulte-Noelke, Munich, 2009, p. 9; for a discussion of these techniques, *see* Alpa & Andenas, *Fondamenti del diritto privato europeo*, Milan, 2005.
310. Principles, *supra*, p. 14.

Instrument in European Contract Law[311] (which dates back to July 2011), does not mention fundamental rights, provides for a few general principles: reasonableness (Article 4), freedom of contract (Article 7), good faith and fair dealing (Article 8); nor does it refer to general or constitutional principles accredited by EU law or national constitutions in the matter of interpretation. The text proposes a *closed system*: 'This instrument is to be interpreted and developed autonomously and in accordance with its objectives and the principles underlying it' (Article 1(1)). The text prohibits the use of national laws (Article 1(2)).

Finally, the draft Regulation on a European Sales Law sets out in its opening some 'general principles' that it identifies in (i) freedom of contract, (ii) good faith and fair dealing, and (iii) cooperation. This, too, is a closed text; it makes no reference to fundamental law, nor to the interpretative rules that convey the values of Community law.

This varied culture, which sustains the editors of the texts, bearers of different linguistic, cultural and technical traditions, is therefore refractory to a strict use of the term 'general principle', but does not reject it, indeed it accredits it. And it accredits it not to be understood as a technical-scientific term to be employed with caution and awareness, but rather as a polyvalent term endowed with an evanescent conventional meaning, a sort of statement formulated with general expressions from time to time alluding to a value, a rule, an interpretative direction, and so on. All jurists can understand the meaning of 'principle' and feel authorised to employ it in the most diverse ways. And since language, fashions, and practices cannot be governed, it is necessary from time to time to verify the meaning of the principle before us in order to fully understand the meaning alluded to by those who employed it.

The sensitivity for this term varies depending on the jurist's culture and matrix of origin. For example, I do not know how well-known outside the borders of Italy is the history of 'general principles' that marks Italian legal culture from the late nineteenth century to the present day. It is a history that does not just stop at investigating the formal legal meaning of this category but delves into its ideological and practical significance.

The jurist bound to the written text finds it difficult to accredit the idea that it is useful to coin provisions with a general tenor, with a very broad scope, and describe the case (*Tatbestand*) in vague terms. And he is therefore inclined to distinguish specific, detailed rules from general rules – in other words, a broad enunciation; and he is inclined to distinguish general rules from general principles, which he has derived by an inductive logical process proceeding from many particular rules to arrive at a general enunciation. The jurist attentive to the normative datum then distinguishes the *supreme* principles of the *State's* legal system from those that emerge from other contexts. And he wonders whether the general principles explicitly formulated in a legal provision have a different role from those that are inductively derived from provisions without being made explicit therein.

---

311. *See* it in *Towards a European Contract Law*, edited by Schulze & Stuyck, Munich, 2011.

This is because there are legal systems, such as the Italian legal system, in which the civil code, the constitution and other important regulatory texts (which we could call the 'tables of the law') often use the term 'principle', and thus bind the interpreter much more than those systems in which principles are scarcely mentioned in the texts, are the result of doctrinal elaboration (logic, axiology, hermeneutics, etc.) or are even proposed, again by doctrine, as 'directive rules' for the harmonisation of a domestic legal system or a supranational system or a system in the making, (called 'law of the land') or are even proposed, again by the doctrine, as 'guiding rules' for the harmonisation of a sector of the domestic legal system or a supranational system or a system in the making, known as 'European private law'. Jurists who are less bound to texts mentioning principles are thus freer, and more casual in inventing, manipulating, inventing, classifying 'principles'.

These are just some of the problems that Italian jurists have debated at length over the course of more than a century: one of the highest peaks of this debate was reached at the Accademia dei Lincei, at a conference organised in Rome on 27-29 May 1991, during which masters from various disciplines identified, catalogued and discussed principles both from a philosophical and historical perspective and from a legal and operational perspective, with regard to the various partitions of law.[312]

Since 1991, 20 years have passed in which, at a pace that is certainly not usual for legal culture, so many studies, guidelines, draft regulatory texts, and jurisprudential orientations have accumulated that have profoundly altered national and what we can – not only geographically – call European legal experiences. These are experiences that cannot be ignored. I am referring in particular to those experiences that constitute the 'humus' in which the new legal culture has taken root and which are therefore not only central to the jurist's discourse but also irreversible.

The events, or rather the cultural trends and events that have gradually established themselves and changed the meaning and role of general principles are essentially three: (i) the definitive overcoming of the distinction between private and public law; (ii) the introduction of the European Charter of Fundamental Rights; (iii) the use of the principles of the ECHR by the European Court of Justice and many constitutional and legitimacy courts.

While normative texts are precise, the texts of judgments and often doctrinal contributions are generic or superficial, so that sometimes the expressions 'general principles', 'values', 'fundamental rights', 'human rights' are used indifferently.

Thanks to these directions and cultural events, the universe of principles was thus further enriched and renewed, demonstrating a vitality that was absolutely unthinkable to imagine at the end of the nineteenth century, when the discussion on principles understood in a modern way had begun.

The new millennium witnessed a very significant turning point, which at the same time affected the evolution of Community law and the process of bringing national legal systems closer together, with the construction of common values, the

---

312. *Atti dei convegni lincei* (96), Conference on: *I principi generali del diritto* (Rome, 27-29 May 1991), Rome, 1992.

reformulation of relations between the citizen and the institutions of the EU, and at the same time with the formation of an essential nucleus of rules (*acquis communautaire*) in which uniform principles of consumer contracts were laid down.[313]

The path that has been taken, based on the close connection between fundamental rights and general principles, has led to the result that Community provisions cannot be applied in conflict with general principles (and thus fundamental rights) and that national authorities, judges, and administrations cannot apply Community-derived rules without applying general principles and thus fundamental rights.[314]

The European Charter of Fundamental Rights, the jurisprudence of the European Court of Justice and the pronouncements of national constitutional courts are the basis of positive law that has accredited the thesis that *fundamental rights are general principles*.

From a formal point of view, if we were to stop and consider only the letter of the Charter, it could be debated whether the fundamental rights of the individual are to be understood as 'principles' of law as such. Reading the Preamble of the Charter, it would seem to be understood that fundamental rights are *values* based on the principles of democracy and the rule of law.[315] Thus the text reads:

> Conscious of its spiritual and moral heritage, the Union is founded on the indivisible and universal values of human dignity, freedom, equality and solidarity; it is based on the principle of democracy and the principle of the rule of law. It places the individual at the heart of its action by establishing the citizenship of the Union and by creating an area of freedom, security and justice.

In another passage of the Preamble, values and principles seem to be transformed into fundamental rights: 'To this end, it is necessary to strengthen the protection of fundamental rights, in the light of the evolution of society, social progress and scientific and technological developments, by making these rights more visible in a Charter.' But the most relevant step concerns the nature of these values/principles/rights: 'The enjoyment of these rights gives rise to responsibilities and duties towards each other as well as towards the human community and future generations. Therefore, the Union recognises the rights, freedoms and principles set out below.' It is therefore not a matter of emphatic enunciations that exhaust their function in painting the ideal image of the Charter: fundamental rights are or express principles that have legal force, which give rise to responsibilities and duties towards the State or the Union and towards *others*.

In 2007, a Resolution of the European Parliament conferred legal value on the Charter, even though the Court of Justice and national courts had long since independently determined to consider the Charter binding and to draw inspiration from it in

---

313. *EC Consumer Law Compendium. The Consumer Acquis and Its Transposition in the Member States*, edited by Schulte-Neolke, Twigg-Flenser, Ebers, Munich, 2008; *Common Frame of Reference and Existing EC Contract Law*, edited by Schulze, Munich, 2009; *The Principles of Community Contract Law: Acquis Communautaire and European Private Law*, Turin, 2009.
314. This is the thesis I argued years ago in *The Applicability of the European Convention on Human Rights to Relations Between Private Persons*, in *Eur.dir.priv.*, 1999, II, p. 873; Wade, *Horizons and Horizontality*, LQR, 11, 2000, 217.
315. Rodotà, *La Carta come atto politico e come atto giuridico*, in *Riscrivere i diritti in Europa*, Bologna, 2001.

resolving issues and deciding disputes.[316] The Charter immediately entered the body of 'living law' and added a legal value to its political value.

More. The Treaty of the European Union was amended by the Lisbon Treaty with the addition of Article 1a, which reads:

> The Union is founded on the values of respect for human dignity, freedom, democracy, equality, the rule of law and respect for human rights, including the rights of persons belonging to minorities. These values are common to the Member States in a society characterised by pluralism, non-discrimination, tolerance, justice, solidarity and equality between women and men.

And Article 6 reads:

> The Union recognises the rights, freedoms and principles set out in the Charter of Rights European Union of 7 December 2000, as adapted on 12 December 2007 to Strasbourg, which has the same legal value as the treaties.

If the legal value of the Charter is reaffirmed – acquired, so to speak, on the ground in the jurisprudential application of the Courts, then affirmed by the 2007 resolution, and now again enshrined in the Treaty – this means that those provisions are binding in nature, must be applied by the Community and national courts, and can be applied not only in vertical relationships (i.e., vis-à-vis States) but also in horizontal relationships. We will return to this point in a moment.

For their part, human rights as recognised and classified in the European Convention received further recognition in the Lisbon Treaty.

In fact, Article 6.3 states:

> 'Fundamental rights, as guaranteed by the European Convention for the Protection of Human Rights and Fundamental Freedoms and as they result from the consti-tutional traditions common to the Member States, shall be part of Union law as *general principles*'. This formula further clarifies the text of the 1992 Maastricht Treaty, according to which 'the Union shall respect fundamental rights (...) as general principles of Community law.'

One could observe that the principles of the Charter and the principles of the Convention now form a whole, based on this double formal recognition.

But the issue is more complex than how it is sometimes portrayed.

The question had also received echoes at the above-mentioned conference of the Lincei. Rodolfo Sacco had spoken about it – with regard to principles in general – citing the EEC's founding treaty (the then Article 215 c.2), which by tabulas inscribed principles among the *sources of* Community law (principles are second-degree legal rules founding the Community legal system);[317] Angelo Falzea had emphasised the high axiological nature of fundamental principles[318] that 'even with their strong ideality they are rules of positive law'; Pietro Rescigno had theorised, with regard to the

---

316. Celotto & Pistorio, *The Legal Effectiveness of the Charter of Fundamental Rights of the European Union* (Case Law Review 2001-2004), Giur.it, 2004.
317. Sacco, *General Principles in European Legal Systems*, in Atti, *supra*, p. 163.
318. Falzea, *Introductory Report*, *supra*, p. 25.

principles included in the Constitution of the Italian Republic, and to the extent that they were recognised by the international community, that they could even constitute a limit to national sovereignty.[319] But above all, Giorgio Oppo and Luigi Mengoni had recognised the rank and role of general principles in fundamental rights. Oppo had emphasised that general principles govern behaviour even in the sphere of private autonomy: 'the highest values are (...) those of liberty, equality and solidarity ("political, economic, social") [citing precisely Article 3 of the Italian Constitutional Charter] and the first principles that follow are those of equal autonomy of citizens and the imputation to the agent of the consequences, active and passive, of behaviour'.[320]

Mengoni had identified inviolable rights with the general principles, specifying, however, that they are to be coordinated with the other norms-principles because the Constitution is a table of values that often have opposite meanings, and therefore they must be balanced with each other. This reaffirmed Ronald Dworkin's distinction between rules and principles made with regard to their function: rules admit only slavish compliance, principles guide the interpreter;[321] these and those are norms that differ not in their structure but in their effects.

All the aforementioned authors considered that the principles should also be applied *horizontally*, i.e., they could be applied not only in relations between the citizen and the State, or between the citizen and the institutions of the EU but also in relations between private parties and thus also to the regulation of contracts. This conclusion is not unambiguous in EU law doctrine, nor in the orientation of the interpreters of civil law and, in general, of European law.

To reason about the production of horizontal effects from fundamental rights/general principles, it is necessary to proceed by successive segments.

Hugh Collins is right when he argues that one can best understand these issues when one comes from experiences in which the distinction between private and public law has lost its centuries-old prominence, and when in those experiences the process of constitutionalising private law has become established.[322]

Generalisations cannot be made.

Experiences in which the phenomenon of the constitutionalisation of private law occurred, even before the formation of a common European law, are one thing. The driving models of this way of constructing the new civil law and modernising it in light of society's founding values were precisely the Italian model, with the process of constitutionalising private law beginning not with the entry into force of the republican constitution (1948), but from the early 1960s; the German model, which also took

---

319. Rescigno, *Concluding Report, supra*, p. 341.
320. Oppo, *Il diritto privato, supra*, p. 227.
321. Mengoni, *I principi generali del diritto e la scienza giuridica, supra*, p. 325.
322. Collins, *The Impact of Human Rights Law on Contract Law in Europe* (edited by Andenas, Andrew and Tamaruya), Legal Studies Research. Paper Series, University of Cambridge, Paper No. 13/2011, but *see also Constitutional Values and European Contract Law*, edited by Grundmann, Alphen aan den Rijn, 2008; Hesselink, Mak, Rutgers, *Constitutional Aspects of European Private Law: Freedoms, Rights and Social Justice in the Draft Common Frame of Reference*, Center for the Study of European Contract Law Working Papers Series No. 2009/05.

shape in the same period (the basic law dates from 1949), and the Spanish model, which started immediately after the introduction of the new constitution of 1978.

Another thing is the experience in which the human rights/principles of the European Convention have been accepted first in terms of the effectiveness of international conventions and then as an integral part of the constitutional order, or in the form of a domestic norm as was the case with the Human Rights Act in England, just to mention the first examples that come to mind.

Yet another account is the experience in which social values have made it possible to go beyond the formally egalitarian bourgeois conception of relations between private individuals, to give access to the values of the person, and thus not only to the protection of the consumer, the worker or the saver (which always refer to a universe of an economic-patrimonial nature) but also to discrimination and differences of sex, language, religion, ethnicity, etc.

I am dealing here with the fundamental rights contained in the Charter, but of course, the discourse encompasses the entire debate on the recognition in the European sphere of the common principles concerning the individual that are widespread and recognised in the constitutional charters of the Member States. And it also concerns the relationship between the Union Charter and the European Charter of Human Rights, as well as the so-called dialogue between the Courts, the multilevel protection of fundamental rights, and the coordination of the pronouncements of the Courts, which, with different competences and a different scope of action, deal with the subject of fundamental rights.

It is precisely the pronouncements of the courts that show that fundamental rights are understood as general principles, presented from time to time in the form of personal values.

Experience teaches us that, beyond the more or less rigorous and technically correct formulas, the function of law is expressed through values-principles-rights and that the legitimisation of a principle can be effected by judges in their *ius dicere* activity so that they in so doing make fundamental rights 'living law'.

The labour market, and thus the employment contract, has been the target most often hit by the Court of Justice of the European Union on the basis of general principles such as the principle of equality (here in the form of equality between men and women in pension treatment), a fundamental right recognised by all modern Constitutions, and by the first declarations of rights. One can also read the text in the opposite sense, namely as an application of the principle of non-discrimination. It is not the case here to review the most striking cases, such as the *Bartsch* case (of 13.9.2008, no. C-46/07), or the cases concerning the application of the principle of personal dignity (C-152/82, 13.11.1990) or the cases concerning the principle of free movement of workers. In the area of contracts, the *Omega Spielhallen* case is exemplary (C-36/02) in which games were prohibited that used electronic devices in which human figures acted as targets (C-36/02).

More recently, in the field of insurance contracts, the Court of Justice ruled that Article 5(2) of Directive 2004/113/EC on the principle of equality between men and women is invalid and therefore clauses in insurance policies that discriminate against women, on the grounds of age, compared to men, are null and void (C-236/09).[323]

A careful analysis of the impact of fundamental rights on the jurisprudence of the courts should include the jurisprudence of the European Court of Human Rights and the jurisprudence of the supreme courts, as well as that of the constitutional courts, of course. However, in the economy of this report, reference can be made to the collections that have accompanied the development of the Strasbourg Court on the subject, without forgetting that the Court tends to consider fundamental rights more as strong subjective positions that individuals are entitled to claim against the states of which they are citizens or guests, obtaining, however, as a remedy for the violation, a compensatory sentence against the violating state.

Is it possible to construct an autonomous body of law, even in the form of a regulation, that deviates from the principles enshrined in the Charter of Fundamental Rights, and thus does not include the principles (even guiding principles) of the Charter among its principles?

There are several possible ways to include the principles of the Charter among the principles of European Contract Law, among the principles of the Common Frame of Reference, among the principles of the Sales Regulation:

(i)   The simplest is direct recall, even without their reproduction.

(ii)  The most natural for the jurist, who prefers to interpret the text rather than rewrite it, is to consider each text (from the PECLs to the Rules) as necessarily interpreted and applied in the light of the principles of the Charter (and of the Convention, which counts as a set of general principles).

(iii) The most traditional one is to consider fundamental principles as mandatory rules, and therefore as rules that must be applied in any case.

In all these cases, the application of these rights/principles/rules to relations between private individuals can be direct.

In doctrine, however, diverse positions can be found.

For example, Collins, on the subject of contractual freedom, argues that the solution can be *bustrofed*: if one places more emphasis on the individual's freedom to bind oneself, then other freedoms can be restricted, such as the one that would require one to observe a timetable that does not respect health; if one places more value on dignity, then work rules that are contrary to health and rest should be disapplied and contractual agreements considered contrary to fundamental rights.

Hans Micklitz[324] points out that among the fundamental rights, social rights must also be taken into account, and that these, however, are not safe: 'the expansion of

---

323. A rich and scholarly collection of annotated cases is now to be found in Cosio and Foglia (cur), *Il diritto europeo nel dialogo delle Corti*, Milan, 2012; on the subject *see Jurisprudence of the European Court of Human Rights and Influence on Domestic Law*, edited by Ruggeri, Naples, 2012.

324. Micklitz, *Failure or Ideological Preconceptions: Thoughts on Two Grand Projects: The European Constitution and the European Civil Code*, EUI Working Papers, Law 2010/04, p. 5.

social rights does not help to overcome the narrow boundaries of the EU competence on The Social'. And in a broader line of reasoning that proposes a revisitation of Community sources, Micklitz sees in the combination of a European Constitution and a European civil code the framework in which an integrated market can truly take place in which not only individual rights but also collective rights are relevant and the principle of solidarity is fully recognised alongside the principle of dignity.

In a more reductive and cautious perspective, Olga Cherednychenco prefers to speak of complementarity between fundamental rights and contract law: 'it is obvious (she says in conclusion of a recent essay) – that the complementarity between fundamental rights and contract law can only be achieved if the ECJ refrains from interfering in such cases by means of the fundamental rights review of the provisions of the CFR or the interpretation of the general clauses contained therein'.[325] But the relevance of fundamental rights in the sphere of European private law and thus of their direct application in contractual law relationships is not denied by the author, who then poses a further question: given this assumption, the problem is not so much their recognition within contract law but *how far* the protection of fundamental rights must go when the conflicting interests of the parties require an acceptable balancing. In this sense the author distinguishes, taking into account the different models established in the European experience, a direct effect, a strong indirect effect, a weak indirect effect.

But here we come to the point. If one starts from the assumption that the Charter of Fundamental Rights underpins the entire Community legal order, then instead of fundamental rights and European Contract Law being complementary, one must speak of the subordination of the latter to the former, as Chantal Mak rightly argues, following extensive and careful comparative research.[326]

At the end of the day, the whole problem of the direct or indirect effect of fundamental or inviolable rights that we have recorded in the experiences of constitutionalisation of private law, as they have developed in Italy and Germany, has been reproduced with many assonances also for the rules of the European Convention on Rights, and the difficult choices made by interpreters are due to several reasons to the fact that the Convention is an international act that does not apply directly in the domestic legal system, that the text did not explicitly mention *dignity* as a value that underpins the entire complex of rights and freedoms of the person, that the freedom of the person includes freedom of contract and this can be seen as an enhancement of or a limit to personal rights.[327]

The modern legislator's dilemma thus lies in this: is it more appropriate, for the purposes of the correct and certain application of the law, to ignore fundamental rights in the provisions regulating the general discipline of the contract, and protect them by

---

325. Cherednychenko, *Fundamental Rights, Policy Issues and the Draft Common Frame of Reference for European Private Law*, in ERPL, 6, 2010, p. 63.
326. Mak, *Fundamental Rights in European Contract Law: A Comparison of the Impact of Fundamental Rights on Contractual Relationship in Germany, the Netherlands, Italy and England*, Alphen aan der Rijn, 2008.
327. Thus Brownsword, *Freedom of Contract, Human Rights and Human Dignity*, in *The Foundations of European Private Law*, edited by R. Brownsword, H.-W. Micklitz, L. Niglia & S. Weatherill, Oxford and Portland, 2011, p. 192.

way of interpretation, or to mention them in such a way that, whatever the process of interpretation, their protection is guaranteed? Obviously, this implies a fundamental choice, namely that freedom of contract cannot go so far as to legitimise the violation of fundamental rights.

The drafters of the DCFR preferred, on the basis of suggestions made by many members of the group, to include the mention of fundamental rights, even if this is not a broad protection and if the remedies granted for their breach of contract consist of damages rather than nullity of the contract.

Among the Principes *directeurs* of the new contract law reform project directed by François Terré is an intermediate formula, whereas in the previous version by Pierre Catala, fundamental rights were ignored. It reads in fact in Article 4 al.2 of Titre I Des Contrats:

> On ne peut porter atteinte aux libertés et droits fondamentaux que dans la mesure indispensable à la protection d'un intérèt sérieux et légitime.

The proposal, coming from Georges Rouhette,[328] is appreciated by Carole Aubert de Vincelles,[329] who points out that it is then specifically applied in Article 59 of the draft on the content of the contract.

---

328. Rouhette, *Regard sur l'avant-projet de réforme de droit des obligations*, in *Rev.dr.comp.*, 4/2007, p. 1393.
329. Aubert de Vincelles, *Les principes généraux relatifs au droit des contrats, in Pour une réforme de droit des contrats*, sous la direction de François Terré, Paris, 2009, p. 115.

CHAPTER 14

# Sustainability and Corporate Governance

Among the new developments in private law in the area of solidarity, one must consider an area that appeared marginal until recently and has now become central in this perspective as well. This is the area of company law and, more specifically, company administration, where the principle of solidarity is expressed in terms of sustainability.

## §14.01 SUSTAINABILITY, A POLITICAL AND ECONOMIC TERM

The term 'sustainability' has only recently been introduced into the legal vocabulary and, like all terms with a verb suffix in '-able', expresses the possibility – or necessity – of what is predicated in the verb. From this point of view, therefore, it is not a term that defines a certain semantic boundary, but, if anything, expresses a path *in progress* and, at the same time, a criterion of judgement, which allows one to verify whether what is stated in the verb has then been fulfilled. By way of example, the term 'possible' is often used in the civil code, which makes it possible to verify, on the basis of the situation in which the subject finds himself, whether he was able to perform what was required by the normative precept, and to measure his behaviour on the basis of standards, such as diligence, declined in its various meanings, or on the basis of general clauses, such as good faith and fairness, possibly taking into account what normally happens in similar situations, and also the behaviour of subjects belonging to the same category. Another significant example is given, in the language of the doctrine, by the term 'enforceable', which implies a check on the performance of obligations: according to the rules of good faith and fair dealing, the debtor may not be required to make an effort that extends to the limit of the 'impossible'.

What is 'sustainable' expresses precisely a yardstick that checks what has been incurred in order to ascertain whether – in the conditions in which the party was placed – a greater effort could have been required of it or whether, under the circumstances, what was performed should be considered sufficient.

The vagueness of the term is inherent in the vagueness and elasticity of general clauses, which are in themselves necessarily undefined.

It is precisely for these reasons that it may be useful to reconstruct its entry into the world of law, given that, from that moment, the term becomes a *normative concept,* and as such expresses a command, which, if not observed, implies a sanction, or as we used to say, a yardstick, on the basis of which to establish whether or not a sanction is applicable.

The first official document in which the subject was enunciated – without, however, claiming to be imperative – was in 1972, at the United Nations Conference on the Human Environment held in Stockholm, in which attention was drawn to the fact that, in order to sustainably improve the living conditions of mankind, natural resources must be safeguarded for the benefit of all; international cooperation is required to achieve this goal. In Stockholm, emphasis was therefore placed on the need to protect the environment in which human beings live and to find a solution to environmental problems, without, however, forgetting the social, economic and developmental aspects of populations.

The premise underlying the Concluding Declaration is that:

> Man has a fundamental right to freedom, equality and satisfactory living condi-
> tions in an environment that allows him to live in dignity and well-being, and is
> highly responsible for the protection and improvement of the environment before
> future generations.

It forms the basis for any programme of action to make the implementation of this right possible. We are in the presence of an *agreement between states,* and precisely the intentions expressed concern the behaviour of states: private individuals, men considered as such, are the recipients of the effects of that behaviour, effects that also include 'future generations'.

The text states, *inter alia,* that:

> (...) 12. Resources shall be made available to conserve and improve the environ-
> ment, taking particular account of the special needs of developing countries, the
> costs they will incur in introducing environmental protection into their develop-
> ment programmes and the need to provide them, if they so request, with
> international technical and financial assistance for this purpose.
> 13. For a more rational management of resources and thus improve the
> environment, States shall, in planning development, take integrated and coordi-
> nated measures to ensure that such development is compatible with the need to
> protect and improve the human environment for the benefit of their peoples.

The environment is the main focus of the Declaration, precisely because, being understood as a human *habit,* it is the framework within which the current and future survival of humanity is at stake.

In 1987, also as part of the UN's work, the President of the *World Commission on Environment and Development* (WCED), Gro Harlem Bruntland presented the report 'Our *common* future'.

The Report spans more than three hundred pages, is divided into three parts (concerns, challenges, commitments) and outlines an agenda that is handed over to states in order to control, improve and save the environment. Businesses are not the recipients of the commitments, yet States, in order to fulfil the commitments, must intervene in the economy in order to achieve 'sustainable development'.

The Brundtland report '*Our Common Future*' notes that the global environmental hotspots and problems are mainly due to the great poverty of the global South and the unsustainable production and consumption patterns of the global North. The report therefore highlights the need to implement a strategy that integrates development and environmental needs. This strategy has been defined in English by the term 'sustainable development', which is currently in wide use:

> Sustainable development is development that enables the present generation to meet its own needs without compromising the ability of future generations to meet their needs (WCED, 1987).

The protection of nature in coordination with the expansion of human rights has been the subject of successive elaborate international documents and conferences that have set out a number of principles and goals to be achieved by governments to promote economic development while protecting the environment. These include:

1992 – in Rio de Janeiro, the UN Conference on Environment and Development (Earth Summit);
2002 – in South Africa, the World Summit on Environmental Sustainability;
2002 – in Monterrey, Mexico, the International Conference on Financing for Development; 2008 – in Doha, Qatar, the Second International Conference on Financing for Development;
2010 – the first European document is the 'Europe 2020' strategy for smart, sustainable and inclusive growth;
2012 – in Rio de Janeiro 'Rio + 20', the World Conference on Sustainable Development (*The Future We Want*);
2015 – in New York, the Summit for the Adoption of the 2030 Agenda for Sustainable Development.

An examination of these documents shows how the strategy that considered only states as recipients of commitments has gradually shifted to a more extensive and all-encompassing strategy, in which companies and individuals are also involved so that the coordinated efforts of public and private institutions can achieve the desired goal. The direct involvement of companies means that this issue does not only develop within the scope of macroeconomic and international policy analyses but extends to encompass economic-business analyses.[330]

The debate on the rational distribution of resources, the costs of environmental protection, and human rights programmes has intensified across the planet.

---

330. *See* for all Perrini, *Sustainability*, Milan, 2018.

In order to emphasise the relevance of the protected interests, some constitutions of less developed countries, such as those of South America, have included protection obligations to be observed with regard to new subjects of law.

The Constitutional Court of the Republic of Colombia recognised the Colombian Amazon Rainforest as a subject of law. In its ruling No. 4360 of 5 April 2018, the Supreme Court of Justice defines nature as a '*sujeto de derechos*' that has been granted the same rights as a natural person, including the right to life. Legal subjectivity has given this vital ecosystem for the world the right to protection, conservation, maintenance and upkeep incumbent on the state and territorial entities of the Amazon basin, and in the ruling, urgent action was ordered to stem the deforestation of the rainforest. The ruling of the Supreme Court of Justice also focuses on analysing the Colombian Constitution from the perspective of environmental protection, considering it as a '*Constitución Ecológica*' or '*Constitución Verde*', and elevating the concept of environmental protection to a fundamental human right. In fact, in the aforementioned judgment, the Supreme Court of Justice emphasises that the environment constitutes a right of constitutional rank, contained in Chapter III of the Colombian Constitutional Magna Carta, under the heading 'collective and environmental rights' (Articles 79 and 80).

In any case, 'the principle of sustainability has become a benchmark for economic and social choices on a global level'.[331]

## §14.02    SUSTAINABILITY AS A NORMATIVE CONCEPT AND THE JOINT-STOCK COMPANY DEBATE

It is more difficult to trace the path on the legal terrain because, beyond the textual relevance of the term, which will be discussed in a moment, sustainability, i.e., the achievement of objectives that make private economic initiative compatible with the protection of human rights and the environment, lies at the heart of a debate that involves corporate *social responsibility*, corporate governance, corporate social responsibility reporting and other technically complex aspects.

On these occasions, the topic 'of sustainability' can be assessed from different perspectives. The first reference is to the 'social theory of business' as a European-style theoretical basis, to be examined in the context of general business discipline.

It was already being discussed before the introduction of the civil code of 1942 (and in particular within the framework of corporate law) and then the discourse became more accentuated during the 1950s. It started from a basic consideration, also accepted in the text of the code, namely the distinction between the interest of the company and the interest of the shareholders.

The analysis of the interests protected in the context of the legal regulation of activities considered it unquestionable that the company had to realise private ends – the realisation of profit – because, in a free market in which private initiative could be carried out without being bent to the interests of the state, the maximisation of profit

---

331. Giovannini, *The Sustainability Principle*, in Aspenia, 2019, p. 76.

was, so to speak, the natural aim of enterprise. Hence the reactions of those who, when faced with programmes to convert private enterprise to the realisation of public interests, spoke out against the 'functionalisation' of private enterprise.[332]

Article 41 of the Constitution was to be understood as a receipt that allowed the legislature to limit economic initiative for reasons of *social utility*, but this did not imply that the individual enterprise should, on its own initiative, set itself objectives to protect interests other than that of the enterprise itself.

If anything, the extent to which shareholders' interests should be taken into account, in particular their right to the division of profits and the dividend, was debated.

To this question, the prevailing doctrine gave an answer that qualified the company as an institution autonomous from the shareholders, the bearer of its own interest, the '*social interest*', to which the shareholders' right to receive profits was conditional on the availability of resources after the needs of the company, functional to the achievement of its purpose, had been satisfied.

This position was superseded in the following period by many scholars who had begun to discuss the meaning and content of the 'social interest' formula.[333]

At the end of the last century, it was agreed that there is no interest of the partners other than that of the company since the partners within the company concur to develop a common interest; if anything, one could argue between the interests of majority and minority partners. And, taking into account the theories based on the economic analysis of law, American style, the conception of the company has prevailed not as a separate entity but as a 'bundle of contracts', i.e., as an expression of the contractual will of the shareholders that manifests itself in the *governance* mechanisms that are being modified to allow for the emphasis to be placed on the particular rights of individuals or groups of shareholders vis-à-vis others with respect to operational management, the definition of strategic objectives, and the company's policy of remuneration for investments.

The doctrine was also implemented in Italy with the 2003 company law reform and the expansion of the protection of the rights of individual shareholders' interests in the management dynamics of the company.

However, the regulatory framework for defining the content of the corporate interest that the company must pursue has become more complicated in relation to the extension of interests external to the shareholder structure that find affirmation and consequent protection in the legal system and that in fact complement the interests of the shareholders. It is increasingly necessary to combine in the management of the company the interest in profit with the protection of widespread interests of the civil community in which the company operates with constant development of the attention due to the care of these external interests as well.

---

332. Minervini, *Contro la funzionalizzazione dell'impresa privata*, in *Riv. dir. civ.*, 1958, I, pp. 618 ff.; Asquini, *I battelli del Reno*, in *Riv. soc.*, 1959, pp. 619 ff.
333. *See*, in particular, Jaeger, *L'interesse sociale*, Milan, 1964, critically reviewed by Ferri G., in *Riv. dir. comm.*, 1965.

It is not yet a theory of the socialisation of the company, but it is certainly an integration of the content of the company's own interest, which therefore stands as an autonomous entity with respect to its shareholders. In this context, the role of subjects external to the corporate structure, generically referred to as *stakeholders*, is also being affirmed, the definition of which has created and continues to create misunderstandings as to the determination of the perimeter of the subjects and interests included therein, so that we have turned towards a very broad vision of the same notion, leaving it to the directors and their discretionary evaluation to define the relative contents according to the company's concrete activity and the scope of its relations with the social and natural environment.

The result was a further evolution of the doctrine, and a return of the 'institutional' conception of the company, understood as an expression of an autonomous entity common not only to the shareholders but also to other stakeholders to be protected in the management of the company.

Recently, it has also been argued that the contractualist theory of society is to be considered abandoned.

The debate is still ongoing between the supporters of prioritising the protection of the interests of the *stockholders*[334] and those who, appealing to *Corporate Social Responsibility* and stakeholder protection, believe that the company, even if it is governed by private law, must take on the protection of interests other than that of the stockholders, who are involved in its activities, such as employees, suppliers, customers, users, and then of course the environment and human rights.[335]

In other words, the *shareholders'* primacy is no longer a dogma[336] and their power must be shared with the holders of 'other' interests than those of the shareholders.

In the 2021 book on '*Stakeholder Capitalism*' by Klaus Schwab, founder of the *World Economic Forum*, a model is promoted according to which private companies are not only profit-seeking entities but also act for the benefit of the wider society (not only the shareholders). Thus, there is a shift from '*shareholder capitalism*' to '*stakeholder capitalism*' *with the* need to provide a more articulated indication of the objectives of business activity.

The debate has also penetrated into Italy, where it has become intertwined with the discussion on the notion of 'company', the purpose of the company, and the categories of protected interests, with the discussion on corporate social responsibility and the contents and prospects of the social business economy.[337]

---

334. Hansmann, *Corporation and Contract*, Working Paper, 2006; Hansmann & Kraakmann, *The End of History for Corporate Law*, Working Paper, 2000.
335. Freeman & Reed, *Stockholders and Stakeholders: A New Perspective on Corporate Governance*, in 25 Calif. Manag. Rev. 1983, pp. 88 ff.
336. Shareholder Theory Summary, Lawteacher.net, July 2021; Smith & Roennegard, *Shareholder Primacy, Corporate Social Responsibility and the Role of Business Schools*, in J. Bus. Ethics, 2014, pp. 1 ff.; Hayden & Boodie, *Reconstructing the Corporation*, Cambridge, 2021.
337. In the large mass of contributions, *see* Angelici, *Divagazioni sulla 'responsabilità sociale' d'impresa*, in *Riv. soc.*, 2018, pp. 3 ff.; Marasà, *Purpose of profit and purpose of common benefit in benefit corporations*, in *Orizzonti del diritto commerciale*, 2017, 2, pp. 8 ff.; Stella Richter Jr, *Benefit and non-benefit companies*, in *Orizzonti del diritto commerciale*, 2017, 2, pp. 1 ff.;

Sustainability goals are now typified on the scale of interests.[338] They are certainly remarkable goals, but it is one thing to regard them as goals that states, on the basis of international cooperation agreements, can achieve, it is quite another to propose them to private individuals.

Certainly, some are already the subject of constitutional provision, others of articulated legislation, e.g., health protection, water or land use; others are not feasible as a goal of private individuals, but *'big corporations'* can help in pursuing them.

Here they are in the order indicated by the 2015 UN Declaration (*Transforming our world: the 2030 Agenda for Sustainable Development*, on the *United Nations – Sustainable Development knowledge platform*).[339]

## §14.03 THE NORMATIVE PATH OF THE CONCEPT OF 'SUSTAINABILITY'

The EU began to address this issue in the early 2000s with documents limited to specific aspects, workers' rights, minority shareholders' rights, consumer rights and environmental protection. This economic and social policy – which goes back to the Germanic convention of the social market economy – is much debated, both by those who consider it restrictive of free economic initiative and by those who see in it an image of capitalism 'with a human face'.[340]

The legal framework that currently informs corporate social responsibility and translates the principle of sustainability into legal terms consists mainly of:

---

Libertini, *Economia sociale di mercato e responsabilità sociale dell'impresa*, in *Orizzonti del diritto commerciale*, 2013, pp. 1 ff.; Conte, *L'impresa responsabile*, Milan, 2018.

338. Barbier & Burgess, *Sustainable Development Goals and the Systems Approach to Sustainability*, in 11 Economics, 2017, pp. 1 ff.; Rolli, *The Impact of ESG Factors on Business: Governance Models and New Responsibilities*, Bologna, 2021.

339. 'Overcoming poverty: end poverty in all its forms, everywhere; overcoming hunger: end hunger, ensure food security, improve nutrition and promote sustainable agriculture; good health: ensure a healthy life and promote wellbeing for all at all ages; quality education: ensure inclusive education for all and promote fair and quality lifelong learning opportunities; gender equality: achieve gender equality through the empowerment of women and girls; clean water and sanitation ensuring the availability and sustainable management of water and sanitation services for all; renewable and affordable energy: ensuring the availability of affordable, reliable, sustainable and modern energy services for all; good jobs and economic growth: promoting inclusive, sustained and sustainable economic growth, full and productive employment and decent work for all; innovation and infrastructure: building sound infrastructure, promoting inclusive and sustainable industrialisation and fostering innovation; reducing inequalities: reduce inequalities within and between countries; sustainable cities and communities: create sustainable cities and human settlements that are inclusive, safe and sound; responsible use of resources: ensure sustainable consumption and production patterns; combating climate change: take urgent action to combat climate change and its consequences; sustainable use of the sea: conserve and sustainably use the oceans, seas and marine resources for sustainable development; sustainable use of land: protecting, restoring and promoting the sustainable use of terrestrial ecosystems, managing forests sustainably, combating desertification, halting and reversing land degradation and halting biodiversity loss; peace and justice: promoting sustainable development; strengthening implementation instruments and revitalising the global partnership for sustainable development.'

340. *See, e.g.*, Somma, *Il diritto privato liberista. Reflections on Private Autonomy*, in *Bul. mex. der. comp.*, p. 101.

(i) Dir. 2014/95/EU (the so-called Non-Financial Reporting Directive), which imposes disclosure requirements with regard to the management of environmental and social risks associated with a company's activities. The related discipline is based on the vision of a global role of the company as an operator that must look at the *long term* and therefore also take care of social and environmental factors in order to gather the trust of investors. It is the application of social market theory and the affirmation of interests that must take into account and be compatible with social and environmental aspects.

(ii) Legislative Decree No. 254 of 2016 (for the implementation of which the Consob Regulation set out in Resolution No. 20267/2018 was also issued) implementing the Non-Financial Reporting Directive (2014/95/EU). The Decree and the provisions contained therein require large companies that qualify as relevant public interest entities to prepare and publish a so-called non-financial statement. This declaration must contain, for each financial year, information relating to environmental, social and personnel issues, respect for human rights and the fight against active and passive corruption, aimed at ensuring an understanding of the company's activity, its performance, results and impact. Thus, specific rules are introduced for the disclosure of information to the public, binding on companies and directors who are required not only to manage their economic and financial activities correctly in the pursuit of profit but also to take responsibility for the external impacts of these management activities and provide adequate external information. Sanctions are foreseen for missing or inaccurate information to the market.

(iii) Dir. 2017/828/EU on shareholders' rights, transposed into our law by Legislative Decree No. 49 of 2019 (the '*Shareholders Rights 2*'), which, with a view to strengthening the pursuit of non-financial objectives, intervenes on the remuneration policies of directors and management with the obligation to give evidence of the connection of such policies with the 'corporate strategy, long-term interests and with the sustainability of the company'.

The introduction of specific regulations concerning the 'non-financial' aspects of company management complements the duties of directors and justifies the use of resources to protect interests other than those of shareholders.

These are interests that, insofar as they are protected, increase the value of the shares in the long run. The regulatory provision makes it possible to exclude the possibility that their protection can be imputed to errors or shortcomings in the management of the company, and thus shields directors and managers from actions brought by shareholders, since in the context of the economic management of the company, the use of funds intended for these purposes cannot be censured.

With the attraction of these interests to the care of the directors, they are called upon to carry out a weighting activity whose evaluation, also by the shareholders and other subjects with protected interests, should be considered as referring to the application of the *'business judgement rule'*. The assessment should in fact only concern the diligence in reasonably evaluating and weighing the elements of risk and opportunity for the care of the social and environmental impact of the business activity.

Recently, a desire has developed in the EU to direct companies more incisively towards taking care of these interests, imposing more specific rules with a focus on the subject that has led to the approval of regulations for the pursuit of 'sustainability' in certain sectors and for financial services and investments. In this context, in harmony with the goals set forth in the UN 2030 Agenda for Sustainable Development, non-financial goals, the Sustainable Development Goals (SDGs), have been defined, on which the activities of companies should focus and which also represent the parameters for evaluating the actions carried out by them in pursuit of these goals, which must be reported in the Non-Financial Document.

The obligation to draw up a social balance sheet, which is reserved by the 2014 directive for listed companies, banks and insurance companies, responds to the need to *inform the market*. There is still no obligation to allocate resources for these purposes, but it is clear that if a 'balance sheet' is to be drawn up, it is necessary to document the initiatives taken by directors and managers to achieve those purposes.

With reference to sustainable finance, the divergence in legislation and application between the various EU Member States led to the approval of the EU Regulation 2020/852 on Taxonomy, ratified on 18 June 2020, which is directly applicable in the Member States, with the establishment of a unified classification system for sustainable activities in which the criteria for determining whether an economic activity can be considered environmentally sustainable are set out.

In March 2021, Assonime produced a document that also contains a summary of the legislation in force in the EU countries with an in-depth discussion of their respective contents. The Assonime document focuses in particular on the directors' responsibility for the pursuit of non-financial objectives and the most appropriate *governance* rules. Two alternative hypotheses are indicated in this regard:

(a) Inclusion of the objectives, or even just the principle of sustainable development, in the corporate purpose stated in the articles of association of the company. This would directly expand the corporate interest or purpose itself and would represent a structural change in the model that binds not only the directors but also the shareholders, to the extent of their respective competences.

(b) Provision for the care of non-financial aspects among the directors' duties. This would add an element affecting the assessment of their diligence in the performance of their duties, but would not affect the company's purpose, which would remain the typical one of pursuing the profit to be distributed among the shareholders.

Assonime favours solution *b)*, which has been incorporated into the new *Corporate Governance* Code, in keeping with the policy of leaving the regulation of corporate *governance* rules to voluntary compliance with recommendations (so-called *soft law*) rather than rigid and binding rules, in order to allow for the best flexibility in defining the organisation of each company and the care of interests, also taking into account the vagueness of the expression 'sustainable success' and the content of the 17 SDGs themselves.

For some of these SDGs goals, it seems difficult to relate their achievement directly to the tasks and responsibilities of individual companies and therefore of individual directors, since in some cases they may represent mere wishes for a better world, such as the desire to end all forms of poverty in the world or to end world hunger, and in other cases, they are an orientation towards concrete actions rather than indications of concrete obligations. Still others require the necessary contribution of public initiatives that are beyond the management or intervention capacities of individual societies.

Therefore, it is a matter of examining on a case-by-case basis how and with what intensity the company's action must take care of the individual aspects of environmental and social impact and the achievement of the related objectives in order to assess whether there can be a liability of the directors for the lack or insufficiency of adequate initiatives in company management.

On 21 April 2021, the European Commission presented a proposal for a directive on the publication of corporate sustainability information amending dir. 2013/34/EU, dir. 2004/109/EU, dir. 2006/43/EU and Reg. (EU) No. 537/2014. The text of the proposal was in consultation until 22 June 2021 and was subsequently transmitted to the European Parliament and the EU Council for adoption under the ordinary procedure. The proposed Directive amends the provisions of the Non-Financial Information Directive and provides, *inter alia, for the* extension of the scope of the preparation of the Non-Financial Document to medium-sized companies.

## §14.04    THREE PARADIGMATIC CASES OF CORPORATE SOCIAL RESPONSIBILITY FOR VIOLATION OF FUNDAMENTAL RIGHTS: VEDANTA, OKPABI, MILIEUDEFENSIE

Within a short period of time, different courts in the United States of America, the United Kingdom and the Netherlands have made relevant decisions on corporate social responsibility, applying rules of domestic law but taking into account resolutions and documents of international organisations, primarily the United Nations and the Organisation for Economic Co-operation and Development (OECD). It could be debated whether the interests affected are, in addition to health and property, those traditionally assigned to individuals – also collectively – living in a given area or whether, in addition to these interests, the measures are concerned with protecting a broader interest aimed at defending the environment and future generations. In any case, it is relevant to emphasise how, following different paths of argumentation, the judges have sought to protect populations once subject to colonial exploitation and today to exploitation by large *corporations* by resorting to the social responsibility of the company, and the responsibility of the parent company for harmful acts of the subsidiary.

Recourse to private law instruments exempts judges from appealing to public law disciplines with detailed prescriptions, the general clauses operating (especially) in the area of civil liability being sufficient to prepare the ground on which to base injunctive or compensatory measures.

The facts of the *Vedanta* case take place in Zambia (the former Rhodesia), a country belonging to the British Commonwealth, and concern villagers who, as a result of the activities of two companies of the Vedanta group, claimed to have suffered personal injury, damage to their property, and loss of profits, together with loss of enjoyment of the environment, as a result of the dumping of copper mine waste managed by a company set up ad hoc on site by the defendant group. The slurry had been pouring onto the soil and into the groundwater for more than a decade.

The question is primarily one of jurisdiction: should villagers turn to Zambian courts or English courts to defend their rights? Does the damage stem from the activity of the subsidiaries, which is carried out locally, and are they based in the country, or can it also involve the parent company?

The subsidiaries are owned by the holding company, which is listed in India but has its registered office in London. The plaintiffs insist on the jurisdiction of the English court on the grounds that Zambian courts are unreliable, and the Zambian court is a *'forum non conveniens'*.

The matter goes through three degrees of judgement.

The High Court upheld the Zambians' action, ruling out the possibility that they had abused EU law: since the local companies do not have adequate resources to compensate for the damage, and it is legitimate to suspect that the holding company had planned the water pollution, the court held that it is possible, in the abstract, to base an action on the non-contractual liability of the holding company since there is a *duty of care* – characterised by foreseeability, proximity and reasonableness – aimed at protecting the plaintiffs' interests. The holding company's liability – *parent liability* – arises from the holding company's control and direction over the companies operating there. And in fact, the court held, the business carried on by the holding company and the subsidiaries was the same, the holding company should reasonably have known how the business carried on by the subsidiaries would be carried on, with serious damage to the inhabitants; the holding company had greater experience and expertise than the subsidiaries, it should have realised the need for greater expertise and experience on the part of the subsidiaries.

Apart from the arguments concerning the application of the principle of *forum non conveniens* linked to Article 4 of the Brussels Convention, the court is concerned with whether the companies operating there are viable, whether they cannot run the risk of bankruptcy, whether the aggrieved populations, living in extreme poverty, are able to have recourse to other courts and whether they can be supported in defending their rights with legal aid. All these reasons militate in favour of rooting the litigation in the United Kingdom.

The Court of Appeal follows the decision of the High Court. Vedanta insists on its arguments.

The matter came before the Supreme Court, which, in a wide-ranging and educated reasoning, confirmed the previous judgments.

It is interesting, to examine, rather than the debated question of the abuse of the application of the Brussels Convention to root the issue in the United Kingdom, to follow the Court's reasoning regarding the liability of the parent company for tortious acts committed by the subsidiary.[341]

The cited precedent – *Chandler v. Cape plc* [2012] EWCA Civ 525 – had upheld the plaintiff's claim for damages, who had been injured by a subsidiary of the defendant. The judges of the Court of Appeal had held that, as a general rule, due to the fact that the two companies are different legal persons, the parent company does not have a duty to monitor the conduct of the subsidiary; however, when it is put in a position to monitor the conduct of *managers*, to express opinions and views on the acts performed, to be informed about the use of assets owned, it is reasonable to place on the parent company the burden of exercising due diligence to prevent the damage.

Well, in the case examined, the Court finds that Vedanta exercised such control over the subsidiary's activity that it was aware of the infiltration that had caused serious damage to the plaintiff populations.

After carefully examining Vedanta's defences, the court finds that the mining company violated local environmental protection regulations. Following a detailed analysis of the precedents, Judge Rapporteur refutes all arguments used by Vedanta and finds that the appeal can be argued.

For our purposes, it is worth considering an aspect of substantive law and an aspect of a formal nature.

The first concerns social justice: we are in the presence of poor populations, whose income comes from livestock and agriculture, from an economic activity that provides simple survival support, and which fits into the biological cycle and adapts to the environment perfectly. It is the outsourcing of mining that alters the environment and makes farming problematic.

It should be noted that the purpose of the action is to obtain compensation for the irreversible transformation of the land caused by the mining activity. Interruption or suspension of the activity is not required.

There is no discussion of the legal nature of the injured interest, nor, as would be the case here, of whether we are in the presence of 'common property', of ad hoc interests, of collective or diffuse interests, it being clear, however, that the mining exploitation of the land is subsequent to its previous use for cultivation and livestock farming.

From a formal point of view, it is interesting to emphasise both the configuration of the facts as damaging protected interests within the scope of civil liability and, above all, to highlight the imputation of liability also to the parent company, on the basis of the exercise of management and *control* powers.

Hence a number of inferences: that the protection of the environment and the orographic consistency of a place can be coordinated with each other, taking into

---

341. *Vedanta Resources plc v. Lungowe*, [2019] 20, 10 April 2019.

account past uses and the generational future; that private law can fill the gaps in the public system, at least in terms of reintegration of patrimonial damage; that risks can be allocated between group companies, overcoming the problems of subjectivity and patrimonial liability, by resorting to *parental liability*.

A rather similar case was recently decided by the English Supreme Court. This time, it concerned a large number of inhabitants of the Niger Delta area. The inhabitants were complaining of very serious damage – to life, health, the environment – resulting from water pollution caused by oil leaking into pipelines by the extracting companies and their subsidiaries. The parent company – *Royal Dutch Shell plc* – is registered in the United Kingdom. The extraction activity and its transportation are carried out by a subsidiary based in Nigeria. Again, the action against the parent company was based on non-contractual tort and the subsidiaries' management and control activities.

The reasoning of the judgment starts from the premise of the Vedanta case, namely the existence of a *duty of care on the part of* the parent company. The premise is not entirely secure, of course, because the existence of the parent company's liability for acts imputed to the subsidiary is still disputed in the United Kingdom. And yet the Supreme Court notes that, in the present case, it was established that the parent company had greater experience than the subsidiary, as well as greater expertise and resources to be able to verify the damage caused to life, health and the environment by the extraction and transportation of oil.

In order to prove the involvement of the parent company – in other words, the *proximity of* the UK-based company to the aggrieved persons residing in Nigeria – the rapporteur carefully examines the defences of the aggrieved persons, concerning the internal structure of the parent company and the acts of the different bodies concerning the mining activity. That is, the deliberations that can be ascribed to the network of controls organised by Shell. It therefore examines the activities of the *corporate governance* body, sustainability reports, with particular emphasis on analyses of the effects of the activity on the environment, and also communications between the parent company and subsidiary.

The facts ascertained by the appellate court and examined by the Supreme Court, however, had shown that the parent company is a holding company with a small number of employees, which does not carry out operational activities and has no particular expertise in oil extraction so that all decisions on how to carry out extraction and pipelines were the responsibility of the subsidiary.

In order to give a correct answer to the question of whether the parent company should be held liable for damages caused by the subsidiary, the relator examines – in fact – five aspects: (i) the existence of mandatory rules imposing on the extractive company particular conduct, (ii) the imposition of obligations to take proceedings, (iii) the imposition of a system of controls, (iv) the imposition of a system of charges, (v) the existence of a system of direction and supervision over the subsidiary.

To these questions, the rapporteur responds to the effect that the *proximity* requirement, although facilitated by the evidence, does not lead to a convincing and persuasive solution in the affirmative, since most of the controls are carried out on the basis of standard procedures, which standardise the activities of all the subsidiaries in the group.

So it is for the requirement of fairness and substantive justice, which does not seem appreciable to the reporting judge.

The opinions expressed by the other two judges are varied and all thoroughly argued. And the dissenting opinion of one of the judges of the panel insists on the existence of proximity and thus the applicability of the precedent (*Vedanta*) also to Shell.

The third court concludes that the proximity requirement is not sufficiently proven, and therefore acquits Shell.

This case also shows how complex the assessment of corporate social responsibility is, and that, although conceivable in the abstract, the parent company's liability cannot be presumed, but must be established in fact, on the basis of *duty of care*.

The third case also shows similarities with the previous ones; it was decided against the parent company Shell by the District Court of The Hague on 26 May 2021; the decision applies to the Dutch Civil Code. The text was also published by the Court in an English version.[342] This is one of the first cases of violation of $CO_2$ emission standards: Shell was not found guilty in the past but was obliged to immediately implement all necessary measures to reduce emissions caused by the group's activities in the future.

Here again, the rules invoked are of private law and generally concern the requirements of the wrongful act.

First, the issues of legal standing. The plaintiff was an environmental protection association and acted on behalf of two other associations and four foundations engaged in the same field. The defendant was the holding company of the Shell group, as seen above, registered in the United Kingdom but with its head office in the Netherlands. As is clear from the reasoning, it is up to the parent company to define the policies of the subsidiaries, which, as operating companies, are engaged worldwide in extracting oil, processing it and distributing it, through a system of service companies coordinated by the parent company. The Court dwells on the side effects of the business activity, pointing out the harmful aspects of $CO_2$, climate change and the progressively deteriorating global situation as represented by the UN studies on the subject. Associated with these effects are the damage to health, the level of livability, and the risks to the entire world population. For pages and pages, the explanatory statement describes the situation around the globe, in Europe and the Netherlands, enumerates all major measures and findings taken by the UN and resolves preliminary legal issues.

First, the legal standing of associations and foundations. This concerns the application of Article III, 305a of the Civil Code, which admits the standing of associations and foundations in the promotion of *class actions*. Having to verify whether the interests defended by these entities could fall within the scope of the provision, the Court asked whether the interests of future generations could be such as

---

342. ECLI:RBDHA:2021:5339.

to ground an obligation attributable to the defendant company as a useful safeguard of the *stakeholders'* interests.

Given the wording of the rule, it excludes that such interests can be protected because populations scattered around the world can be harmed at different times by climate change and in different ways. However, with regard to Dutch residents, the Court considers that some of the associations may be considered legitimate, taking into account their statutory purposes. The Court then wonders whether the harm suffered should be that which aggregates to the $CO_2$ situation worldwide or only concerns the population residing in the Netherlands and inclines towards this alternative.

Very interesting are the arguments concerning the configuration of the tort, since the holding company had contested its liability, assuming that the definition of the '*corporate policy*' was to be considered only a preparatory act that went beyond the boundaries of the tort, since corporate policy definitions are not in themselves a cause of immediate harm. In the Court's view, it is precisely the definition of company policy that must be regarded as constituting an independent wrongful act in itself. In other words, the definition of company policy constitutes a wrongful act if it contradicts an (unwritten) standard against which to measure the diligence required to administer a company.

The examination of the factual findings concerning the $CO_2$ emissions in the region of the residents belonging to the plaintiff association showed, in the Court's assessment, that the activity of the Shell group was potentially harmful.

But what interests have been harmed?

The plaintiff identified the infringement of human and fundamental rights such as respect for life, *privacy* and family: these are Articles 2 and 8 of the European Convention and the Charter of Fundamental Rights of the Union, as well as Articles 6 and 17 of the International Covenant on Civil and Political Rights approved by the United Nations in 1966 and entered into force in 1976.

Corroborating the series of documents and measures useful for the configuration of the illicit act, the Court recalls the determinations of the UN Committee on Human Rights on the deterioration of the climate and the environment, the UN Guiding Principles in which the responsibility of States is distinguished from the responsibility of companies, so that the distinction does not imply an absolution of companies, but rather their 'individual responsibility' also in monitoring the measures adopted by States. This obligation also emerges from the OECD Guide for Multinational Enterprises (Principle No. 23), which reminds companies of the necessary protection of fundamental rights, 'in order to protect the environment and health in the places where they operate by contributing to the achievement of sustainable development objectives'. Hence the obligation of companies to respect fundamental rights and to take all necessary measures to achieve this, which does not imply a passive attitude, but if anything an active cooperation. This obligation applies to all companies of all sizes, subject of course to the principle of proportionality.

This obligation must be observed by all companies in the production and distribution chain, according to the criteria developed by the Report prepared by Oxford University in 2020.

On the basis of the factual data collected in the course of the procedure concerning the $CO_2$ emissions of the entire Shell group, the Court considers that the parent company has a *result obligation* (paragraph 4.4.23) to prevent and reduce the risks associated with its activity, and this in respect of the entire group over which the holding company exercises its power of direction and control. Hence, a series of measures of a technical nature is indicated by the Court to the parent company to achieve that result.

But the Court does not stop there. It also takes into account an acute argument raised by the defendant's defence, namely the futility of the measures taken because, in the oil market, the space freed up by Shell in complying with its obligation to perform will be occupied by its competitors. The Court does not fall into the trap: it reiterates the usefulness of the measures and the irrelevance of the conduct of competing companies in relieving Shell of its obligation. After all, individual cooperation contributes to collective welfare.

It is through the cooperation of public bodies – states *first and foremost* – and private entities that the goals set by researchers to halt the degradation of the planet can be realised.

To achieve this, the obligations imposed on companies must be *appropriate* and *proportional*. Hence the need for Shell to adapt its corporate policies, and the order to reduce emissions proportionally immediately enforceable.

However, the Court ruled out damages as it did not consider the group's emissions up to that point to be illegal.

# Leave

The principle of solidarity is an *open work; it is the* note of a symphony that can be variously retraced, and the symphony can take soft or stronger tones. It is a constant in the sources of law, constitutional, civil and commercial. It is up to the jurist with his culture and civil commitment, with his competence and constancy, to express its full potential. It is an imperative legal concept. And as such, it is a precept not confined to the ideal world nor entrusted to hope or goodwill, but part of the 'Western canon'. None of us, let alone those who are jurists, can escape it.

This book has no conclusion. The path of solidarity is long and winding, and without end.

The pandemic and the war between Russia and Ukraine on the Union's doorstep have raised sensitive issues and serious problems also in terms of solidarity.

Even if, reductively, solidarity is in most cases taken as the summary principle of the welfare state, given the disappointing results to which the use of the euro has led, the failure of the neo-liberal economic model, the immorality of the prevalence of economic interests over the values of the person, we are led to believe that the text of the treaties needs to be reconsidered in order to achieve in the near future a level of social life in which the differences between classes and individuals are reduced, and the principle of inclusion is accepted; a future in which the hopes and expectations raised by the imperative words of law are etched in stone rather than written on water.

# Bibliography

AA.VV., *I Grundriss di Karl Marx: Fundamental Outlines of Political Criticism 150 Years Later*, Pisa, 2015

AA.VV., *Le libertà fondamentali dell'Unione europea e il diritto privato*, edited by F. Mezzanotte, Introduction by A. Zoppini, Rome, 2016

AA.VV., *Perseguire il bene comune: come solidarietà e sussidiarietà possono operare insieme*, Pontif. Acc. Sc. Soc., Acta, no. 14, Vatican, 2008

AA.VV., *Social Justice in European Contract Law: A Manifesto*, in E.L.Journal, 10, no. 6. 2004, pp. 653 ff.

AA.VV., *Solidarities Ancient and Modern*, edited by P. Merlin, Rome, 2017

Addis Saba, *Partigiane: Le donne della Resistenza*, Milan, 2007

Agulon M. *The Republican Experiment, 1848–1852*, The Cambridge History of Modern France, 1983

Alexy R., *Theorie der juristischen Argumentation*, Berlin, 1978, translated into Italian, Teoria dell'argomentazione giuridica, edited by M.La Torre, Milan, 1998

Alford H., *Corporate Social Responsibility and the Social Doctrine of the Catholic Church*, Milan, 2009

Alpa G. & Andenas, M. *Fondamenti del diritto privato europeo*, Milan, 2005 (trans.into English, European Private Law, Pisa, 2022)

Alpa G. & Conte, G. *Fundamental Rights and Freedoms in Contractual Relations*, Turin, 2018

Alpa G., *Diritto civile. Due secoli di storia*, Bologna, 2018

Alpa, G., *I principi generali*, Milano, 1993 (3d ed. 2023)

Alpa G., Il *danno biologico. Percorso di un' idea*, Padua, 1987

Alpa G. *La responsabilità civile*, Milan, 2018

Andler Ch., Du quasi-contrat social et de M. Léon Bourgeois, Revue de Métaphysique et de Morale T. 5, no. 4 (Juillet 1897), pp. 520

Angelici, C., Caravale M. & Moscati L., *Negozianti e imprenditori.200 anni dal Code de commerce*, Milano, 2008

Angelici C., *Divagazioni sulla 'responsabilità sociale' d'impresa*, in *Riv. soc.*, 2018, pp. 3 ff.

Antonini, B., *Ferdinand Lasalle et les deux internationale*, Cahiers Jaurès 2014/2-3 (N° 212-213), p. 153 ff.

Arendt H. *Men in Dark Times*, Bakersfield (CA), 1970

Arfé G., *Storia del socialismo italiano* (1892-1926), Turin, 1965

Asquini A., *I battelli del Reno*, in *Riv. soc.*, 1959, pp. 619 ff.

Aubert de Vincelles C., *Les principes généraux relatifs au droit des contrats*, in *Pour une réforme de droit des contrats, sous la direction de François Terré*, Paris, 2009, p. 115

AubryCh., et Rau, Ch.Fed., *Cors de droit civil français d'aprs la méthode de Zachariae*, Paris, 1897-1922

Austin J.L., *How to Do Things with Words (1962)*, transl. into It., Genoa, 2019

Azam J.P., *A Theory of Poverty Aversion and Civil Society Development* 2003 https://doi.org/10.1111/1468-0343.00115

Ballestrero M.V., *Dalla tutela alla parità. La legislazione italiana sul lavoro delle donne*, Bologna, 1979

Ballestrero M.V., *Donne (Lavoro delle)*, Digesto, IV edizione, UTET, Torino, 1990

Banakar R. & Travers M., eds, *Feminist Legal Theory: An Introduction to Law and Social Theory*, London, 2002

Bar (von) Clive, E. & Schulte-Noelke H. (eds), *Principles, Definitions and Model Rules of European Private Law: Draft Common Frame of Reference*, Outline edition, Munich, 2009

Banti A.M., *La Nazione del Risorgimento. Parentela, santità e onore alle origini dell'Italia unita*, Turin, 2000

Banti A.M. *L'onore della nazione. Identità sessuali e violenza nel nazionalismo europeo dal XVIII secolo alla Grande Guerra*, Turin, 2005

Banti A.M. & P. Ginsborg (eds) Storia d'Italia. Annali 22. *Il Risorgimento*, Turin, 2007

Barbagallo F., *Limiti costituzionali alla libertà contrattuale e sindacato giurisdizionale : un nuovo caso di rilettura costituzionalmente orientata del canone di buona fede*, in *Forum Quaderni costituzionali*, 3, 2020, pp. 151 ss.

Barbier E., & Burgess J., *Sustainable Development Goals and the Systems Approach to Sustainability*, in *Economics*, 11, 2017, pp. 1 ff.

Barroso L.R., *A dignidade da pessoa humana no direito constitucional contemporaneo*, Belo Horizonte, 2014, p. 62

Bartlett C. & Kennedy R., *Feminist Legal Theory: Readings in Law and Gender*, London, 1991

Basedow J., *EU Private Law: Anatomy of a Growing Legal Order*, Cambridge-Antwerpen-Chicago, 2021

Baurmann M., *Solidarity as a Social Norm and as a Constitutional Norm*, in Bayertz K., (ed.) *Solidarity*, N.Y., 1999 pp. 243 ff.

Bayertz K., (ed.) *Solidarity*, Dordrecht, 1999

Benamozegh E., *Israele e l 'umanità (1914)*, Turin, 2016

Benditt Th.M., *Law as Rule and Principle*, Stanford, 1976

Berenson E., *Populist Religion and Left-Wing Politics in France, 1830-1852*, Princeton, 2014

Bessone M., *La famiglia nella Costituzione*, sub art. 29 Cost., in Branca G., *Commentario alla Costituzione*, Bologna-Roma, 1976,

Beveridge W., *Full Employment in a Free Society*, London, 1944

Biagini F.A. *Il tema della fraternità nel'Ebraismo*, in www.etzhaim.eu/frternità

Biondi A. & Dagilyté E., *Solidarity in EU Law: Legal Principle in the Making*, Northampton (MA), 2018

Blais M.C., *Au Principe de la République: le cas Renouvier*, Paris, 2000

Blais M.C., *La solidaritè. Historie d'unn idée*, Paris, 2007

Blanc L., *De l'Humanité*, Paris, 1839

Bobbio N., *Scienza del diritto e analisi del linguaggio*, in *Riv. trim. dir. proc. civ.*, 1950, pp. 342 ff.

Bohm, F. *La società di diritto privato e l' economia di mercato*, in Forte, F. *L'economia sociale di mercato e i suoi nemici*, Soveria Mannelli, 2012, pp. 67 ff.

Boll F., Prost A., & Robert J.L., *L'invention des syndacalismes*, Paris, 2020

Borger, V. *The Currency of Solidarity*, Cambridge, 2020

Borgetto, M., *La notion de fraternité en droit public français: Le passé, le present et l'avenir de la solidarité*, Paris, 1993

Borzaga C. & Ianes, A. *L'economia della solidarietà*, Rome, 2006

Braudel F., *Civilisation matérielle, économie et capitalisme*, Paris, 1967

Brownsword R., *Freedom of Contract, Human Rights and Human Dignity*, in *The Foundations of European Private Law*, R. Brownsword, H.-W. Micklitz, L. Niglia and S. Weatherill eds, Oxford and Portland, 2011

Brunot F., *Histoire de la langue française*, Paris, 1905

Busnelli F.D., *Il principio di solidarietà e l'attesa delle poveri gente, oggi*, in *Persona e mercato*, 2012, pp. 101 ff.

Busnelli F.D., *Solidarietà: aspetti di diritto privato*, in *Iustitia*, 1999, pp. 435 ff.

Bydlinsky F., *Juristische Methodenlehre und Rechtsbegriff*, Munich, 1991

Cabo Martin C., *Teoria constitucional de la solidaridad*, Madrid, 2006

Calandri E., Guasconi M. & Ranieri, R, *Storia politica e economica dell'integrazione europea*: dal 1945 ad oggi, Milan, 2015

Canon Ortegon L., *La solidaridad como fundamento del Estado social de derecho,de la seguridad social y la protecciòn social en Colombia*, in Paginas de Solidaridad social, 2017, 1, pp. 5 ff.

Cantisani S., *Il volto sociale dell' Europa la compenetrazione tra le carte dei diritti e il ruolo delle corte e dei giudici nazionali*, in *Dir.amm.* 2022, n. 1

Caretti P., *Discutere del linguaggio dei giuristi per riflettere sul loro ruolo oggi: qualche considerazione a conclusione del convegno 'la lingua dei giuristi'*, in *Osservatorio sulle fonti*, no. 3/2015

Carlassare L., *Solidarietà: un progetto politico*, www.Constitutionalismi.it, 2016, no. 1

Cau M., *La via maestra alla giustizia sociale. Alcide De Gasperi tra solidarismo e corporativismo*, in 21 *Scienza e politica*, 2009

Cazzetta G., *Leggi sociali, cultura giuridica e origini della scienza giuslavoristica in Italia fra Otto e Novecento*, in Quaderni fiorentini, 1988, no. 17, pp. 154 ss.

Celotto A. & Pistorio, *L'efficacia giuridica della Carta dei diritti fondamentali dell'Unione europea* (Case Law Review 2001-2004), *Giur.it*, 2004

Cherednychenko O., *Fundamental Rights, Policy Issues and the Draft Common Frame of Reference for European Private Law*, in E. Rev. Private L., 6, 2010, p. 63

Chevallier J., *Essai d'analyse structurale du Preambule*, Hal. Archives – ouvertes. Fr./hal – 01728071/ document

Ciancio A., *Alle origini dell'interesse dell' Unione europea per i diritti sociali*, in *Federalismi.it*, 14.9.2018

CIRIEC, *Recent Developments in the Social Economy in the European Union*, Brussels, 2016

CIRIEC, *The Social Economy in the European Union*, Brussels, 2012

Collins H., *The Impact of Human Rights Law on Contract Law in Europe*, edited by M. Andenas, Paper Series, University of Cambridge, Paper no. 13/2011

Comte A., *Cours de philosophie positive*, Paris, 1830-42

Comte A., *Système de politique positive*, Paris, 1851-54

Conte G., *L'impresa responsabile*, Milan, 2018

Cordoba, M., *La solidaridad como un principio general del derecho in Argentina, Seminario permanente sobre investigaciòn del derecho de la persona humana, familia y sucesiones*, 29 May 2019. Buenos Aires, 2019

Cosio R. & Foglia R. (cur), *Il diritto europeo nel dialogo delle Corti*, Milan, 2012

Costa, P. *Cittadinanza*, voce dell'Enciclopedia del Novecento, III Appendice, Rome, 2004

Cozzolino, A., Forte, F., Palazzi J., *Europa:che fare?*, Naples, 2019

Culmann, *Cattolici e Protestanti: Un progetto di solidarietà cristiana*, Bologna, 1962

Cunico G. & Bruzzone A. (eds), *Solidarietà: una prospettiva etica*, Sesto S. Giovanni (Mi), 2017

De Felice R., *Mazzini e il socialismo*, Rome, 1972

De Francesco A., *Democratici e socialisti in Francia dal 1830 al 1851*, Il Politico, 51(3), 1986, pp. 459-494

Dell'Erba N. *Giuseppe Mazzini*, in *Il contributo italiano alla storia del pensiero*, Rome, 2013

Denninger E., *Constitutional Law and Solidarity*, in *Solidarity*, K. Bayertz ed., Dordrecht, 1999

Dirri, A., *La Corte di Giustizia torna sul meccanismo di ricollocazione dei migranti tra rivendicazioni identitarie e tenuta dei valori fondanti dell'Unione europea*, in AIC, 2020, no. 5

Dobuzinskis L., *Defenders of Liberal Individualism: The Forgotten Intellectual Founders of the French Third Republic*, European Journal of Political Theory, 7 (2008)

Dohet J., *Le mouvement coopératif : histoire, questions et renouveau*, in Courier hebd.du CRISP, 2018, 5-6, pp. 58 ff.

Duràn, M.A. *Los limites de la solidaridad*, Digital Csic, 2003

Duguit L., *L'Etat,le droit objective et la loi positive*, Paris, 1901, repr. Dalloz, 2003

Dworkin R., *Taking Rights Seriously*, Cambridge (Mass,), 1977, transl. into It. Bologna, 1982

Dyzenhaus D., *Legal Theory in the Collapse of Weimar: Contemporary Lessons?*, in The American Political Science Review 91(1) (March 1997), pp. 121-134

Eichner M., *On Postmodernist Feminist Legal Theory*, Harv. C.R.-C.L. L. Rev., 36(1) (2001)

Eucken E., *Die Grundlagen der Nationaloeconomie*, Berlin, 1939 (8th ed., 1989)

European Union, *Social Economy and Social Entrepreneurship*, Brussels, 2014

Della Peruta F., *Nazionalità e Risorgimento fino alla rivoluzione del '48*, in *Niccolò Tommaseo e Firenze. Atti del Convegno di studi* (Florence, 12-13 February 1999), R. Turchi and A. Volpi eds, Florence, 2000, p. 9

Falzea A., *Relazione introduttiva*, in I principi generali del diritto, Atti dell' Accademia Nazionale dei Lincei, Rome, 1992

Federico V. & Lahusen Chr., eds, *Solidarity as a Public Virtue? Law and Public Policies in the European Union*, London, 2018

Fernandes Mendonça S.M., *Deveres Fundamentais de Solidariedade* in *Rev.de Derecho*, 2018, no. 18, pp. 91 ff.

Fernandez Segado F.F., *La solidaridad como principio constitucional*, in *Theoria y Realidad Constitucional*, 2012, no. 30, pp. 142 ff.

Ferrando G., *Note sull'uguaglianza morale e giuridica dei coniugi*, in: *Politica del Diritto*, 1990, pp. 509 ff.

Ferrando G., *Diritto di Famiglia*, IV ed., Bologna, 2020

Ferraris P., *Saggi su Roberto Michels*, Neaples, 1993

Ferri G.B., *Il potere e la parola e altri scritti di diritto civile*, Padua, 2008

Ferrone V., *Il problema Rousseau e i diritti dell'uomo. La pratica politica dei diritti tra natura e cultura, individuo e comunità, 'stato di pura natura' e società civile*, in Studi francesi, 2012, pp. 167 ss. https://doi.org/10.4000/studifrancesi.3931

Fiorelli P., *Storia giuridica e storia linguistica*, Milan, 1957

Frader L., *Femmes, genre et mouvement ouvrier en France aux XIXe et XXe siècles : bilan et perspectives de recherche,in Clio*, 1996, p. 3, https://doi.org/10.4000/clio.472

Francesco V. & Zaccaria G., *Diritto e interpretazione. Lineamenti di teoria ermeneutica del diritto*, Rome-Bari 1999

Freeman R.E. & Reed D.L., *Stockholders and Stakeholders: A New Perspective on Corporate Governance*, in Calif. Manag. Rev. 25, 1983, pp. 88 ff.

Galante Garrone A., *L'incontro con il sansimonismo*, in *Giuseppe Mazzini*, Roma, 1972

Galante Garrone A., *Filippo Buonarroti e i rivoluzionari dell'Ottocento*, Torino, 1972

Galgano F., *Lex mercatoria.Storia del diritto commerciale*, Bologna, 1993

Garcia Ramìrez J., *La solidaridad como deber: texto y contexto del enunciado constitucional*. VI Jornadas de Jóvenes Investigadores. Instituto de Investigaciones Gino Germani, Facultad de Ciencias Sociales, Universidad de Buenos Aires, Buenos Aires

Gay P., *La cultura di Weimar.L'oursider come insider*, Bari, 1978

Gay P., Illuminations *by Walter Benjamin, Hannah Arendt, Harry Zohn*, in *The Hudson Review* 22(1) (Spring, 1969), pp. 165-171

Genre E., *Diaconia e solidarietà. I valdesi dalla borsa dei poveri all'Otto per mille*, Turin, 2017

Gény F., *Méthode d'interprétation et sources de droit privé positif*, Paris, 1899

Gerber D., *Law and Competition in Twentieth Century Europe: Protecting Prometheus*, Oxford, 1998

Giarrizzo G., *Massoneria e Risorgimento*, 'Hiram', 1999, no. 2, pp. 43-46

Giovannini E., *Il principio di sostenibilità*, in *Aspenia*, 2019, p. 76

Giubboni S., *I diritti sociali nell' Unione europea dopo il Trattato di Lisbona. Paradossi, rischi e opportunità*, in *Persona e mercato*, 2011, pp. 3 ss.

Giubboni S., *Solidarietà. Un itinerario di ricerca*, Napoli, 2022

Goldschmidt N., *Alfred Müller-Armack and Ludwig Erhard: Social Market Liberalism*, Freiburg Discussion Papers on Constitutional Economics 04/12, 2004

Gordon P.E. & McCormick J.P. (eds), *Weimar Thought: A Contested Legacy*, Princeton, 2013

Grimmel A. (ed.), *The Crisis of the European Union*, London and New York, 2018

Grimmel A. & My Giang (eds), *Solidarity in the European Union*, Berlin, 2017

Grossi P., *Un dialogo con i comparatisti su lingua e diritto*, in *Riv. int. fil. dir*, 2014, pp. 412 ff.

Grossi P., *L'invenzione del diritto*, Roma-Bari, 2017

Grossi P., *Ritorno al diritto*, Roma-Bari, 2015

Grossi P., *Introduzione al Novecento giuridico*, Roma-Bari, 2012

Grundmann S. (ed.), *Constitutional Values and European Contract Law*, Alphen aan den Rijn, 2008

Guastini R., *Dovere giuridico*, in *Enc.giur.Treccani*, Roma, 1990, XXI, 4

Guastini R., *Le fonti del diritto e l'interpretazione*, Milano, 1993

Guastini R., *L'interpretazione dei documenti normativi*, Milano, 2004

Gueli V., *Recensione*, in *Riv.dir.comm.* 1937, II, 111

Gurvitch G., *Sociology of Law* (N.Y. 1942), transl. into it., Milan, 1957

Habermas J., *Solidarietà fra estranei. Interventi su 'Fatti e norme'*, Milano, 1999

Habermas J., *Questa Europa è in crisi*, Roma-Bari, 2012

Hamon F. & Troper F., *Droit consititutionnel*, 41 ed., 2020-2021, Paris, 2020

Hansmann H., *Corporation and Contract*, Working Paper, 2006

Hansmann H. & Kraakmann R., *The End of History for Corporate Law*, Discussion Paper no. 280 3/2000 Harvard Law School Cambridge, MA

Hawkins M., *Charles Renouvier and the 'Conservative Republic' in France*, History of Political Thought, 33(1) (Spring 2012), p. 145

Hayden G.M. & Boodie M.T., *Reconstructing the Corporation*, Cambridge, 2021

Herrera C.M., *El concepto de solidaridad y sus problemas politico-consitucionales. Una perspectiva iusfilosofica*, Rev. Est.soc., 2013, no. 46, p. 63

Herrera C.M., *Socialisme juridique et droit naturel. À propos d'Emmanuel Lévy*, in *Les jurists face au politique*, Paris, 2003, pp. 69 ff.

Hesselink M.W., Mak Ch. & Rutgers G.W., *Constitutional Aspects of European Private Law: Freedoms, Rights and Social Justice in the Draft Common Frame of Reference*, Center for the Study of European Contract Law Working Papers Series no. 2009/05

Hosbawn E., *Preface (1965) in Marx, Forme economiche precapitalistiche*, trans. into. It., Roma, 1967, pp. 7 ff.

Ignace, A.C. *Giuseppe Mazzini et les démocrates français: débats et reclassements au lendemain du 'printemps des peuples'*, in Revue d'histoire du XIXe siècle, 2008, pp. 36 ff.

Irti N., *Diritto agrario italiano*, Torino, 1978

Jaeger P.G., *L'interesse sociale*, Milan, 1964

Jimena Quesada L., *Social Rights in the Case Law of the Court of Justice of the European Union: The Opening to the Turin Process, Conference on Social Rights in Today's Europe*, Nicosia, 24 February 2017

Joerges Ch., *Will the Welfare State Survive the European Integration?*, in E.J. *Conflict and Transformation*, Oxford, 2022

*Judaism and Universal Fraternity*, edited by the Franciscan Study Centre for Interreligious Dialogue and Cultures, Rome, 2019

Kant I., *Per la pace perpetua. Progetto filosofico* (1795), in I. Kant, *Scritti politici*, Turin, 1956, pp. 283-336

Kelly D. (ed.), *Feminist Legal Theory: Foundations*, Philadelphia, 1993

Köhler E.A. & Nientiedt D., *The Muthesius Controversy: A Tale of Two Liberalisms*, Freiburg, 2015

Koubi G., *Le Préambule de la Constitution de 1946 : antinomies juridiques et contradictions politiques*, Paris, 1996

Lacey N., *Feminist Legal Theory*, in 9 Oxford J. Legal Stud. 383 (1989)

Lahusen Ch. & Grasso M.T., *Solidarity in Europe: Citizens' Response in Time of Crisis*, London, 2018

Laitinen A., *Solidarity*, in *Enc. of Philosophy and Social Science*, London, 2013

Lama E., *Cooperazione*, Enc. Italiana Treccani, Rome 1948

Lanchester F., *Le costituzioni tedesche da Francoforte a Bonn*, Milan 2002

Lapide P., *Predicava nelle loro sinagoghe*, Brescia 2001

Lapide P., *Il discorso della Montagna*, Brescia 2001

Laquer W., *La Repubblica di Weimar. Vita e morte di una società permissiva*, Milan, 1977

Lassalle F., *System der erworbenen Rechte* (1861), Berlin, 2011

Levi A., *La filosofia politica di Giuseppe Mazzini*, Bologna, 1917

Levit V., *Minow, Feminist Legal Theory: A Primer*, New York, 2016

Lévy, E., *Les fondements du droit*, Paris, 19933

Libertini M., *Economia sociale di mercato e responsabilità sociale dell'impresa*, in Orizzonti del diritto commerciale, 2013, pp. 1 ff.

Lipari N., *Diritto e valori sociali*, Roma, 2004

Lombardi G., *Doveri pubblici* (dir.cost.), voce dell' *Enc.dir.,aggiorn.*, VI, Milan, 2002, pp. 357 ff.

Logue W., *Charles Renouvier, Philosopher of Liberty*, Baton Rouge (LA), 1993

Lòpez E.J.V., *Solidaridad y deber jurìdico.Aportes para la fundamentaciòn jurìdica de la responsabilidad social corporativa*, Ius, 2020-12-31, pp. 1 ss.

Losano M., *Le costituzioni della Germania post-bellica e i diritti fondamentali*, in Rev.Fac.Derecho, n. 32, Montevideo, Enero-Junio 2021, pp. 225 ff.

Louvrier J., *Marx, le marxisme et les historiens de la Révolution française au XXE siècle*, Cahiers d'histoire, 2007, pp. 102 ff.

Maine H.S., *Ancient Law: Its Connection with the Early History of Society and its Relation to Modern Ideas*, London, 1861

Mak Ch., *Fundamental Rights in European Contract Law: A Comparison of the Impact of Fundamental Rights on Contractual Relationship in Germany, the Netherlands, Italy and England*, Alphen aan der Rijn, 2008

Marasà G., *Purpose of Profit and Purpose of Common Benefit in Benefit Corporations*, in Orizzonti del diritto commerciale, 2017, 2, pp. 8 ff.

Marshall T.H., *Citizenship and Social Class, and Other Essays*, Cambridge, 1950 (tr. it.: *Cittadinanza e classe sociale*, edited by S. Mezzadra, Roma-Bari: Laterza, 2002)

Martinelli, *Economia e società*, Milan, 1986

Marx and Engels, *Opera* Omnia, Rome 1960, vol. VII, p. 21

Mattei U. & Quarta A., *Three Types of Solidarity: Beyond the Crisis in Contract Law*, in Giust.civ.com, 2020, n. 5

Mattioni A. & Marzanti A., *La fraternità come principio di diritto pubblico*, Rome, 2007

Max Planck, *Encyclopedia of European Private Law*, Oxford, 2012

Mazzini G., *Dei doveri dell' uomo*, (1860), Milan, 2010

Mengoni L., *Diritto e valori*, Bologna, 1985

Michels R., *L'imperialismo italiano. Studi politico-demografici*, Milano, 1914

Michels R., *Probleme der Sozialphilosophie*, Leipzig, 1914

Micklitz, H.-W., *Failure or Ideological Preconceptions – Thoughts on Two Grand Projects: The European Constitution and the European Civil Code*, EUI Working Papers. Law 2010/04

Micklitz, H.-W., *Judical Activism of the European Court of Justice and the Development of the European: Social Mode in Anti-discrimination and Consumer Law,* in EUI Law, 2009, 19

Micklitz, H.-W., *The Visible Hand of European Private Law in Regulatory Matters*, in *EUI Waking Papers*, Florence, 2010

Micklitz H.-W., *Il fascino del diritto privato europeo*, in Contr. Impr. Europa, 2021, p. 103

Minervini G., *Contro la funzionalizzazione dell'impresa privata*, in Riv. dir. civ., 1958, I, pp. 618 ff.

Morelli M.T.A. (ed.), *Le donne della Costituente*, Rome_Bari, 2007

Mortati C., *La Costituzione di Weimar*, (1946) repr. Milan, 2019

Mossman F.J., *Feminism and Legal Method*, Australian Journal of Law and Society, 3, 1986, pp. 30-52

Navarretta E., *Il contratto democratico e la giustizia contrattuale*, in Riv. Dir. civ., 2016, pp. 1262 ff.

Nencioni G., *Idealismo e realismo nella scienza del linguaggio*, Firenze 1946

Novarino M. & Rosso S., *Solidarietà e percorso iniziatico*, Rome, 2018

Obradovic D., *Cases C-643 and C-647/15: Enforcing Solidarity in EU Migration Policy*, europeanlawblog, 2 October 2017

Olivi B. & Santaniello R., *Storia dell'Integrazione europea*, Bologna 2015

Oppo G., Scritti giuridici. Vol. 6: Principi e problemi del diritto privato, Padua, 2000

Orestano R., *Realtà, parole, valori nella scienza del diritto, in Riv. dir. civ.*, 1985, pp. 461 ff.

Piovani P., *Mobilità, sistematicità, istituzionalità della lingua e del diritto*, Milano, 1962

Paugam S. (ed.), *Repenser la solidaritè*, Paris, 2007

Peces-Barba, Martinez G., *Sucuritad juridica y solidaridad como valores de la Constitucion espanola*, Funciones y fines del derecho. Murcia, 1992

Peraldi Leneuf, F. *'Solidarité(s) : perspectives juridiques'* – Actes de colloques de l'IFR n°6 sous la direction de Maryvonne Hecquard-Théron le 22 juillet 2009

Péraldi Leneuf F., *Solidarity, a Legal Concept? Study of the Concept in the Charter of Fundamental Rights of the European Union*, in ERPL, 26, 2014, pp. 91 ff.

Perrini A., *Sustainability*, Milan, 2018

Pino A., *Diritti sociali. Per una critica ad alcuni luoghi comuni, Ragion pratica*, 2016, no. 2 pp. 795 ff.

Pinelli C., Il discorso sui diritti sociali tra Costituzione e diritto europeo, http://www.europeanrights.eu/public/commenti/Pinelli_relazione_convegno1

Pontifical Council for Justice and Peace, Compendium of the Social Doctrine of the Church, Rome, 2004

Pugliatti S., *Grammatica e diritto*, Milan, 1978

Radisson M., *La philosophie en France au XIX e siecle*, Paris, 1867, repr. 1889

Reich N., *General Principles of EU Civil Law*, Cambridge-Antwerpen-Portland, 2013, repr. 2017

Report of the Minister of Justice, Dino Grandi, to the King of Italy, Rome, 194

Rescigno P., Persona e comunità: Saggi di diritto privato, Padua, 1987

Ridola P., *Stato e costituzioni in Germania*, Turin, 2016, pp. 1 ff.

Rizza L., Obbligo di solidarietà e perdita di valori, *Diritto, Immigrazione e Cittadinanza Fascicolo n. 2/2018*

Rodotà S., *Il terribile diritto*, Bologna, 2012

Rodotà S., *La Carta come atto politico e come atto giuridico*, in *Riscrivere i diritti in Europea*, Bologna, 2001

Rodotà S., *Solidarietà. Un utopia necessaria*, Roma-Bari, 2014

Rodotà S., *Il problema della responsabilità civile* Milan, 1964

Rolli R., *L'impatto dei fattori ESG sull'impresa, Modelli di governance e nuove responsabilità*, Bologna, 2021

Romano S., *Doveri, obblighi, in Frammenti di un dizionario giuridico*, (1947) rit.inalt .Macerata, 2019

Rorty R., *Contingency, Irony and Solidarity*, Cambridge, 1989

Rosenberg A., *Origini della Repubblica di Weimar*, (1928), transl. into It, Florence, 1972

Rosenthal J.L., The *Fruits of Revolution: Property Rights, Litigation and French Agriculture* (1770-1860), Cambridge, 1992

Ross M. & Borgmann-Prebil Y., *Promoting Solidarity in the European Union*, Oxford, 2010

Rouhette G., *Regard sur l'avant-projet de réforme de droit des obligations*, in Rev.dr.comp., 4/2007, p. 1393

Rousseau E., *Discorso sull'origine e i fondamenti della disuguaglianza fra gli uomini* (1755) in *Discorsi*, L. Luporini ed., Milan, 1997, p. 128

Rousseau E., *Del contratto sociale* (1792) Milan, 2014, p. 294

Ruggeri A., *Linguaggio della Costituzione e linguaggio delle leggi*, in *Osservatorio delle fonti*, 2015, no. 3, pp. 1 ff.

Russo A., *Antiche e moderne vie della solidarietà*, Milan, 2021

Sabatini F., *Il linguaggio normativo come uso prototipico della lingua*, in *Le parole giuste*, Atti del convegno organizzato dal Senato della Repubblica con l' Università di Pavia, Rome, 2017

Sacco R., *General Principles in European Legal Systems,* in Atti, cit., p. 163

Sacco, R. *Lingua e diritto*, in *Ars interpretandi*, 2000, pp. 117 ff.

Salvemini, G. *Mazzini*, Roma, 1925

Sangiovanni A., *Solidarity in the European Union*, in *Oxford J. Leg Stud.*, 33(2), 2013, pp. 213 ff.

Sbriccoli M., *Elementi per una bibliografia del socialismo giuridico italiano*, Milan, 1976

Scarpelli U., *Filosofia analitica e giurisprudenza*, Milano, 1953

Scharpf F.W., *The Asymmetry of European Integration*, Working Paper, Freie Universitaet Berlin, 2009, no. 6

Schiek D., *Solidarity in the Case Law of the European Court of Justice-Opportunities Missed?*, in *Transnational Solidarity. Concept, Challenges and Opportunities (Chapter 12)*, H. Runke, H. Petersen & I. Manners ed., Cambridge University Press, 2020

Schulze R., *Common Frame of Reference and Existing EC Contract Law*, Munich, 2009

Schulte Noelke H., Twigg-Flesner Chr. & Ebers M. (eds), *EC Consumer Law Compendium: The Consumer Acquis and Its Transposition in the Member States*, Munich, 2008

Schulze R. & Stuyck R. (eds), *Towards a European Contract Law,* Munich, 2011

Sciarra, S. *L'Europa e il lavoro. Solidarietà e conflitto in tempo di crisi*, Roma-Bari, 2013

Smith N.C. & Roennegard D., *Shareholder Primacy, Corporate Social Responsibility and the Role of Business Schools*, in J. of Bus. Ethics, 2014, pp. 1 ff.

Soldani S., *La duplice sconfitta della Seconda Repubblica in Francia,* Studi Storici, 20, no. 3 (July-September, 1979), pp. 667-677

Somek A., *Solidarity Decomposed: Being and Time in European Citizenship*, U. of Iowa College of Law, Legal Studies Research Papers, no. 07-13, May 2007

Somma A., *Contro Ventotene*, Rome, 2021

Somma A., *La dittatura dello spread*, in www.sossanita.it

Somma A., *Il diritto privato liberista. Riflessioni sull'autonomia privata*, in *Bul. mex. der. comp.*, p. 101

Soret J.-H., *Philosophies de l'Action catholique: Blondel-Maritain*, Paris, 2007

Sorge B., *Introduzione alla dottrina sociale della Chiesa*, Brescia, 2009

Sorrentino F., *I diritti fondamentali dopo Lisbona*, in *Corriere giuridico*, 2010, n. 2, 145 ss.

Smithies A., *Full Employment in a Free Society*, in *The American Economic Review*, 35(3), June 1945, pp. 355-367

Sperber J., *Karl Marx homme du XIX siècle*, Paris, 2007

Sparti D., Difficili convivenze. Una nota su Habermas e il multiculturalismo, in *Quad. Sociologia*, 2002, pp. 29 ff.

Spinelli A. & Rossi E.G., *Per un' Europa libera e unita* (Il Manifesto di Ventotene, reprinted by the Senate of the Republic of Italy), Rome, 2017

Stein P., *Regulae juris. From juristic rules to legal maxims*, Edinburgh, 1966

Stella Richter Jr, M., Società benefit e società non benefit, *in Orizzonti del diritto commerciale*, 2017, 2, pp. 1 ff.

Stjerno S. *Solidarity in Europe*, Cambridge, 2005

Supiot A. (cur.), *La Solidarité. Enquête sur un principe juridique*, Paris, 2015

Szasz A., *The Road to European Monetary Union*, Basingstoke, Hampshire, 1999

Tridimas T., *The General Principles of EC Law*, Oxford, 1999

Trimarchi P., *Rischio e responsabilità oggettiva*, Milan, 1961

Twining W. & Miers D., *How to Do Things with Rules*, Cambridge, 2012

Vanberg V.J., *The Freiburg School: Walter Eucken and the Ordoliberalism*, Freiburger Diskussionspapiere zur Ordnungsökonomik, no. 04/11

Vidal Gil E.J., *Solidaridad y derechos humanos, Diccionario crítico de los derechos humanos*, Sevilla, 2000

Wade H.W.R., Horizons and Horizontality, in *Law Quarterly Review* 11 (2000), 217

Wirsching A., *Weimar, cent anni dopo, La storia e l'eredità: bilancio di un'esperienza controversa*, Rome, 2019

Zoll, *La solidarietà.Eguaglianza e differfenza*, Bologna, 2003

# Table of Cases

# Index

1. Lammy Betten (ed.), *The Future of European Social Policy*, 1991 (ISBN 90-654-4585-4).
2. Annemarie Loman, Kamiel Mortelmans, Harry H.G. Post & Stewart Watson, *Culture and Common Law: Before and After Maastricht*, 1992 (ISBN 90-654-4638-9).
3. John A.E. Vervaele, *Fraud against the Community: The Need for European Fraud Legislation*, 1994 (ISBN 90-654-4634-6).
4. Philip Raworth, *The Legislative Process in the European Community*, 1993 (ISBN 90-654-4690-7).
5. Jules Stuyck, *Financial and Monetary Integration in the European Economic Community*, 1993 (ISBN 90-654-4718-0).
6. Jules Stuyck & A.J. Vossestein (eds), *State Entrepreneurship, National Monopolies and European Community Law*, 1993 (ISBN 90-654-4773-3).
7. Jules Stuyck & A. Looijestijn-Clearie (eds), *The European Economic Area EC-EFTA*, 1994 (ISBN 90-654-4815-2).
8. Rosita B. Bouterse, *Competition and Integration: What Goals Count?*, 1995 (ISBN 90-654-4816-0).
9. René Barents, *The Agricultural Law of the EU, 2nd Edition*, 2022 (ISBN 978-94-035-4411-3).
10. Nicholas Emiliou, *Principles of Proportionality in European Law: A Comparative Study*, 1996 (ISBN 90-411-0866-1).
11. Eivind Smith, *National Parliaments as Cornerstones of European Integration*, 1996 (ISBN 90-411-0898-X).
12. Jan H. Jans, *European Environmental Law*, 1996 (ISBN 90-411-0877-7).
13. Síofra O'Leary, *The Evolving Concept of Community Citizenship: From the Free Movement of Persons to Union Citizenship*, 1997 (ISBN 90-411-0878-5).
14. Laurence W. Gormley (ed.), *Current and Future Perspectives on EC Competition Law*, 1983 (ISBN 90-411-0691-X).
15. Simone White, *Protection of the Financial Interests of the European Communities: The Fight against Fraud and Corruption*, 1998 (ISBN 90-411-9647-1).
16. Morten P. Broberg, *Broberg on the European Commission's Jurisdiction to Scrutinise Mergers*, 4th Edition, 2013 (ISBN 978-90-411-3339-7).
17. Doris Hildebrand, *The Role of Economic Analysis in the EC Competition Rules: The European School*, 2nd Edition, 2002 (ISBN 90-411-1706-7).
18. Christof R.A. Swaak, *European Community Law and the Automobile Industry*, 1999 (ISBN 90-411-1140-9).

19. Dorthe Dahlgaard Dingel, *Public Procurement: A Harmonization of the National Judicial Review of the Application of European Community Law*, 1999 (ISBN 90-411-1161-1).

20. John A.E. Vervaele (ed.), *Compliance and Enforcement of European Community Law*, 1999 (ISBN 90-411-1151-4).

21. Martin Trybus, *European Defence Procurement Law: International and National Procurement Systems as Models for a Liberalized Defence Procurement Market in Europe*, 1999 (ISBN 90-411-1167-0).

22. Helen Staples, *The Legal Status of Third Country Nationals Resident in the European Union*, 1999 (ISBN 90-411-1277-4).

23. Damien Geradin (ed.), *The Liberalization of State Monopolies in the European Union and Beyond*, 1999 (ISBN 90-411-1264-2).

24. Katja Heede, *European Ombudsman: Redress and Control at Union Level*, 2000 (ISBN 90-411-1413-0).

25. Ulf Bernitz & Joakim Nergelius (eds), *General Principles of European Community Law*, 2000 (ISBN 90-411-1402-5).

26. Michaela Drahos, *Convergence of Competition Laws and Policies in the European Community*, 2002 (ISBN 90-411-1562-5).

27. Damien Geradin (ed.), *The Liberalization of Electricity and Natural Gas in the European Union*, 2001 (ISBN 90-411-1560-9).

28. Gisella Gori, *Towards an EU Right to Education*, 2001 (ISBN 90-411-1670-2).

29. Brendan P.G. Smith, *Constitution Building in the European Union*, 2001 (ISBN 90-411-1695-8).

30. Friedl Weiss & Frank Wooldridge, *Free Movement of Persons within the European Community*, 2nd Edition, 2007 (ISBN 978-90-411-2545-3).

31. Ingrid Boccardi, *Europe and Refugees: Towards an EU Asylum Policy*, 2002 (ISBN 90-411-1709-1).

32. John A.E. Vervaele & André Klip (eds), *European Cooperation Between Tax, Customs and Judicial Authorities*, 2001 (ISBN 90-411-1747-4).

33. Wouter P.J. Wils, *The Optimal Enforcement of EC Antitrust Law: Essays in Law and Economics*, 2002 (ISBN 90-411-1757-1).

34. Damien Geradin (ed.), *The Liberalization of Postal Services in the European Union*, 2002 (ISBN 90-411-1780-6).

35. Nick Bernard, *Multilevel Governance in the European Union*, 2002 (ISBN 90-411-1812-8).

36. Jill Wakefield, *Judicial Protection through the Use of Article 288(2) EC*, 2002 (ISBN 90-411-1823-3).

37. Sebastiaan Princen, *EU Regulation and Transatlantic Trade*, 2002 (ISBN 90-411-1871-3).

38. Amaryllis Verhoeven, *The European Union in Search of a Democratic and Constitutional Theory*, 2002 (ISBN 90-411-1872-1).

39. Paul L.C. Torremans, *Cross Border Insolvencies in EU, English and Belgian Law*, 2002 (ISBN 90-411-1888-8).

40. Malcolm Anderson & Joanna Apap (eds), *Police and Justice Cooperation and the New European Borders*, 2002 (ISBN 90-411-1893-4).
41. Christin M. Forstinger, *Takeover Law in EU and USA: A Comparative Analysis*, 2002 (ISBN 90-411-1919-1).
42. Antonio Bavasso, *Communications in EU Antitrust Law: Market Power and Public Interest*, 2003 (ISBN 90-411-1974-4).
43. Fiona G. Wishlade, *Regional State Aid and Competition Policy in the European Union*, 2003 (ISBN 90-411-1975-2).
44. Gareth Davies, *Nationality Discrimination in the European Internal Market*, 2003 (ISBN 90-411-1998-1).
45. René Barents, *The Autonomy of Community Law*, 2003 (ISBN 90-411-2251-6).
46. Gerhard Dannecker & Oswald Jansen (eds), *Competition Law Sanctioning in the European Union*, 2004 (ISBN 90-411-2100-5).
47. Nauta Dutilh (ed.), *Dealing with Dominance: The Experience of National Competition Authorities*, 2004 (ISBN 90-411-2211-7).
48. Stefaan van den Bogaert, *Practical Regulation of the Mobility of Sportsmen in the EU Post Bosman*, 2005 (ISBN 90-411-2327-X).
49. Katalin Judit Cseres, *Competition Law and Consumer Protection*, 2005 (ISBN 90-411-2380-6).
50. Philipp Kiiver, *The National Parliaments in the European Union: A Critical View on EU Constitution Building*, 2006 (ISBN 978-90-411-2452-4).
51. Alexander Turk, *The Concept of Legislation in European Community Law*, 2006 (ISBN 978-90-411-2472-2).
52. Dimitrios Sinaniotis, *The Interim Protection of Individuals before the European and National Courts*, 2006 (ISBN 978-90-411-2498-2).
53. M. Holoubek & D. Damjanovic, M. Traimer (eds), *Regulating Content: The European Regulatory Framework for the Media and Related Creative Sectors*, 2006 (ISBN 978-90-411-2597-2).
54. Anneli Albi & Jacques Ziller (eds), *The European Constitution and National Constitutions: Ratification and Beyond*, 2006 (ISBN 978-90-411-2524-8).
55. Gustavo E. Luengo, *Regulation of Subsidies and State Aids in WTO and EC Law: Conflicts in International Trade Law*, 2007 (ISBN 978-90-411-2547-7).
56. Eniko Horvath, *Mandating Identity: Citizenship, Kinship Laws and Plural Nationality in the European Union*, 2007 (ISBN 978-90-411-2662-7).
57. Rass Holdgaard, *External Relations Law of the European Community: Legal Reasoning and Legal Discourses*, 2007 (ISBN 978-90-411-2604-7).
58. Jill Wakefield, *The Right to Good Administration*, 2007 (ISBN 978-90-411-2697-9).
59. Dimitry Kochenov, *EU Enlargement and the Failure of Conditionality: Pre- accession Conditionality in the Fields of Democracy and the Rule of Law*, 2008 (ISBN 978-90-411-2696-2).
60. Despina Mavromati, *The Law of Payment Services in the EU: The EC Directive on Payment Services in the Internal Market*, 2008 (ISBN 978-90-411-2700-6).

61. Anne Meuwese, *Impact Assessment in EU Lawmaking*, 2008 (ISBN 978-90-411-2720-4).

62. Ulf Bernitz, Joakim Nergelius & Cecilia Cardner (eds), *General Principles of EC Law in a Process of Development*, 2008 (ISBN 978-90-411-2705-1).

63. Johan van de Gronden (ed.), *The EU and WTO Law on Services: Limits to the Realisation of General Interest Policies within the Services Markets?*, 2008 (ISBN 978-90-411-2809-6).

64. Alina Tryfonidou, *Reverse Discrimination in EC Law*, 2009 (ISBN 978-90-411-2751-8).

65. Mikael Berglund, *Cross-Border Enforcement of Claims in the EU: History Present Time and Future*, 2014 (ISBN 978-90-411-4564-2).

66. Theodore Konstadinides, *Division of Powers in European Union Law: The Delimitation of Internal Competence between the EU and the Member States*, 2009 (ISBN 978-90-411-2615-3).

67. Mattias Derlén, *Multilingual Interpretation of European Union Law*, 2009 (ISBN 978-90-411-2853-9).

68. René Barents, *Directory of EU Case Law on the Preliminary Ruling Procedure*, 2009 (ISBN 978-90-411-3150-8).

69. Yan Luo, *Anti-dumping in the WTO, the EU and China: The Rise of Legalization in the Trade Regime and Its Consequences*, 2010 (ISBN 978-90-411-3207-9).

70. Patrick Birkinshaw & Mike Varney (eds), *The European Union Legal Order after Lisbon*, 2010 (ISBN 978-90-411-3152-2).

71. Thomas Gr. Papadopoulos, *EU Law and Harmonization of Takeovers in the Internal Market*, 2010 (ISBN 978-90-411-3340-3).

72. Bas van Bockel, *The Ne Bis In Idem Principle in EU Law*, 2010 (ISBN 978-90-411-3156-0).

73. Veljko Milutinović, *The 'Right to Damages' under EU Competition Law: From Courage v. Crehan to the White Paper and Beyond*, 2010 (ISBN 978-90-411-3235-2).

74. Amandine Garde, *EU Law and Obesity Prevention*, 2010 (ISBN 978-90-411-2706-8).

75. Leonard Besselink, Frans Pennings & Sacha Prechal (eds), *The Eclipse of the Legality Principle in the European Union*, 2011 (ISBN 978-90-411-3262-8).

76. Sacha Garben, *EU Higher Education Law: The Bologna Process and Harmonization by Stealth*, 2011 (ISBN 978-90-411-3365-6).

77. Dimitry Kochenov (ed.), *EU Law of the Overseas: Outermost Regions, Associated Overseas Countries and Territories, Territories Sui Generis*, 2011 (ISBN 978-90-411-3445-5).

78. Pablo Ibáñez Colomo, *European Communications Law and Technological Convergence: Deregulation, Re-regulation and Regulatory Convergence in Television and Telecommunications*, 2012 (ISBN 978-90-411-3829-3).

79. Elise Muir, *EU Regulation of Access to Labour Markets: A Case Study of EU Constraints on Member State Competences*, 2012 (ISBN 978-90-411-3823-1).

80. Tim Corthaut, *EU Ordre Public*, 2012 (ISBN 978-90-411-3232-1).

81. Oana Ştefan, *Soft Law in Court: Competition Law, State Aid and the Court of Justice of the European Union*, 2013 (ISBN 978-90-411-3997-9).
82. Francesco Rossi dal Pozzo, *Citizenship Rights and Freedom of Movement in the European Union*, 2013 (ISBN 978-90-411-4660-1).
83. Jens Hartig Danielsen, *EU Agricultural Law*, 2013 (ISBN 978-90-411-3280-2).
84. Ulf Bernitz, Xavier Groussot & Felix Schulyok (eds), *General Principles of EU Law and European Private Law*, 2013 (ISBN 978-90-411-4683-0).
85. Michelle Everson, Cosimo Monda & Ellen Vos (eds), *European Agencies in between Institutions and Member States*, 2014 (ISBN 978-90-411-2843-0).
86. Stefan Leible & Matthias Lehmann (eds), *European Contract Law and German Law*, 2014 (ISBN 978-90-411-2588-0).
87. Piero Leanza & Ondrej Pridal, *The Right to a Fair Trial: Article 6 of the European Convention on Human Rights*, 2014 (ISBN 978-90-411-4855-1).
88. Patrick J. Birkinshaw, *European Public Law: The Achievement and the Brexit Challenge*, 3rd Edition, 2020 (ISBN 978-90-411-9751-1).
89. George Cumming, *Expert Evidence Deficiencies in the Judgments of the Courts of the European Union and the European Court of Human Rights*, 2014 (ISBN 978-90-411-4123-1).
90. Vesna Rijavec, Tomaž Keresteš & Tjaša Ivanc (eds), *Simplification of Debt Collection in the EU*, 2014 (ISBN 978-90-411-4854-4).
91. Nina Półtorak, *European Union Rights in National Courts*, 2015 (ISBN 978-90-411-5863-5).
92. Kyriaki-Korina Raptopoulou, *EU Law and Healthcare Services: Normative Approaches to Public Health Systems*, 2015 (ISBN 978-90-411-5013-4).
93. Torsten Frank Koschinka & Piero Leanza, *Preliminary Injunctions: Germany, England/Wales, Italy and France*, 2015 (ISBN 978-90-411-5833-8).
94. Vesna Rijavec, Tomaž Keresteš & Tjaša Ivanc (eds), *Dimensions of Evidence in European Civil Procedure*, 2016 (ISBN 978-90-411-6662-3).
95. Stefan Leible (ed.), *General Principles of European Private International Law*, 2016 (ISBN 978-90-411-5955-7).
96. Patrick J. Birkinshaw & Andrea Biondi (eds), *Britain Alone!: The Implications and Consequences of United Kingdom Exit from the EU*, 2016 (ISBN 978-90-411-5832-1).
97. René Barents, *Remedies and Procedures before the EU Courts*, 2nd Edition, 2020 (ISBN 978-94-035-1140-5).
98. Luca Prete, *Infringement Proceedings in EU Law*, 2017 (ISBN 978-90-411-6900-6).
99. Robert van den Hoven van Genderen, *Privacy Limitation Clauses: Trojan Horses under the Disguise of Democracy*, 2017 (ISBN 978-90-411-8599-0).
100. Mariusz Krzysztofek, *Post-Reform Personal Data Protection in the European Union: General Data Protection Regulation (EU) 2016/679*, 2017 (ISBN 978-90-411-6237-3).
101. Gianni Lo Schiavo, *The Role of Financial Stability in EU Law and Policy*, 2017 (ISBN 978-90-411-8230-2).

102. Emmanuel Guinchard & Marie-Pierre Granger (eds), *The New EU Judiciary: An Analysis of Current Judicial Reforms*, 2017 (ISBN 978-90-411-6834-4).

103. Kirsten Henckel, *Cross-Border Transfers of Undertakings: A European Perspective*, 2017 (ISBN 978-90-411-9227-1).

104. Vesna Rijavec, Wendy Kennett, Tomaž Keresteš & Tjaša Ivanc, *Remedies Concerning Enforcement of Foreign Judgements: Brussels I Recast*, 2018 (ISBN 978-90-411-9416-9).

105. Albert Sanchez-Graells & Constant De Koninck, *Shaping EU Public Procurement Law: A Critical Analysis of the CJEU Case Law 2015–2017*, 2018 (ISBN 978-94-035-0160-4).

106. Andrea Biondi, Patrick J. Birkinshaw & Maria Kendrick, *Brexit: The Legal Implications*, 2019 (ISBN 978-90-411-9540-1).

107. Mariusz Krzysztofek, *GDPR: General Data Protection Regulation (EU) 2016/679: Post-Reform Personal Data Protection in the European Union*, 2019 (ISBN 978-94-035-0594-7).

108. Giovanni Bassani, *The Legal Framework Applicable to the Single Supervisory Mechanism: Tapestry or Patchwork?*, 2019 (ISBN 978-94-035-0872-6).

109. Piotr Staszczyk, *A Legal Analysis of NGOs and European Civil Society*, 2019 (ISBN 978-94-035-1251-8).

110. Patrizio Messina, *Finance for SMEs: European Regulation and Capital Markets Union – Focus on Securitization and Alternative Finance Tools*, 2019 (ISBN 978-94-035-0161-1).

111. Jacques H.J. Bourgeois (ed.), *EU Framework for Foreign Direct Investment Control*, 2020 (ISBN 978-94-035-1883-1).

112. Ulf Bernitz, Xavier Groussot, Jaan Paju & Sybe de Vries (eds), *General Principles of EU Law and the EU Digital Order*, 2020 (ISBN 978-94-035-1165-8).

113. Aleksandra Drożdż, *Protection of Natural Persons with Regard to Automated Individual Decision-Making in the GDPR*, 2020 (ISBN 978-94-035-2045-2).

114. Mariusz Krzysztofek, *GDPR: Personal Data Protection in the European Union*, 2021 (ISBN 978-94-035-3270-7).

115. Katarzyna Gromek-Broc (ed.), *Public Law in a Troubled Era: A Tribute to Professor Patrick Birkinshaw*, 2023 (ISBN 978-94-035-3576-0).

116. Guido Alpa, *Solidarity: A Normative Principle*, 2023 (ISBN 978-94-035-3596-8).